Think

Think

A compelling introduction to philosophy

SIMON BLACKBURN

OXFORD
UNIVERSITY PRESS

OXFORD
UNIVERSITY PRESS

Great Clarendon Street, Oxford OX2 6DP

Oxford University Press is a department of the University of Oxford.
It furthers the University's objective of excellence in research, scholarship,
and education by publishing worldwide in

Oxford New York

Athens Auckland Bangkok Bogotá Buenos Aires Calcutta
Cape Town Chennai Dar es Salaam Delhi Florence Hong Kong Istanbul
Karachi Kuala Lumpur Madrid Melbourne Mexico City Mumbai
Nairobi Paris São Paulo Singapore Taipei Tokyo Toronto Warsaw

with associated companies in Berlin Ibadan

Oxford is a registered trade mark of Oxford University Press
in the UK and in certain other countries

© Simon Blackburn 1999

The moral rights of the author have been asserted

Database right Oxford University Press (maker)

First published 1999

British Library Cataloguing in Publication Data

Data available

Library of Congress Cataloging in Publication Data

Data available

ISBN 0-19-210024-6 (hbk.)
ISBN 0-19-969087-1 (pbk.)

1 3 5 7 9 10 8 6 4 2

Typeset by Invisible Ink
Printed in Great Britain
on acid-free paper by
T. J. International Ltd.,
Padstow, Cornwall

Preface

THIS BOOK GREW FROM years of wrestling with the problems of trying to interest people in ideas. I have done this as a teacher, but also as someone who has tried to explain the value of the humanities in general, and philosophy in particular, to a wider audience. Indeed my first debt is to the climate of the times, whose scepticism about the value of higher education made it evident to me just how urgent this task is. A second, more serious debt is to all the students of many years, whose nods and frowns eventually shaped the book. I also owe a debt to teaching assistants here at the University of North Carolina, who had first-hand experience of engaging students in earlier versions of the work. I would never have taken the plunge, however, had it not been for the generous encouragement of Catherine Clarke and Angus Phillips, at Oxford University Press. Angus has closely monitored the progress of the work, and I owe much to his support and advice.

Earlier versions of the material have been read by Huw Price and

Ralph Walker, who each provided invaluable suggestions. Yuri Balashov and Dan Ryder gave me help with specific topics. For the sake of brevity I have not included a glossary of philosophical terms, which would in any case have echoed definitions found in my *Oxford Dictionary of Philosophy*.

The superb editing of Maura High and Angela Blackburn gave me an uncomfortable sense of my shortcomings as a writer, while happily disguising them from the wider public. Angela, of course, had also to suffer the usual burdens of having a writing husband, and without her support nothing would have been possible.

Simon Blackburn

Contents

Introduction

THIS BOOK IS FOR people who want to think about the big themes: knowledge, reason, truth, mind, freedom, destiny, identity, God, goodness, justice. These are not the hidden preserve of specialists. They are things that men and women wonder about naturally, for they structure the ways we think about the world and our place in it. They are also themes about which thinkers have had things to say. In this book I try to introduce ways of thinking about the big themes. I also introduce some of the things thinkers have had to say about them. If readers have absorbed this book, then they should be on better terms with the big themes. And they should be able to read many otherwise baffling major thinkers with pleasure and reasonable understanding.

The word 'philosophy' carries unfortunate connotations: impractical, unworldly, weird. I suspect that all philosophers and philosophy students share that moment of silent embarrassment when someone innocently asks us what we do. I would prefer to introduce myself as doing conceptual engineering. For just as the engineer studies the structure of material things, so the philosopher studies the structure of thought. Understanding the structure involves seeing how parts function and how they interconnect. It means knowing what would happen for better or worse if changes were made. This is what we aim at when we investigate the structures that shape our view of the world. Our concepts or ideas form the mental housing in which we live. We may end up proud of the structures we have built. Or we may believe that they need dismantling and starting afresh. But first, we have to know what they are.

The book is self-standing and does not presuppose that the reader has any other resources. But it could be augmented. For example, it could be read alongside some of the primary source materials from which I frequently quote. These are readily available classics, such as Descartes's *Meditations*, or Berkeley's *Three Dialogues*, or Hume's *Enquiry Concerning Human Understanding*, or his *Dialogues Concerning Natural Religion*. But it can equally well be read on its own without the texts to hand. And after finishing it, the reader should pick up the classics, and other things like logic texts or writings on ethics, with a mind prepared.

WHAT ARE WE TO THINK ABOUT?

Here are some questions any of us might ask about ourselves: What am I? What is consciousness? Could I survive my bodily death? Can I be sure that other people's experiences and sensations are like mine? If I can't share the experience of others, can I communicate with them? Do we always act out of self-interest? Might I be a kind of puppet, programmed to do the things that I believe I do out of my own free will?

Here are some questions about the world: Why is there something and not nothing? What is the difference between past and future? Why does causation run always from past to future, or does it make sense to think that the future might influence the past? Why does nature keep on in a regular way? Does the world presuppose a Creator? And if so, can we understand why he (or she or they) created it?

Finally, here are some questions about ourselves *and* the world: How can we be sure that the world is really like we take it to be? What is knowledge, and how much do we have? What makes a field of inquiry a science? (Is psychoanalysis a science? Is economics?) How do we know about abstract objects, like numbers? How do we know about values and duties? How are we to tell whether our opinions are objective, or just subjective?

The queer thing about these questions is that not only are they baffling at first sight, but they also defy simple processes of solution. If someone asks me when it is high tide, I know how to set about getting an answer. There are authoritative tide tables I can consult. I may know roughly how they are produced. And if all else fails, I could go and measure the rise and fall of the sea myself. A question like this is a matter of experience: an *empirical* question. It can be settled by means of agreed procedures, involving looking and seeing, making measurements, or applying rules that have been tested against experience and found to work. The questions of the last paragraphs are not like this. They seem to require more reflection. We don't immediately know where to look. Perhaps we feel we don't quite know what we mean when we ask them, or what would count as getting a solution. What would show me, for instance, whether I am not after all a puppet, programmed to do the things I believe I do freely? Should we ask scientists who specialize in the brain? But how would they know what to look for? How would they know when they had found it? Imagine the headline: 'Neuroscientists discover human beings not puppets.' How?

So what gives rise to such baffling questions?

In a word, self-reflection. Human beings are relentlessly capable of reflecting on themselves. We might do something out of habit, but then we can begin to reflect on the habit. We can habitually think things, and then reflect on what we are thinking. We can ask ourselves (or sometimes we get asked by other people) whether we know what we are talking about. To answer that we need to reflect on our own positions, our own understanding of what we are saying, our own sources of authority. We might start to wonder whether we know what we mean. We might wonder whether what we say is 'objectively' true, or merely the outcome of our own perspective, or our own 'take' on a situation. Thinking about this we confront categories like knowledge, objectivity, truth, and we may want to think about them. At that point we are *reflecting* on concepts and procedures and beliefs that we normally just *use*. We are looking at the scaffolding of our thought, and doing conceptual engineering.

This point of reflection might arise in the course of quite normal discussion. A historian, for example, is more or less bound at some point to ask what is meant by 'objectivity' or 'evidence', or even 'truth', in history. A cosmologist has to pause from solving equations with the letter *t* in them, and ask what is meant, for instance, by the flow of time or the direction of time or the beginning of time. But at that point, whether they recognize it or not, they become philosophers. And they are beginning to do something that can be done well or badly. The point is to do it well.

How is philosophy learned? A better question is: how can thinking skills be acquired? The thinking in question involves attending to basic structures of thought. This can be done well or badly, intelligently or ineptly. But doing it well is not primarily a matter of acquiring a body of knowledge. It is more like playing the piano well. It is a 'knowing how' as much as a 'knowing that'. The most famous philosophical character of the classical world, the Socrates of Plato's dialogues, did not pride himself on how much he knew. On the contrary, he prided himself on being the only one who knew how little he knew (reflection, again). What he was good at—supposedly, for estimates of his success differ—was exposing the weaknesses of other peoples' claims to know. To process thoughts well is a matter of being able to avoid confusion, detect ambiguities, keep things in mind one at a time, make reliable arguments, become aware of alternatives, and so on.

To sum up: our ideas and concepts can be compared with the lenses through which we see the world. In philosophy the lens is itself the topic of study. Success will be a matter not of how much you know at the end, but of what you can do when the going gets tough: when the seas of argument rise, and confusion breaks out. Success will mean taking seriously the implications of ideas.

WHAT IS THE POINT?

It is all very well saying that, but why bother? What's the point? Reflection doesn't get the world's business done. It doesn't bake bread or fly aeroplanes. Why not just toss the reflective questions aside, and get on with other things? I shall sketch three kinds of answer: high ground, middle ground, and low ground.

The high ground questions the question—a typical philosophical strategy, because it involves going up one level of reflection. What do we mean when we ask what the point is? Reflection bakes no bread, but then neither does architecture, music, art, history, or literature. It is just that we want to understand ourselves. We want this for its own sake, just as a pure scientist or pure mathematician may want to understand the beginning of the universe, or the theory of sets, for its own sake, or just as a musician might want to solve some problem in harmony or counterpoint just for its own sake. There is no eye on any practical applications. A lot of life is indeed a matter of raising more hogs, to buy more land, so we can raise more hogs, so that we can buy more land ... The time we take out, whether it is to do mathematics or music, or to read Plato or Jane Austen, is time to be cherished. It is the time in which we cosset our mental health. And our mental health is just good in itself, like our physical health. Furthermore there is after all a payoff in terms of pleasure. When our physical health is good, we take pleasure in physical exercise, and when our mental health is good, we take pleasure in mental exercise.

This is a very pure-minded reply. The problem with it is not that it is wrong. It is just that it is only likely to appeal to people who are half-convinced already—people who didn't ask the original question in a very aggressive tone of voice.

So here is a middle-ground reply. Reflection matters because it is *continuous* with practice. How you think about what you are doing affects how you do it, or whether you do it at all. It may direct your research, or your attitude to people who do things differently, or indeed your whole life. To take a simple example, if your reflections lead you to believe in a life after death, you may be prepared to face persecutions that you would not face if you became convinced—as many philosophers are—that the notion makes no sense. Fatalism, or the belief that the future is fixed whatever we do, is a purely philosophical belief, but it is one that can paralyse action. Putting it more politically, it can also express an acquiescence with the low status accorded to some segments of society, and this may be a pay-off for people of higher status who encourage it.

Let us consider some examples more prevalent in the West. Many people reflecting on human nature think that we are at bottom entirely selfish. We only look out for our own advantage, never really caring about anyone else. Apparent concern disguises hope of future benefit. The leading paradigm in the social sciences is *homo economicus*—economic man. Economic man looks after himself, in competitive struggle with others. Now, if people come to think that we are all, always, like this, their relations with each other become different. They become less trusting, less cooperative, more suspicious. This changes the way they interact, and they will incur various costs. They will find it harder, and in some circumstances impossible, to get cooperative ventures going: they may get stuck in what the philosopher Thomas Hobbes (1588–1679) memorably called 'the war of all against all'. In the market-place, because they are always looking out to be cheated, they will incur heavy transaction costs. If my attitude is that 'a verbal contract is not worth the paper it is written on', I will have to pay lawyers to design contracts with penalties, and if I will not trust the lawyers to do anything except just enough to pocket their fees, I will have to get the contracts checked by other lawyers, and so on. But all this may be based on a philosophical mistake—looking at human motivation through the wrong set of categories, and hence misunderstanding its nature. Maybe people can care for each other, or at least care for doing their bit or keeping their promises. Maybe if a more optimistic self-image is on the table, people can come to live up to it. Their lives then become better. So this bit of thinking, getting clear about the right categories with which to understand human motivation, is an important *practical* task. It is not confined to the study, but bursts out of it.

Here is a very different example. The Dutch astronomer Nicholas Copernicus (1473–1543) reflected on how we *know* about motion. He realized that how we perceive motion is *perspectival*: that is, whether we see things as moving is the result of how we ourselves are placed and in particular whether we ourselves are moving. (We have mostly been subject to the illusion in trains or airports, where the next-door train or aeroplane seems to move off, and then we realize with a jolt that it is we who are moving. But there were fewer everyday examples in the time of Copernicus.) So the apparent motions of the stars and planets might arise because they are not moving as they appear to do, but we observers move.

And this is how it turned out to be. Here reflection on the nature of knowledge—what philosophers call an *epistemological* inquiry, from the Greek *episteme*, meaning knowledge—generated the first spectacular leap of modern science. Einstein's reflections on how we know whether two events are simultaneous had the same structure. He realized that the results of our measurements would depend upon the way we are travelling compared to the events we are clocking. This led to the Special Theory of Relativity (and Einstein himself acknowledged the importance of preceding philosophers in sensitizing him to the epistemological complexities of such a measurement).

For a final example, we can consider a philosophical problem many people get into when they think about mind and body. Many people envisage a strict separation between mind, as one thing, and body, as a different thing. When this seems to be just good common sense, it can begin to infect practice in quite insidious ways. For instance, it begins to be difficult to see how these two different things interact. Doctors might then find it almost *inevitable* that treatments of physical conditions that address mental or psychological causes will fail. They might find it next to impossible to see how messing with someone's mind could possibly cause changes in the complex physical system that is their body. After all, good science tells us that it takes physical and chemical causes to have physical and chemical effects. So we might get an a priori, armchair certainty that one kind of treatment (say, drugs and electric shocks) has to be 'right' and others (such as treating patients humanely, counselling, analysis) are 'wrong': unscientific, unsound, bound to fail. But this certainty is premised not on science but on a false *philosophy*. A better philosophical conception of the relation between mind and body changes it. A better conception should enable us to see how there is nothing *surprising* in the fact of mind–body interaction. It is the most commonplace fact, for instance, that thinking of some things (mental) can cause people to blush (physical). Thinking of a future danger can cause all kinds of bodily changes: hearts pound, fists clench, guts constrict. By extrapolation there should be nothing difficult to comprehend about a mental state such as cheerful optimism affecting a physical state like the disappearance of spots or even the remission of a cancer. It becomes a purely *empirical* fact whether such things happen. The armchair certainty that they could not happen is itself revealed as dependent on bad understanding of the structures of thought, or in other words bad philosophy, and is in that sense unscientific. And this realization can change medical attitudes and practice for the better.

So the middle-ground answer reminds us that reflection is continuous with practice, and our practice can go worse or better according to the value of our reflections. A system of thought is something we live in, just as much as a house, and if our intellectual house is cramped and confined, we need to know what better structures are possible.

The low-ground answer merely polishes this point up a bit, not in connection with nice clean subjects like economics or physics, but down in the basement where human life is a little less polite. One of the series of satires etched by the Spanish painter Goya is entitled 'The Sleep of Reason Produces Monsters'. Goya believed that many of the follies of mankind resulted from the 'sleep of reason'. There are always people telling us what we want, how they will provide it, and what we should believe. Convictions are infectious, and people can make others convinced of almost anything. We are typically ready to believe that *our* ways, *our* beliefs, *our* religion, *our* politics are better than theirs, or that *our* God-given rights trump theirs or that *our* interests require defensive or pre-emptive strikes against them. In the end, it is ideas for which people kill each other. It is because of ideas about what the others are like, or who we are, or what our interests or rights require, that we go to war, or oppress others with a good conscience, or even sometimes acquiesce in our own oppression by others. When these beliefs involve the sleep of reason, critical awakening is the antidote. Reflection enables us to step back, to see our perspective on a situation as perhaps distorted or blind, at the very least to see if there is argument for preferring our ways, or whether it is just subjective. Doing this properly is doing one more piece of conceptual engineering.

Since there is no telling in advance where it may lead, reflection can be seen as dangerous. There are always thoughts that stand opposed to it. Many people are discomfited, or even outraged, by philosophical questions. Some are fearful that their ideas may not stand up as well as they would like if they start to think about them. Others may want to stand upon the 'politics of identity', or in other words the kind of identification with a particular tradition, or group, or national or ethnic identity that invites them to turn their back on outsiders who question the ways of the group. They will shrug off criticism: their values are 'incommensurable' with the values of outsiders. They are to be understood only by brothers and sisters within the circle. People like to retreat to within a thick, comfortable, traditional set of folkways, and not to worry too much about their structure, or their origins, or even the criticisms that they may deserve. Reflection opens the avenue to criticism, and the folkways may not like criticism. In this way, ideologies be-come closed circles, primed to feel outraged by the questioning mind.

For the last two thousand years the philosophical tradition has been the enemy of this kind of cosy complacency. It has insisted that the unexamined life is not worth living. It has insisted on the power of rational reflection to winnow out bad elements in our practices, and to replace them with better ones. It has identified critical self-reflection with freedom, the idea being that only when we can see ourselves properly can we obtain control over the direc-tion in which we would wish to move. It is only when we can see our situation steadily and see it whole that we can start to think what to do about it. Marx said that previous philosophers had sought to understand the world, whereas the point was to change it—one of the silliest famous remarks of all time (and absolutely belied by his own intellectual practice). He would have done better to add that without understanding the world, you will know little about how to change it, at least for the better. Rosencrantz and Guildenstern admit that they cannot play on a pipe but they seek to manipulate Hamlet. When we act without understanding, the world is well prepared to echo Hamlet's response: ' 'Sblood, do you think I am easier to be played on than a pipe?'

There are academic currents in our own age that run against these ideas. There are people who question the very notion of truth, or reason, or the possibility of disinterested reflection.

Mostly, they do bad philosophy, often without even knowing that this is what they are doing: conceptual engineers who cannot draw a plan, let alone design a structure. We return to see this at various points in the book, but meanwhile I can promise that this book stands unashamedly with the tradition and against any modern, or postmodern, scepticism about the value of reflection.

Goya's full motto for his etching is, 'Imagination abandoned by reason produces impossible monsters: united with her, she is the mother of the arts and the source of her wonders.' That is how we should take it to be.

CHAPTER ONE

Knowledge

PERHAPS THE MOST unsettling thought many of us have, often quite early on in childhood, is that the whole world might be a dream; that the ordinary scenes and objects of everyday life might be fantasies. The reality we live in may be a virtual reality, spun out of our own minds, or perhaps injected into our minds by some sinister Other. Of course, such thoughts come, and then go. Most of us shake them off. But why are we right to do so? How can we know that the world as we take it to be, is the world as it is? How do we begin to think about the relation between appearance and reality: things as we take them to be, as opposed to things as they are?

LOSING THE WORLD

We might say: it all began on 10 November 1619.

On that date, in the southern German town of Ulm, the French mathematician and philosopher René Descartes (1596–1650) shut himself away in a room heated by a stove, and had a vision followed by dreams, which he took to show him his life's work: the unfolding of the one true way to find knowledge. The true path required sweeping away all that he had previously taken for granted, and starting from the foundations upwards.

Of course, it didn't, really, begin in 1619, for Descartes was not the first. The problems Descartes raised for himself are as old as human thought. These are problems of the self, and its mortality, its knowledge, and the nature of the world it inhabits; problems of reality and illusion. They are all raised in the oldest philosophical texts we have, the Indian Vedas, stemming from about 1500 BC. The generation immediately before Descartes had included the great French essayist Montaigne, whose motto was the title of one of his great essays: 'Que sais-je?'—what do I know?

Nor did Descartes come to his enterprise with a totally innocent mind: he himself had an intense education in the prevailing philosophies of the time, at the hands of Jesuit teachers. But by Descartes's time things were changing. The Dutch astronomer Copernicus had discovered the heliocentric (sun-centred) model of the solar system. Galileo and others were laying the foundations of a 'mechanical' science of nature. In this picture the only substances in space would be material, made up of 'atoms', and caused to move only by mechanical forces which science would eventually discover. Both Copernicus and Galileo fell foul of the guardians of Catholic orthodoxy, the Inquisition, for this scientific picture seemed to many people to threaten the place of human beings in the cosmos. If science tells us all that there is, what becomes of the human soul, human freedom, and our relationship with God?

Descartes was smart. He invented standard algebraic notation; and Cartesian coordinates, which enable us to give algebraic equations for geometrical figures, are named after him. He himself was one of the leaders of the scientific revolution, making fundamental advances not only in mathematics but also in physics, particularly optics. But Descartes was also a pious Catholic. So for him it was a task of great importance to show how the unfolding scientific world—vast, cold, inhuman, and mechanical—nevertheless had room in it for God and freedom, and for the human spirit.

Hence his life's work, culminating in the *Meditations*, published in 1641, 'in which are demonstrated the existence of God and the distinction between the human soul and the body', according to the subtitle. But the subtext is that Descartes also intends to rescue the modern world view from the charge of atheism and materialism. The scientific world is to be less threatening than was feared. It is to be made safe for human beings. And the way to make it safe is to reflect on the foundations of knowledge. So we start with Descartes because he was the first great philosopher to wrestle with the implications of the modern scientific world view. Starting with the medievals or Greeks is often starting so far away from where we are now that the imaginative effort to think in their shoes is probably too great. Descartes is, comparatively, one of us, or so we may hope.

There is a danger in paraphrasing a philosopher, particularly one as terse as Descartes. I am going to present some of the central themes of the *Meditations*. This is in the spirit of a sportscast showing only the 'edited highlights' of a game. Closer acquaintance with the text would uncover other highlights; closer acquaintance with its historical context would uncover yet others. But the highlights will be enough to illuminate most of the central issues of subsequent philosophy.

THE EVIL DEMON

There are six *Meditations*. In the first, Descartes introduces the 'method of doubt'. He resolves that if he is to establish anything in the sciences that is 'stable and likely to last' he must demolish all his ordinary opinions, and start right from the foundations.

For he has found that even his senses deceive him, and it is 'prudent never to trust completely those who have deceived us even once'. He puts to himself the objection that only madmen ('who say that they are dressed in purple when they are naked, or that their heads are made of earthenware, or that they are pumpkins or made of glass'—madmen were evidently pretty colourful in the seventeenth century) deny the very obvious evidence of their senses.

In answer to that, he reminds us of dreams, in which we can represent things to ourselves just as convincingly as our senses now do, but which bear no relation to reality

Still, he objects to himself, dreams are like paintings. A painter can rearrange scenes, but ultimately depicts things derived from 'real' things, if only real colours. By similar reasoning, says Descartes, even if familiar things (our eyes, head, hands, and so on)

are imaginary, they must depend on some simpler and more universal things that are real.

But what things? Descartes thinks that 'there is not one of my former beliefs about which a doubt may not properly be raised'. And at this stage,

> I will suppose therefore that not God, who is supremely good and the source of truth, but rather some malicious demon of the utmost power and cunning has employed all his energies in order to deceive me. I shall think that the sky, the air, the earth, colours, shapes, sounds and all external things are merely the delusions of dreams which he has devised to ensnare my judgment.

This is the Evil Demon. Once this frightening possibility is raised, his only defence is resolutely to guard himself against believing any falsehoods. He recognizes that this is hard to do, and 'a kind of laziness' brings him back to normal life, but intellectually, his only course is to labour in the 'inextricable darkness' of the problems he has raised. This ends the first *Meditation*.

COGITO, ERGO SUM

The second *Meditation* begins with Descartes overwhelmed by these doubts. For the sake of the inquiry he is supposing that 'I have no senses and no body'. But:

> Does it now follow that I too do not exist? No: if I convinced myself of something then I certainly existed. But there is a deceiver of supreme power and cunning who is deliberately

and constantly deceiving me. In that case I too undoubtedly exist, if he is deceiving me; and let him deceive me as much as he can, he will never bring it about that I am nothing so long as I think that I am something. So after considering everything very thoroughly, I must finally conclude that this proposition, I am, I exist, *is necessarily true whenever it is put forward by me or conceived in my mind.*

This is the famous 'Cogito, ergo sum': 'I think, therefore I am.'

Having saved his 'self' out of the general seas of scepticism, Descartes now asks what this self *is*. Whereas formerly, he thought he knew what his body was, and thought of himself by way of his body, now he is forced to recognize that his knowledge of his self is not based on knowledge of his embodied existence. In particular, he is going to meet problems when he tries to *imagine* it. Imagination is a matter of contemplating the shape or image of a corporeal thing (a body, or thing extended in space). But at this stage, we know nothing of corporeal things. So 'imagining' the self by imagining a thin or tubby, tall or short, weighty bodily being, such as I see in a mirror, is inadequate.

So what is the basis of this knowledge of the self?

Thinking? At last I have discovered it—thought; this alone is inseparable from me. I am, I exist—that is certain. But for how long? For as long as I am thinking. For it could be, that were I totally to cease from thinking, I should totally cease to exist. . . . I am, then, in the strict sense only a thing that thinks.

The inquiry now takes a slightly different course. Descartes recognizes that a conception of oneself as an embodied thing, living in an extended spatial world of physical objects, will come back almost irresistibly. And he realizes that the 'I' he is left with is pretty thin: 'this puzzling I that cannot be pictured in the imagination'. So 'let us consider the things which people commonly think they understand most distinctly of all; that is the bodies we touch and see'. He considers a ball of wax. It has taste and scent, and a colour, shape, and size 'that are plain to see'. If you rap it, it makes a sound. But now he puts the wax by the fire, and look:

> [T]he residual taste is eliminated, the smell goes away, the colour changes, the shape is lost, the size increases; it becomes liquid and hot; you can hardly touch it, and if you strike it, it no longer makes a sound. But does the same wax remain? It must be admitted that it does; no one denies it, no one thinks otherwise. So what was it in the wax that I understood with such distinctness? Evidently none of the features which I arrived at by means of the senses; for whatever came under taste, smell, sight, touch or hearing has now altered—yet the wax remains.

Descartes glosses the result of this example as showing that there is a perception of the wax that is 'pure mental scrutiny', which can become 'clear and distinct' depending on how careful he is to concentrate on what the wax consists in. So, by the end of the second *Meditation*, he concludes:

> I now know that even bodies are not strictly perceived by the senses or the faculty of imagination but by the intellect alone, and that this perception derives not from their being touched or seen but from their being understood; and in view of this I know plainly that I can achieve an easier and more evident perception of my own mind than of anything else.

MOTIVATIONS, QUESTIONS

How are we to read a piece of philosophy like this? We start by see-ing Descartes trying to motivate his method of extreme doubt (also known as Cartesian doubt, or as he himself calls it, 'hyper-bolic', that is, excessive or exaggerated doubt). But is the motiva-tion satisfactory? What exactly is he thinking? Perhaps this:

> The senses sometimes deceive us. *So* for all we know, they always deceive us.

But that is a bad argument—a fallacy. Compare:

> Newspapers sometimes make mistakes. *So* for all we know, they always make mistakes

The starting point or premise is true, but the conclusion seems very unlikely indeed. And there are even examples of the argument form where the premise is true, but the conclusion *cannot* be true:

> Some banknotes are forgeries. *So* for all we know, they all are forgeries.

Here, the conclusion is impossible, since the very notion of a forgery presupposes valid notes or coins. Forgeries are parasitic upon the real. Forgers need genuine notes and coins to copy.

An argument is *valid* when there is *no way*—meaning no *pos-sible* way—that the premises, or starting points, could be true without the conclusion being true (we explore this further in Chapter 6). It is *sound* if it is valid and it has true premises, in which case its conclusion is true as well. The argument just identified is clearly invalid, since it is no better than other examples that lead us from truth to falsity. But this in turn suggests that it is uncharitable to interpret Descartes as giving us such a sad offering. We might interpret him as having in mind something else, that he regrettably does not make explicit. This is called looking for a *suppressed premise*—something needed to buttress an argument, and that its author might have presupposed, but does not state. Alternatively we might *reinterpret* Descartes to be aiming at a weaker conclusion. Or perhaps we can do both. The argument might be:

> The senses sometimes deceive us. We cannot distinguish occasions when they do from ones when they do not. *So* for all we know, any particular sense experience may be deceiving us.

This seems to be a better candidate for validity. If we try it with banknotes and forgeries, we will find that the conclusion seems to follow. But the conclusion is a conclusion about *any particular* experience. It is no longer the conclusion that *all* our experience (en bloc, as it were) may be deceiving us. It is the difference between 'for all we know any particular note may be a forgery' and 'for all we know all notes are forgeries'. The first may be true when the second is not true.

Still, perhaps at this stage of the *Meditations* the weaker conclusion is all Descartes wants. But we might also turn attention to the second premise of this refined argument. Is this premise true? Is it true that we cannot distinguish occasions of error—things like illusions, delusions, misinterpretations of what we are seeing—from others? To think about this we would want to introduce a distinction. It may be true that we cannot detect occasions of illusion and error *at a glance*. That is what makes them illusions. But is it true that we cannot do so *given time*? On the contrary, it seems to be true that we can do so: we can learn, for instance, to mistrust images of shimmering water in the desert as typically misleading illusions or mirages—tricks of the light. But worse, the fact that we can detect occasions of deception is surely *presupposed* by Descartes's own argument. Why so? Because Descartes is presenting the first premise as a place to start from—a known truth. But we only *know* that the senses sometimes deceive us because further investigations—using the very same senses—*show* that they have done so. We find out, for instance, that a quick glimpse of shimmering water misled us into thinking there was water there. But we discover the mistake by going closer, looking harder, and if necessary touching and feeling, or listening. Similarly, we only know, for instance, that a quick, off-the-cuff opinion about the size of the Sun would be wrong because further laborious observations show us that the Sun is in fact many times the size of the Earth. So the second premise only seems true in the sense of 'we cannot distinguish *at a glance* whether our senses are deceiving us'. Whereas to open the way to Descartes's major doubts, it would seem that he needs 'we cannot distinguish *even over time and with care* whether our senses are deceiving us'. And this last does not seem to be true. We might try saying that the senses are 'self-corrective': further sense experience itself tells us when a particular sense experience has induced us to make a mistake.

Perhaps anticipating this kind of criticism Descartes introduces the topic of dreams. 'Inside' a dream we have experiences which bear some resemblance to those of ordinary living, yet nothing real corresponds to the dream. Is Descartes's idea here that the whole of experience may be a dream? If so, once again we might use a distinction like the one we just made: perhaps we cannot distinguish immediately or 'at a glance' whether we are dreaming, but using our memory, we seem to have no trouble distinguishing past dreams from past encounters with reality.

Still, there is something troubling about the idea that all experience might be a dream. For how could we set about determining whether that is true? Sometimes people 'pinch themselves' to ensure that they are not dreaming. But is this really a good test? Might we not just dream that the pinch hurts? We might try from within a dream to discover whether it is a dream. Yet even if we think up some cunning experiment to determine whether it is, might we not just dream that we conduct it, or dream that it tells us the answer that we are awake?

We might try saying that events in everyday life exhibit a scale and a sheer coherence that dreams do not exhibit. Dreams are jerky and spasmodic. They have little or no rhyme or reason. Experience, on the other hand, is large and spacious and majestic. It goes on in regular ways—or at least we think it does. However, it is then open for Descartes to worry whether the scale and coherence is itself deceptive. That takes him to the Evil Demon, one of the most famous thought-experiments in the history of philosophy. It is a thought-experiment designed to alert us to the idea that, so far as truth goes, all our experience might be just like a dream: totally disconnected from the world.

It is important to seize on two things at the outset. First, Descartes is perfectly well aware that as active, living, human agents we do not bother ourselves about such an outlandish possibility. In fact, we cannot: as many philosophers have pointed out, it is psychologically impossible to keep doubt about the external world alive outside the study. But that does not matter. The doubt is worth bothering about because of the task he is engaged upon. This is the task of finding foundations of knowledge, of ensuring that his beliefs are built on a sound footing. Descartes's inquiry is made for purely intellectual reasons. Second, Descartes is not asking you to *believe* in the possibility of the Evil Demon. He is only asking you to consider it—en route to getting clear how to dismiss it. That is, he thinks (not unreasonably, surely?) that unless this possibility can be dismissed, there remains a challenge of *scepticism*: the possibility that we have no knowledge, but that all our beliefs are entirely delusive.

We can appreciate the thought-experiment by reminding ourselves how very 'realistic' a virtual reality can become. Here is an updated variant of the thought-experiment. Imagine an advance in science that enables a mad scientist to extract your brain, and then to maintain it in a vat of chemicals that sustain its normal functioning. Imagine that the scientist can deliver inputs to the normal information channels (the optic nerve, the nerves that transmit sensations of hearing and touch and taste). Being good-natured, the scientist gives information *as if* the brain were lodged in a normal body and living a reasonable life: eating, playing golf, or watching TV. There would be feedback, so that for instance if you deliver an 'output' equivalent to raising your hand, you get 'feedback' as if your hand had risen. The scientist has put you into a virtual reality, so your virtual hand rises. And, it seems, you would have no way of knowing that this had happened, since to you it would seem just as if a normal life was continuing.

Descartes's own version of the thought-experiment does not cite brains and vats. In fact, if you think about it, you will see that he does not need to do so. Our beliefs about the brain and its role in generating conscious experience are beliefs about the way the world works. So perhaps they too are the result of the Evil Demon's inputtings! Perhaps the Demon did not need to get his hands (?) dirty messing around in vats. He just inputs experiences in whatever way is made appropriate by the *real* reality. Brains and nerves themselves belong to the *virtual* reality.

This thought-experiment does not cite actual illusions of sense, or actual dreams. It simply sets experience as a whole against a very different and potentially disturbing reality. Notice as well that it is not obviously useful to argue against the Evil Demon hypothesis by citing the coherence and scale of everyday experience. For we do not know of any reason why the Demon could not input experience as coherent as he wishes, and of whatever scale or extent he wishes.

So how could we possibly rule out the Evil Demon hypothesis? Once it is raised, we seem to be powerless against it.

Yet, in this sea of doubt, just when things are at their darkest, Descartes finds one certain rock upon which he can perch. 'Cogito, ergo sum': I think, therefore I am. (A better translation is 'I am thinking, therefore I am'. Descartes's premise is not 'I think' in the sense of 'I ski', which can be true even if you are not at the moment skiing. It is supposed to be parallel to 'I am skiing'.)

Even if it is a virtual reality that I experience, still, it is I who experience it! And, apparently I know that it is I who have these experiences or thoughts (for Descartes, 'thinking' includes 'experiencing').

Why does this certainty remain? Look at it from the Demon's point of view. His project was to deceive *me* about everything. But it is not logically possible for him to deceive *me* into thinking that I exist when I do not. The Demon cannot simultaneously make both these things true:

> I think that I exist.
> I am wrong about whether I do.

Because if the first is true, then I exist to do the thinking. Therefore, I must be right about whether I exist. So long as I think that (or even think that I think it), then I exist.

I can think that I am skiing when I am not, for I may be dreaming, or deluded by the Demon. However, I cannot think that I am thinking when I am not. For in this case (and only this case) the mere fact that I think that I am thinking *guarantees* that I am thinking. It is itself an example of thinking.

THE ELUSIVE 'I'

Outside the context of the doubt, the 'I' that thinks is a *person* that can be described in various ways. In my case, I am a middle-aged professor of philosophy, with a certain personality, a history, a network of social relations, a family, and so on. But in the context of the doubt, all this is swept away: part of the virtual reality. So what is the 'I' that is left? It seems very shadowy—a pure subject of thought. It might not even have a body! This takes us to the next twist.

You might try peering into your own mind, as it were, to catch the essential 'you'. But, remembering that the 'you' (or the 'I', from your point of view) is here separated from normal marks of identity (your position in space, your body, your social relations, your history), it seems there is *nothing to catch*. You can become aware of your own experiences, but never, it seems, aware of the 'I' that is the subject of those experiences. Or you can try to imagine the self, to frame a picture of it, as it were. But as Descartes remarks, imagination seems good at framing pictures of things that have shape and size, and are found in space ('extended things'). The self that remains as the rock in the seas of doubt may not *be* an extended thing. For we can be certain of it when we are still uncertain about extended things, since we are taking seriously the possibility of the Evil Demon.

One reconstruction of this point of the argument presents Descartes thinking like this:

> I cannot doubt that I exist. I can doubt whether things extended in space ('bodies') exist. *Therefore,* I am not a body.

In a nutshell, souls are certain, bodies are doubtful, so the soul is distinct from the body. If this is Descartes's argument, then it is superficially plausible, but can be seen to be invalid. For consider the parallel:

> I cannot doubt that I am here in the room. I can doubt whether a person who will get bad news tomorrow is in the

room. *Therefore,* I am not a person who will get bad news tomorrow.

A nice proof with a welcome result! The fallacy is often called the 'masked man fallacy': I know who my father is; I do not know who the masked man is; *so,* my father is not the masked man.

I myself doubt if Descartes committed this fallacy, at least in this *Meditation.* At this point he is more concerned with the way in which we know *anything* about souls and bodies. He is not concerned to prove that they are distinct, but more concerned to show that knowledge of the self is not dependent upon knowledge of bodies. Because the one can be certain, even when the other is not. Nevertheless, what are we left really knowing about the self?

In the following century the German philosopher Georg Christoph Lichtenberg (1742–99) remarked: 'We should say, "it thinks" just as we say, "it thunders". Even to say "cogito" is too much, if we translate it with "I think".' (Lichtenberg liked pithy aphorisms, and was an important influence on a yet later figure, Friedrich Nietzsche [1844–1900].)

The idea is that the apparent reference to an 'I' as a 'thing' or subject of thought is itself an illusion. There is no 'it' that thunders: we could say instead just that thunder is going on. Similarly Lichtenberg is suggesting, at least in the context of the doubt, that Descartes is not entitled to an 'I' that is thinking. All he can properly claim is that 'there is a thought going on'.

This seems a very bizarre claim. For surely there cannot be a thought without someone thinking it? You cannot have thoughts floating round a room waiting, as it were, for someone to catch them, any more than you can have dents floating around waiting to latch onto a surface to be dented. We return to this in Chapter 4. But then why isn't Lichtenberg right? If Descartes cannot confront a self that is doing the thinking, cannot experience it, cannot imagine it, then why is he entitled to any kind of certainty that it exists? Indeed, what can it mean to say that it exists?

Descartes adroitly puts this problem to one side, by raising a parallel difficulty about 'things which people commonly think they understand most distinctly of all'—ordinary bodies, or things met with in space. This is what was aimed at by the ball of wax example. Here is a possible reconstruction of the argument:

> At a particular time, my senses inform me of a shape, colour, hardness, taste that belong to the wax. But at another time my senses inform me of a different shape etc. belonging to the wax. My senses show me *nothing but* these diverse qualities (which we can call 'sensory qualities', since our senses take them in). I nevertheless make a judgement of identity: it is the same piece of wax on the earlier and the later occasion. So, it is the nature of the ball of wax that it can possess different sensory qualities at different times. So, to understand what the wax *is* I must use my understanding, not my senses.

If this is a good reconstruction, we should notice that Descartes is not denying that it is by means of the senses that I know that the wax is there in the first place (assuming we have got rid of the Evil Demon, and are back to trusting our senses). In fact, he goes on to say as much. Rather, he is suggesting that the senses are like *messengers* that deliver information that needs *interpreting*. And this interpretation, which is here a question of identifying the one object amongst the many successive appearances, is the work of the understanding. It is a matter of employing principles of classification, or categories, whose credentials we can also investigate.

So, all we can understand by the wax is that it is some elusive 'thing' that can take on different bodily properties, such as shape, size, colour, taste. And we understand by the self, the 'I', just some equally elusive 'thing' that at different times thinks different thoughts. So maybe the self should not be regarded as especially mysterious, compared with everyday things like the ball of wax. Perhaps selves are no harder to understand than bodies, and we only think otherwise because of some kind of prejudice. We return to the wax in Chapter 7.

CLEAR AND DISTINCT IDEAS

The first two *Meditations* deserve their place as classics of philosophy. They combine depth, imagination, and rigour, to an extent that has very seldom been paralleled. So one is left with bated breath, waiting for the story to unfold. Here is Descartes left perching on his one minute rock, surrounded by a sea of doubt. But it seems he has denied himself any way of getting off it. Life may still be a dream. To use the metaphor of foundations: he is down to bedrock, but has no building materials. For the very standards he set himself, of 'demon-proof' knowledge, seem to forbid him even from using 'self-evident' or natural means of reasoning, in order to argue that he knows more than the Cogito. There is nothing difficult about the Demon deceiving us into listening to delusive pieces of reasoning. Our reasonings are apt to be even more fallible than our senses.

Curiously, he does not see it quite like that. What he does is to reflect on the Cogito, and ask what makes it so especially certain. He convinces himself that it is because he has an especially transparent 'clear and distinct' perception of its truth. It is generally agreed that Descartes, the mathematician, had a mathematical model of clarity in mind. Suppose, for instance, you think about a circle. Imagine a diameter, and draw chords from the opposite ends to a point on the circumference. They meet at a right angle. Draw others, and they always seem to do so. At this point, you might have a not very clear sense that perhaps there is a reason for this. But now, suppose you go through a proof (drawing the line from the centre of the circle to the apex of the triangle, and solving the two triangles you create). After that you can just *see* that the theorem *has* to hold. This may come as a 'flash': a blinding certainty, or insight into this particular piece of geometrical truth. This is just a random geometrical example of a procedure that can make you 'see' something that you might only dimly have grasped. But if only we could see the rest of reality, mind, body, God, freedom, human life, with the same rush of clarity and understanding! Well, one philosophical ideal is that we can. This is the ideal of *rationalism*: the power of pure unaided reason. For the rationalist can see from her armchair that things must be one way and cannot be other ways, like the angle in the semicircle. Knowledge achieved by this kind of rational insight is known as 'a priori': it can be seen to be true immediately, without any experience of the way of the world.

THE TRADEMARK ARGUMENT

Trusting clarity and distinctness, Descartes indulges a piece of reasoning. Looking into his own 'self', which is all that he has at this point, Descartes discovers that he has an idea of perfection. He then argues that such an idea implies a cause. However, the thing that caused it must have as much 'reality', and that includes perfection, as the idea itself. This implies that only a perfect cause, that is, God, will do. Hence God exists, and has left the idea of perfection as an innate sign of his workmanship in our minds, like a craftsman leaving a trademark stamped in his work.

Once Descartes has discovered God, the seas of doubt subside in a rush. For since God is perfect, he is no deceiver: deceiving is clearly falling short of goodness, let alone perfection. Hence, if we do our stuff properly, we can be sure that we will not be the victims of illusion. The world will be as we understand it to be. Doing our stuff properly mainly means trusting only clear and distinct ideas.

What are we to make of the 'trademark' argument? Here is a reconstruction:

> I have the idea of a perfect being. This idea must have a cause. A cause must be at least as perfect as its effect. So something at least as perfect as my idea caused it. Therefore such a thing exists. But that thing must be perfect, that is, God.

Suppose we grant Descartes the idea mentioned in the first premise. (There are theological traditions that would not even do that. They would say that God's perfection defies understanding, so that we have no idea of it, or him.) Still, why is he entitled to the premise that his idea must have a cause? Might not there be events that have simply no cause? Events that, as we might say, 'just happen'? After all, sitting on his rock, Descartes cannot appeal to any normal, scientific, experience. In his bare metaphysical solitude, how can he deny that events might just happen? And if he thinks the contrary, shouldn't he then worry whether the Demon might be working on him, making him think this although it is not true?

However, it gets worse when we arrive at the next step. Consider my idea of someone who is perfectly punctual. Does this need a perfectly punctual cause? Surely a better thing to think would be this. I can simply define what it is for someone to be perfectly punctual. It means that they are never late (or perhaps, never early and never late). To understand what it would be for someone to be like that, I do not have to have come across such a person. I can describe them in advance. I understand what condition they have to satisfy without any such acquaintance, and indeed even if nobody is ever like that.

Probably Descartes would reject the analogy. Perhaps he thinks of it more like this. Do I have an idea of a perfect mathematician? Well, I can start by thinking of a mathematician as one who never makes mistakes. But that is hardly adequate. A perfect mathematician would be imaginative and inventive as well. Now, with my very limited knowledge of mathematics, I only have a very confused understanding of what that would be like. In general, I cannot clearly comprehend or understand inventions before they come along— otherwise, I would be making the inventions myself! So perhaps it would take a perfect mathematician to give me a good idea (a 'clear and distinct' idea) of what a perfect mathematician would be like.

Well, perhaps; but now it becomes doubtful whether I do have a clear and distinct idea of a perfect mathematician, and analogously, of a perfect being. Generally, what happens if I frame this idea is that I think more as I did when thinking of someone perfectly punctual. I think of an agent who never makes mistakes, never behaves unkindly, never finds things he cannot do, and so on. I might add in imagination something like a kind of glow, but it is clear that this will not help. It surely seems presumptuous, or even blasphemous, to allow myself a complete, clear, comprehension of God's attributes.

In fact, elsewhere in his writings Descartes gives a rather lovely analogy, but one which threatens to undermine the trademark argument:

> [W]e can touch a mountain with our hands but we cannot put our arms around it as we could put them around a tree or something else not too large for them. To grasp something is to embrace it in one's thought; to know something it is sufficient to touch it with one's thought.

Perhaps we can only touch God's supposed qualities by way of definition, but cannot comprehend them. In that case we cannot argue back to an ideal or archetype that enabled us to comprehend them.

So, the trademark argument is one that strikes most of us as far from demon-proof—so far, in fact, that it seems pretty easy to resist even if we are not at all in the grip of extreme doubt. At this point some suppressed premises suggested by the history of ideas may be used to excuse Descartes. He was undoubtedly more optimistic about the trademark argument than we can be because he inherited a number of ideas from previous philosophical traditions. One very important one is that genuine causation is a matter of the cause *passing on* something to an effect. Causation is like passing the baton in a relay race. So, for example, it takes heat to make something hot, or movement to induce motion. This is a principle that surfaces again and again in the history of philosophy, and we shall encounter it more than once. Here it disposed Descartes to think that the 'perfection' in his idea needed to be secreted into it, as it were, by a perfect cause.

But this principle about causation is scarcely demon-proof. In fact, it is not even true. We have become familiar with causes that bear no resemblance to their effects. The movement of a piece of iron in a magnetic field bears no resemblance to an electric current, but that is what it causes. In fact, it seems as though Descartes (once more influenced by ideas from previous philosophical traditions) may have slipped into thinking that an idea of X actually shares X. So an idea of infinity, for instance, would be an infinite idea. (Would an idea of something solid be a solid idea?) Similarly an idea of perfection would be a perfect idea, and would require a perfect cause. But again, it might be the Demon that makes you think any such thing, and again there is no good reason to follow him.

THE CARTESIAN CIRCLE

Descartes convinced himself that the argument was good: every step in it was 'clear and distinct'. So now he has God, and God is no deceiver. Still, remember that to do this he had to trust his clear and distinct ideas as sources of truth. Nevertheless, isn't there an awful hole in his procedure? What happened to the Demon? Might not even our clear and distinct ideas lead us astray? To close off this possibility, it seems, Descartes turns round and uses God—the God whose existence he has just proved—as the guarantor that what we perceive clearly and distinctly must be true.

It was one of his contemporaries, Antoine Arnauld (1612–94), who cried 'foul' most loudly at this point, accusing Descartes of arguing in a circle, the infamous 'Cartesian circle'. Descartes seems committed to two different priorities. Consider the view that if we clearly and distinctly perceive some proposition p, then it is true that p. Let us abbreviate this to ($CDp \rightarrow Tp$), reading that if p is clear and distinct ('CD'), then it is true ('T'). And suppose we symbolize 'God exists and does not deceive us' by 'G'. Then the circle is that at some points it seems that Descartes holds: I can know that ($CDp \rightarrow Tp$) only if I *first* know G. But at other points he holds: I can know that G only if I *first* know ($CDp \rightarrow Tp$). It is like the familiar impasse in the morning, when you need to have some coffee to get out of bed, and you need to get out of bed to fix the coffee.

One or the other has to come first. There is a whole literature trying to understand whether Descartes actually falls into this trap. Some commentators cite passages in which it seems that he does not really hold the first. The major suggestion is that G is necessary only to validate *memory* of proofs. So while you actually clearly and distinctly perceive something, you do not need to trust anything at all, even G, to be entitled to assert its truth. But later, when you have forgotten the proof, only G underwrites your title to say that you once proved it, so it must be true.

Other commentators suggest that Descartes does not need the second. He sees that God exists, clearly and distinctly, but does not need a general rule, of the kind $(CDp \rightarrow Tp)$, to underwrite this perception. He can be certain of this instance of the rule, without being sure about the rule itself. This is itself an interesting form of suggestion, and introduces a very important truth, which is that very often we are more certain of particular verdicts than we are of the principles that we might cite when we try to defend them. For example, I might know that a particular sentence is grammatical, without being sure of any general rule of grammar that allows it. Philosophers have often been rather hard on this possibility. The admired character Socrates, in Plato's *Dialogues*, is infuriatingly fond of getting his stooges to say something, showing that they cannot defend it by articulate general principles, and concluding that they didn't really have any right to claim what they did. However, the case of grammatical knowledge suggests that this is a bad inference. Consider as well how in perception, I may recognize something as a Pomeranian, or a member of the Rolling Stones, or my wife, without knowing any general principles that 'justify' the verdict. My perceptual system may operate according to some general principles or 'algorithms' for translating visual input into verdicts, but I have no idea what they are. So I couldn't answer a Socrates who asked for general principles underlying my recognition. I could only flounder and splutter. But I recognize the Pomeranian, or Rolling Stone, or my wife, for all that. Socrates' procedure is only apt to give philosophers a bad name.

Still, we are bound to ask *why* Descartes thinks he can be certain of this instance of the rule. Why is his 'seeing' that God exists clearly and distinctly also a clear and distinct case of seeing the truth? Some of us may have the dark suspicion that it is because mention of God clouds the mind rather than clarifying it.

For our purposes, we can leave this issue. What remains clear is that there is a distinct whiff of double standards here. The kind of sceptical problem embodied in the Evil Demon is somehow quietly forgotten, while Descartes tries to engineer his way off the lonely rock of the Cogito. And this might suggest that he has put himself on a desert island from which there is no escape.

FOUNDATIONS AND WEBS

The great Scottish thinker David Hume (1711–76) criticized Descartes like this:

> There is a species of scepticism, antecedent to all study and philosophy, which is much inculcated by Descartes and others, as a sovereign preservative against error and precipitate judgment. It recommends an universal doubt, not only of all our former opinions and principles, but also of our very faculties; of whose veracity, say they, we must assure ourselves, by a chain of reasoning, deduced from some original principle, which cannot possibly be fallacious or deceitful. But neither is there any such original principle, which has a prerogative above others, that are self-evident and convincing: Or if there were, could we advance a step beyond it, but by the use of those very faculties, of which we are supposed to be already diffident. The Cartesian doubt, therefore, were it ever possible to be attained by any human creature (as it plainly is not) would

> *be entirely incurable; and no reasoning could ever bring us to*
> *a state of assurance and conviction upon any subject.*

If Descartes's project is to use reason to fend off universal doubt about the truthfulness of reason, then it has to fail.

Hume's challenge seems convincing. It looks as though Descartes was doomed to failure. So what should be the outcome? General scepticism, meaning pessimism about whether there is any harmony at all between the way we believe things to be and the way they are? Or something else? Other possibilities need introduction.

One way of thinking—Hume's own—accepts the view that our system of belief needs some kind of foundation. However, it denies that that foundation could have the kind of rational status that Descartes wanted. The veracity (truthfulness) of our senses and reasonings is itself *part* of the foundation. It cannot itself be demonstrated by standing on some *other* 'original principle'. For all of us, outside the philosophical study, it comes naturally to trust our common experience. We grow up doing so, and as we grow up we become good at recognizing danger areas (illusions, mirages) against the background of natural beliefs we all form. The self-corrective nature of our systems of belief, mentioned above, is all we need. We could call this approach non-rational or *natural* foundationalism. (Not of course implying that there is anything *irrational* about it. It is just that the things in the foundation do not have the demon-proof way of 'standing to reason' that Descartes had hoped for.) Hume himself gave a number of arguments for side-lining any appeal to rationality, and we visit some of them in due course.

The emphasis on natural ways of forming belief chimes in with another strand in Hume and other British philosophers of the seventeenth and eighteenth centuries, which is their distrust of the power of unaided reason. For these philosophers, the best contact between mind and the world is not the point at which a mathematical proof crystallizes, but the point at which you see and touch a familiar object. Their paradigm was knowledge by sense experience rather than by reason. Because of this, they are labelled *empiricists*, whereas Descartes is a card-carrying *rationalist*. The labels, however, conceal a lot of important detail. For example, at some points when he gets under pressure, Descartes himself appears to say that the really good thing about clear and distinct ideas is that you can't doubt them when you have them. This is not really a certification by reason, so much as the very same kind of natural potency that Hume himself attaches to basic empirical beliefs. And soon we visit an area where the champion of British empiricism, John Locke (1632–1704), is as rationalist as the best of them. Great philosophers have a disturbing habit of resisting labelling.

On this view, Descartes's problem was that he relied too much on the powers of reason. Instead, we can appeal to nature, here meaning our natural propensities to form beliefs and to correct them. And what of the Evil Demon? On this story, the true moral of Descartes's struggles is that if we raise the question whether our experience and reasoning (en bloc) accords with the way the world is (en bloc), it will take an act of faith to settle it. 'God' simply labels whatever it is that ensures this harmony between belief and the world. But, as Hume says in the passage just quoted, we do not find a need to raise this question in normal life. The hyperbolic doubt, and the answer to it, is in this sense unreal.

This may sound sensible, or it may just sound complacent. But to blunt the charge of complacency, we can at least notice this. Regarding the doubt as unreal does not have to mean that we simply turn our backs on the problem of harmony between appearance and reality: how we think and how things are. We can approach it from *within* our normal framework of beliefs. In fact, when Hume himself approached it in this way, he became overwhelmed by difficulties in our ordinary ways of thinking about things: difficulties strong enough to reintroduce scepticism about our ability to know anything about the world. This is the topic of Chapter 7.

However, one piece of optimism is available to us, two centuries later. We might thus suppose that evolution, which is presumably responsible for the fact that we have our senses and our reasoning capacities, would not have selected for them (in the shape in which we have them) had they not *worked*. If our eyesight, for example, did not inform us of predators, food, or mates just when predators, food, and mates are about, it would be of no use to us. So it is built to get these things right. The harmony between our minds and the world is due to the fact that the world is responsible for our minds. Their function is to represent it so that we can meet our needs; if they were built to represent it in any way other than the true way, we could not survive. This is not an argument designed to do away with the Evil Demon. It is an argument that appeals to things we take ourselves to know about the world. Unfortunately, we have to visit in time the area of Hume's doubts, where things we take ourselves to know about the world also serve to make that knowledge seem doubtful.

A rather different response shrugs off the need for any kind of 'foundations', whether certified by reason, as Descartes hoped, or merely natural, as in Hume. This approach goes back to emphasizing instead the *coherent structure* of our everyday system of beliefs: the way they hang together, whereas the sporadic experiences or beliefs we get in dreams are fragmentary and incoherent. It then points out an interesting feature of coherent structures, namely that they do not need foundations. A ship or a web may be made up of a tissue of interconnecting parts, and it derives its strength from just those interconnections. It does not need a 'base' or a 'starting point' or 'foundation'. A structure of this kind can have each bit supported by other bits without there being any bit that supports all the others without support itself. Similarly, if any one belief is challenged, others can support it, unless, of course, it turns out that nothing else supports it, in which case it should be dropped. The Austrian philosopher Otto Neurath (1882–1945) used this lovely metaphor for our body of knowledge:

> We are like sailors who on the open sea must reconstruct their
> ship but are never able to start afresh from the bottom.

Any part can be replaced, provided there is enough of the rest on which to stand. But the whole structure cannot be challenged en bloc, and if we try to do so, we find ourselves on Descartes's lonely rock.

This approach is usually called 'coherentism'. Its motto is that while every argument needs premises, there is nothing that is the premise of every argument. There is no foundation on which everything rests. Coherentism is nice in one way, but dissatisfying in another. It is nice in what it does away with, namely the elusive foundations. It is, however, not clear that it offers us enough to replace them. This is because we seemed able to understand the possibility represented by the Evil Demon—that our system of belief should be extensive and coherent and interlocking, but all completely wrong. As I said in the introduction to this chapter, even as children we fall naturally into wondering whether all experience might be a dream. We might sympathize with Descartes's thought that if the options are coherentism or scepticism, the more honest option would be scepticism.

It is good, then, to remember four options in epistemology (the theory of knowledge). There is rational foundationalism, as attempted by Descartes. There is natural foundationalism, as attempted in Hume. There is coherentism. And brooding over all of them, there is scepticism, or the view that there is no knowledge. Each of these has had distinguished defenders. Whichever the reader prefers, he or she will find good philosophical company. One might think that Descartes got almost everything right, or that he got almost everything wrong. The baffling thing is to defend whichever answer commends itself.

LOCAL SCEPTICISMS

Scepticism can be raised in particular areas, as well as in the global fashion of Descartes. Someone might be convinced that we have, say, scientific knowledge, but be very doubtful about knowledge in ethics or politics or literary criticism. We find particular areas shortly where it does not take hyperbolic doubt, only a bit of caution, for us to become insecure. However, there are other nice examples of highly general areas where scepticism is baffling. The philosopher Bertrand Russell (1872–1970) considered the example of time. How do I know that the world did not come into existence a very few moments ago, but complete with delusive traces of a much greater age? Those traces would include, of course, the modifications of the brain that give us what we take to be memories. They would also include all the other things that we interpret as signs of great age. In fact, Victorian thinkers struggling to reconcile the biblical account of the history of the world with the fossil record had already suggested much the same thing about geology. On this account, around 4,000 years ago God laid down all the misleading evidence that the earth is about 4,000 million years old (and, we can now add, misleading signs that the universe is about 13,000 million years old). This was never a popular move, probably because if you are sceptical about time, you quickly become sceptical about everything, or maybe because it presents God as something like a large-scale practical joker. Russell's possibility sounds almost as far-fetched as Descartes's Evil Demon.

However, there is one highly intriguing thing about Russell's scenario. This is that it can actually be argued to be scientifically more *probable* than the alternative we all believe in! This is because science tells us that 'low-entropy' or, in other words, highly ordered systems are more improbable. In addition, as physical systems like the cosmos evolve, entropy or disorder increases. The smoke never returns into the cigarette; the toothpaste never goes back into the tube. The extraordinary thing is that there was ever *enough* order in things for the smoke to be in the cigarette or the toothpaste to be in the tube in the first place. So, one might argue, it is 'easier' for a moderately disordered world, such as the world is now, to come into existence, than it is for any lower-entropy, more orderly ancestor. Intuitively, it is as if there are more ways this can happen, just as there are more ways you can get four-letter or five-letter words in an initial hand of seven letters in Scrabble, than there are in which you can get a seven-letter word. It is much more probable that you get a four-letter word than a seven-letter word. Similarly, the argument goes, it is as if God or Nature had less to do, to make the world as it is today out of nothing, than to make the lower-entropy world as it is supposed to have been some thirteen billion years ago out of nothing. Therefore, it is more probable that it happened like that. In a straight competition for probability between Russell's outlandish hypothesis and common sense, Russell wins. I leave this for the reader to ponder.

THE MORAL

How then should we regard knowledge? Knowledge implies *authority*: the people who know are the people to whom we should listen. It implies reliability: the people who know are those who are reliable at registering the truth, like good instruments. To *claim* knowledge implies claiming a sense of our own reliability. And to *accord* authority to someone or some method involves seeing it as reliable. The unsettling scenarios of a Descartes or a Russell unseat our sense of our own reliability. Once we have raised the outlandish possibilities, our sense of a reliable connection between the way things are and the ways we take them to be goes dim. We could regain it, if we could argue that the scenarios are either impossible, or at least have no real chance of being the way things are. The difficulty is that it is hard to show them to be impossible, and in these abstract realms we have no very good sense of probabilities or chances. So it is difficult to argue that they have no chance of being true without relying on the very opinions that they query. Hence, scepticism permanently beckons, or threatens, us. We *may* be tracking the world reliably, but we may not. To revert to the engineering analogy I used in the Introduction, the structure of our thought seems to span large gaps: here, the gap between how things appear and how they might be. We hand ourselves the right to cross those gaps. But if we do this trailing no very good sense of our own reliability or harmony with the truth, then that right seems ill-founded. And this is what the sceptic insists upon. Any confidence in a harmony between the way we take things to be, and the way they are, will seem to be a pure act of faith.

Descartes left us with a problem of knowledge. He also left us with severe problems in understanding the place of our minds in nature. And finally the entire scientific revolution of which he was such a distinguished parent left us with profound problems of understanding the world in which we are placed. We have seen something of the problem of knowledge. The next chapter turns to problems of mind.

CHAPTER TWO

Mind

SUPPOSE WE PUT ON ONE SIDE the general problem of harmony between the way we take the world to be and the way the world is. We shall keep our fingers crossed, supposing that we do really know what we naturally take ourselves to know. But how well do our views hang together? Descartes left us with our own selves and our own minds as special, intimate, objects of immediate knowledge. Or rather, each of us is left with his or her own mind as a special, intimate, object of immediate knowledge. For even if I can climb out of the seas of doubt onto the Cogito, I cannot climb out onto the nature of *your* mind. So how then do I know anything about your mental life? How do I know, for instance, that you see the colour blue the way that I do? Might it be that some of us feel pain more, but make less fuss about it, or that others feel pain less, but make more fuss? How do we begin to think about mind and body, brains and behaviour?

THE GHOST IN THE MACHINE

We have seen how Descartes's strategy led him to regard knowledge of our own minds as more secure and certain than knowledge of the rest of the world. But Descartes was also a scientist. He made foundational discoveries in optics. He practised dissections, and knew a fair amount about the transmission of impulses through the nerves to the brain. He knew this took place by means of a physical transmission, a 'pull' or 'violent motion' of the nerves, or as we would now think, an electrochemical impulse transmitted through the nervous system. The ordinary senses of sight, touch, taste, smell, and hearing activate the nervous system, which transmits messages to the brain. The brain is not, of course, an undifferentiated lump. Bits of the brain transmit signals to other parts of the brain and back to the body: whole patterns of activation get set up. All this is part of neurophysiology. These events can in principle be seen in public: with the right instruments, the patterns of activation can be shown to a classroom.

And then what?

Well, then there is the magic moment. The 'mind' (the thinking thing, or 'res cogitans') gets affected as well, and the whole world of experience opens up. The subject sees colours, hears sounds, feels textures and temperatures, and has sensations of taste and smell. This world of experience is composed of mental events or events within subjective consciousness. These events in the subject's consciousness cannot be seen in public. They are private. The whole classroom may see some neurones firing, but only the one person feels the pain. Descartes actually located the place where the magical event takes place. For quite sensible neurophysiological reasons he thought that the pineal gland, a structure lying centrally within the brain, must be the place where messages were conducted from the realm of physics to the realm of the mental.

For Descartes it is not only that mental events are distinct from physical events. They also belong to a distinct kind of substance— immaterial substance—a kind of ghost-stuff or ectoplasm. Strictly speaking if I say, 'I thought of the Queen and I saluted,' there is a kind of ambiguity: the 'I' that is the subject of the thought is not the 'I', the body, that salutes. Thoughts and experiences are modifications in one kind of stuff; movement and position belongs to the other. This part of Descartes's doctrine marks him as a 'substance dualist'. It is not just that there are two kinds of properties (mental properties and physical properties) and that persons can have both. It is that there are two kinds of bearers of properties as well. Of course this is theologically convenient: it opens the way to the immortality of the soul, since there is no reason for soul-stuff to have the same life span as anything like a physical body. But substance dualism is not compulsory. One could hold that mental and physical properties are very different but that the one organized body has them both—after all, mass and velocity are two very different kinds of property, but projectiles have them both. People who hold that there are two kinds of property (mental and physical) but that they can belong to the one kind of stuff (whatever large animals are made of) are called property dualists.

Descartes leads us to the view neatly summed up by Gilbert Ryle (1900–76) as holding that the human being is a 'ghost in a machine'.

Events in the machine, the physical body, are like other events in the physical world. They consist in the interactions of familiar kinds of stuff: molecules and atoms, electrical fields and forces. Events in the ghostly part, the mind, are altogether different. Perhaps they are events in some kind of ghost-stuff—ectoplasm, or the non-physical stuff that spirits and angels are made of. Spirits and angels do without the physical embodiment altogether, in the popular mind. But in the normal human being there is a close correlation between events of the one kind and those of the other: sticking a pin in someone makes physical changes, but it also cause a mental event of feeling pain. And vice versa: the mental event of remembering a blunder may cause physical events such as groaning and blushing. So events in the one realm may affect those in the other. But in principle the two realms are entirely distinct.

ZOMBIES AND MUTANTS

Of course, this view is not peculiar to Descartes. It is the view presupposed by many of the world's great religions: it is part of any doctrine holding that we can survive bodily death, or that our soul can go one way while our body goes another. Yet it is a view that faces enormous, and arguably insurmountable, problems.

The first family of problems is epistemological. I just said that in the normal human being there is a close correlation between events of the one kind and those of the other. But how are we entitled to believe that? Here is one way things might be:

The Zombie Possibility. Zombies look like you and me, and behave like you and me. Their physical natures are indistinguishable. If you opened a Zombie brain, you would find that it functions exactly the same way as your brain or mine. If you prick a Zombie, he or she will go 'ouch', just like you or me. *But* Zombies are not conscious. There is no ghost within.

Because Zombies look and behave just like you and me, there is no way of telling which of us are Zombies and which are conscious in the way that you and I are. Or at any rate, in the way that I am. For now I have raised the Zombie possibility, I see that I can't really be sure about you or anyone else. Perhaps consciousness is an extremely rare correlate of a complex system of brain and body. Perhaps I am the only example of it: perhaps the rest of you are all Zombies.

Here is another way things might be:

The Mutant Possibility. Mutants look like you and me, and behave like you and me. Their physical natures are indistinguishable. If you opened a Mutant brain, you would find that it functions exactly the same way as your brain or mine. If you prick a Mutant, he or she will go 'ouch', just like you or me.

Unlike Zombies, Mutants are conscious. There is a ghost within. But the events in the Mutant ghost are not like those we expect. A Mutant who is pricked, for instance, may experience a mental event like hearing middle C on a clarinet. She still goes 'ouch', for, since her brain functions like ours and she behaves like us, being pricked with a pin starts processes that cause changes that eventually end up with her saying 'ouch', just like the rest of us. Perhaps when she does instead hear middle C on a clarinet, she feels awful pain, but it only makes her smile beatifically. A Mutant who sees British post-boxes may see them as yellow; one who sees daffodils may see them as blue. Events in the Mutant's consciousness bear no relation to the events in your mind or mine. Or at any rate, no relation to the events in my mind. For now I have raised the Mutant possibility, I see that I can't really be sure about you or anyone else. Perhaps the rest of you are all Mutants, compared with me.

The point about these possibilities is that they seem to be wide open, on the Cartesian dualist account of mind and body. They are unnerving possibilities, and ones we do not normally consider (although I suspect that they cross our minds *more* often than the outlandish possibilities of the first chapter).

One way to react to them is to bite the bullet. You might say: all right, let us suppose these are wide-open possibilities. Perhaps I can never really know what the mind of another person is like, what mental events occur within it, or even whether there is any mental life going on at all. But can't I still *suppose* that other people's mental lives are much like mine? Can't I reasonably use myself as a model for all the rest? It would be not so much a case of *knowledge* as of a hypothesis or *conjecture*, but it perhaps it is a *reasonable* conjecture to make. This is called the argument from analogy to the existence of other minds.

The problem with this argument is that it seems incredibly weak. As the great Austrian philosopher Ludwig Wittgenstein (1889–1951) dismissively asked: 'And how can I generalize the *one* case so irresponsibly?' The mere fact that in *one* case—my own—

perhaps as luck has it, there is a mental life of a particular, definite kind, associated with a brain and a body, seems to be very flimsy ground for supposing that there is just the same association in all the other cases. If I have a box and it has a beetle in it, that gives me only very poor grounds for supposing that everyone else with a box has a beetle in it as well.

Perhaps worse, it gives me very poor grounds for denying that there are beetles anywhere else than in boxes. Maybe then things that are very *different* from you and me physically are conscious in just the way that I am: rocks or flowers, for example.

You might be inclined just to 'shrug off' the Zombie and Mutant possibilities. You might reflect that they are pieces of philosophical fantasy, unreal or at any rate unverifiable. But that is not an intelligent reaction. The possibilities are indeed unverifiable. Neurophysiologists, for instance, cannot find conscious experience in the way they can find neurones and synapses and patterns of brain activity—as we put it, they cannot display it on the screen to their students in the lecture theatre. But then, on Cartesian dualism, the possibilities we all naturally believe in, namely that other people are *not* Zombies, and *not* Mutants, are *themselves* unverifiable! They amount to blind articles of faith. Someone holding the Zombie possibility is no worse off than the rest of us in that respect.

In fact, if our conception of mind allows the Zombie and Mutant possibilities, we might even suppose them quite probable, or at least as probable as anything else. For if it is not a priori false that other people are Zombies, why should it be a priori less probable than that they are conscious like me?

Why do philosophers talk so much about bizarre possibilities that other people happily ignore (one of the things that gives the subject a forbidding look and a bad name)? The reason is that the possibilities are used to test a conception of how things are. Here they are being used to test the conception of mind and matter that gives rise to them. The argument is that *if* mind and matter are thought of in the Cartesian way, *then* there would be wide-open possibilities of a bizarre kind, about which we could know nothing. *So*, since this is intolerable, we should rethink the conception of how things are (this is called the metaphysics). A better conception of mind and its place in nature should foreclose these possibilities. The aim is not to wallow in scepticism, but to draw back from any philosophy that opens up the sceptical possibilities. We would say: according to Cartesian dualism the Zombie possibility and the Mutant possibility are both wide open. But that just shows there is something wrong about Cartesian dualism. The mental and the physical just aren't as distinct as it is claiming. Because it really is *not* possible that (say) someone who has just stubbed their toe and is howling with pain is doing so *because* they are in a mental state like that which I get into by hearing middle C on a clarinet. *That* mental state just cannot be expressed by howling or groaning. The tie between the intrinsic nature of the mental state—what it feels like—and its expression is closer than that. We *know* that someone who has just stubbed their toe is *not* howling because they have an experience just like the one I have when I hear middle C on a clarinet. We know that they are experiencing something very like what I experience when I stub my toe.

The argument from analogy to other minds was the particular target of Wittgenstein. Wittgenstein's main objection to the 'argument from analogy' is not simply that it is so weak. He tries to show that if you learned about mental events entirely from your own case, it would not be possible for you even to think in terms of other peoples' consciousness at all. It would be as if, were I to drop a brick on your toe, there is simply no pain about—I feel none— and that is the end of it. But since we *do* think in terms of other minds and their experiences, we have to conceptualize them some other way.

On this account, the way forward is to reject the picture of mind and body given to us by Cartesian dualism. And we should be encouraged to reject Cartesian dualism by *metaphysical* as well as *epistemological* pressures. Can we really get a possible picture of how the world is from Cartesian dualism, never mind about whether we know it is like that? Consider the Zombie again. His physical functioning is identical with ours. He responds to the world in the same way. His projects succeed or fail in the same way: his health depends on the same variables as ours. He may laugh at the right places, and weep at appropriate tragedies. He may be good fun to be with. So what is the lack of consciousness *doing*? Or, putting it the other way round, what is consciousness supposedly *doing* for us? Are we to conclude that in us, non-Zombies, mental events exist but do not *do* anything? Is consciousness like the whistle on the engine: no part of the machinery that makes things happen? (This is the doctrine known as epiphenomenalism.) But if minds do not do anything, why did they evolve? Why did nature go in for them? And if mental states really don't do anything, how do they enter memory, for example?

This is the problem of brain–mind interaction, as it presents itself to Cartesian dualism.

LOCKE AND LEIBNIZ AND GOD'S GOOD PLEASURE

The issue here is beautifully summed up in a debate between John Locke and his contemporary, the great mathematician and philosopher Gottfried Wilhelm Leibniz (1646–1716). Locke was another seventeenth-century thinker who worried about the implications of the modern scientific view of the world. In particular, he worried about the point of causation, at which the motions of particles in the brain give rise to ideas, such as those of colour, in the mind. In the following passage he is talking of the way in which bombardments of small atomic particles give rise to things like smells, tastes, sounds, and colours:

> Let us suppose at present, that the different motions and figures, bulk, and number of such particles, affecting the several organs of our senses, produce in us those different sensations, which we have from the colours and smells of bodies, v.g. that a violet, by the impulse of such insensible particles of matter of peculiar figures, and bulks, and in different degrees and modifications of their motions, causes the ideas of the blue colour, and sweet scent of that flower to be produced in our minds. It being no more impossible, to conceive, that God should annex such ideas to such motions, with which they have no similitude; than that he should annex the idea of pain to the motion

*of a piece of steel dividing our flesh, with which that idea hath
no resemblance.*

Locke shared the view we have already met in Newton and
Descartes, that some causal processes were relatively intelligible,
notably those in which one quality, like motion, is passed on from
one particle to another by impact. But the moment of body-to-
mind causation, in which motions in the brain produce something
entirely different, the sensations of smell or colour, or pain, was entirely obscure. It is just an amazing fact that the mental events
occur when they do. It is due to what Locke elsewhere calls the 'arbitrary will and good pleasure' of God, 'the wise architect' who 'an-
nexes' particular modifications of consciousness to particular
physical events. In Descartes's terms, Locke thinks we have no 'clear
and distinct' idea of just what kinds of system God might choose as
suitable places for him to superadd consciousness. It would just be
a brute fact that the universe is organized so that some kinds of system do, and others do not, possess consciousness at all. And it is
just a brute fact that their consciousnesses change and acquire definite properties at the time that their physical selves change and acquire particular properties. The contrast is between a rational and
intelligible connection, such as we find in the a priori discipline of
mathematics, and the fact that certain 'motions' just do produce
the sensations in us that they do. This is the brute fact, the consequence of God's good pleasure.

Actually Locke is not so far here from the doctrine known as *oc-
casionalism*, which was embraced by another contemporary,
Nicolas Malebranche (1638–1715). According to this, physical

events do not strictly cause or bring about mental events at all. Rather, they provide the occasions upon which God himself inserts mental events of appropriate kinds into our biographies. Strictly speaking, our bodies do not affect our minds, but only provide occasions on which God does. Locke himself does not say this, but we might reflect that there is precious little difference between, on the one hand, God intervening at his good pleasure to make it that the dividing of the flesh by the steel brings about a sensation of pain, and, on the other hand, God directly injecting a sensation of pain into the soul whenever there is a dividing of flesh by the steel.

Locke's doctrine deeply upset Leibniz. In the following passage from his *New Essays*, which are a blow-by-blow commentary on Locke, Philalethes is Locke's spokesman, and Theophilus is Leibniz's. Note the direct quotation from the passage from Locke above:

> PHILALETHES. *Now, when certain particles strike our organs in various ways they cause in us certain sensations of colours or of tastes, or of other secondary qualities which have the power to produce those sensations. 'It being no more impossible, to conceive, that God should annex such ideas [as that of heat] to such motions, with which they have no similitude; than that he should annex the idea of pain to the motion of a piece of steel dividing our flesh, with which that idea hath no resemblance.'*
>
> THEOPHILUS. *It must not be thought that ideas such as those of colour and pain are arbitrary and that between them and their causes there is no relation or natural connection: it is not God's way to act in such an unruly and unreasoned fashion. I would say, rather, that there is a resemblance of a kind—not a*

perfect one which holds all the way through, but a resemblance in which one thing expresses another through some orderly relationship between them. Thus an ellipse, and even a parabola or hyperbola, has some resemblance to the circle of which it is a projection on a plane, since then there is a certain precise and natural relationship between what is projected and the projection which is made from it, with each point on the one corresponding through a certain relation with a point on the other. This is something which the Cartesians have overlooked; and on this occasion, sir, you have deferred to them more than is your wont and more than you had grounds for doing. . . . It is true that pain does not resemble the movement of a pin; but it might thoroughly resemble the motions which the pin causes in our body, and might represent them in the soul; and I have not the least doubt that it does.

Where Locke sees only 'God's good pleasure', Leibniz seems to be insisting there must be a rational connection. The events in the soul must bear some quasi-mathematical relationship to the 'motions' in the brain and body that bring them about.

We can put the issue like this. Imagine God creating the universe. How much does he have to do? One attractive doctrine would be this: he has to create the physical stuff and the laws of physics, and then everything else follows. On this view, by fixing the *physical* state of the universe at all times, a creating God fixes everything at all times. If he had wanted to make a world in which something was different—say, one in which pinpricks were not painful—then he would have to have tinkered with the *physical* facts so that this did not come about. He would have had to fix up different nerves and pathways in the body and brain. There is no *independent* variation whereby the physical could stay the same, but the mental be different. This is Leibniz's position, at least as it appears in this passage. (A different interpretation of Leibniz has him thinking that there is independent variation but God has, of course, chosen the *best* way of associating mental and physical events.)

Locke, on the other hand, thinks that God has two different things to do. First, fix all the physics and laws of physics. But second, decide how to 'annex' mental events to physical events, fixing up psycho-physical relations. It is as if the world has two different biographies, one of its physical happenings and one of its mental happenings, and God had to decide how to relate them. On this account, there could be independent variation. God could have kept the physics just the same, but decided not to annex pain to pinpricks.

Consider now a person (yourself) and a physical duplicate of that person (a twin). If Locke is right, then it is in principle possible that the twin is a Zombie or a Mutant. Although his or her physical self is just like yours, it would be an arbitrary exercise of God's bounty to make their mental life similar as well. This is especially obvious on the 'occasionalist' version of the view: perhaps for his own inscrutable reasons God treats my stubbing my toe as an occasion on which to insert pain into my mental biography, but not so for you. On the other hand, if Leibniz is right, there is no such possibility. If you and your twin both stub your toes with the same force, and react physically in the same ways, then the 'expression' of the physical events in your minds must also be the same, just as the figures projected by two identical shapes on a plane at an angle must be the same.

It is interesting that Leibniz uses a mathematical analogy. It is not just that he was an even better mathematician than Descartes, and amongst other things invented the calculus. It is rather that for Leibniz the whole order of nature must eventually be transparent to reason. When things fall out one way or another it is not just that they happen to do so. There must be, if we could only see far enough, a reason why they do. Things have to make sense. When Leibniz says God does nothing in an arbitrary or unprincipled way he is not really expressing a piece of theological optimism, so much as insisting that we ought to be able to *see* why things are one way or another. This is his 'principle of sufficient reason'. In Descartes's terms, we ought to be able to achieve a clear and distinct idea of why things fall out as they do. We should be able to gain insight into why the way things *are* is the way they *must* be. It is this confidence in what ought to be possible to reason that makes Leibniz, like Descartes, a 'rationalist'.

In the philosophy of mind the Leibnizian must deny the possibility of Zombies and Mutants. If the physical biography is fixed, then the mental biography is fixed thereby. There is no independent variation, actual or possible. The *philosophical* problem is that of understanding why this is so. It is a question of how to understand the *way* in which the entire physical story makes true the mental story.

Locke thought he could leave it open whether it is an immaterial 'thing' (a ghost) within us that does the thinking, or whether it is the physical system itself, since God can superadd thought to anything he likes. But he is abundantly clear that it takes a mind to make a mind. It takes a special dispensation: thought cannot arise naturally (or, as Leibniz has it, in a rationally explicable way) from matter.

> *For unthinking particles of matter, however put together, can have nothing thereby added to them, but a new relation of position, which it is impossible should give thought and knowledge to them.*

It is this kind of a priori certainty about what can and cannot cause other things that marks Locke, like everyone else of his time, as fundamentally a rationalist, albeit one who is more nervous about our powers of reason than Descartes and Leibniz.

Thinkers about mind and matter have not got much beyond Locke and Leibniz. Today as well there are thinkers (sometimes called 'new mysterians') who think we shall never understand the relationship between mind and matter. It remains as Locke left it, a rationally inexplicable matter—God's good pleasure. There are even philosophers who think that some kind of Cartesian dualism is true, and that the mind really is epiphenomenal—never causes any physical events at all. They say this because they recognize that the physical is a *closed system*. If there is a process that begins with a pin being stuck in you and ends with a wince, then there is an entire physical chain from pin to wince that explains the wince. So, they think, it has to be *false* that you wince because you are in pain. This bit of common sense has to be given up. You wince because of the physical pathways, not because of a mental add-on. These thinkers are in fact stuck with the same problem of interaction that faces Locke. We discuss it more in the next chapter.

But there are other thinkers who think that a rational relationship can be made out. I shall introduce two broad approaches. The first tries to give an 'analysis' of the mental, in terms that enable us to see it as a Leibnizian expression of the physical. The second tries for a scientific kind of reduction or identity of the mental to the physical.

ANALYSIS

Analysis, as philosophers aim at it, attempts to say what makes true some mysterious kinds of statement, using terms from some less mysterious class. Analysis is easily illustrated by a homely example. Suppose someone becomes perplexed by that icon of modern Western life, the average man, with his 2.4 children and 1.8 automobiles. How can this joke figure be of any real interest? The answer is given by showing what makes true statements couched in terms of him: here that, across families, the total number of children divided by number of progenitors is 2.4, and automobiles divided by number of owners is 1.8. This information is succinctly presented in terms of the average man. He is what Russell called a 'logical construction' out of aggregates of facts. (This does not mean that all statements about the average are sensible or useful: as has been said, the average person has one testicle and one breast.) Philosophers also talk of a *reduction* of statements of one kind to those of another. Analyses provide the reductions.

Analysis tells us what is meant by statements made in one form of words, in terms of statements made in other words. Its credentials as an intellectual tool have themselves been the topic of a great deal of philosophical controversy, and its status has varied over the last hundred years. Some, such as Russell and G. E. Moore (1873–1958), thought of it as the essential goal of philosophy. Later, its prospects were queried by the leading American thinker of the mid-twentieth century, W. V. Quine (1908–), and by others, and their pessimism was given some credibility by the depressing fact that very few philosophical analyses seemed successful. Currently analysis is enjoying something of a cautious revival. But for our purposes these methodological questions can be set aside. The point is that if we can analyse mental ascriptions in physical terms, then the Leibnizian dream of a rational or a priori way of seeing *how* the physical gives rise to the mental is vindicated.

Let us take pain as an example of a mental state. Suppose now we try to analyse what it is for someone to be in pain. We identify pain primarily in terms of what pain makes us *do* (which is also what it is *for*, in evolutionary terms). Pain makes us do a variety of things. It demands attention, it causes us to immobilize parts of the body, distracts us from other things, and of course it is unpleasant. Suppose we can sum these consequences in terms of tendencies or dispositions to behaviour. Then the suggestion is that to be in pain just is to be disposed in these ways. This is the analysis of what it means, or what makes it true, that a person is in pain. This result would be an a priori exercise of reason, brought about by thinking through what is really intended by statements about this kind of mental event. Then the mystery of consciousness disappears. You and your twin, since you share dispositions (you verifiably tend to behave the same way), share your sensations, because this is what sensations are.

This doctrine is called logical behaviourism. I believe there is something right about it, but there are certainly difficulties. We might object that we are familiar with the idea that people can share the same sensation although they react somewhat differently. One can stub one's toe one day, and make a fearful fuss about it, but do the same thing, and feel the same pain, another day and bravely smile and carry on. Behaviour is not a transparent guide to sensations, thoughts, or feelings. (That is the point of the joke about two behaviourists in bed: 'That was great for you, how was it for me?') So, at the very least, complications must be added. Perhaps we could salvage the analysis in terms of dispositions to behaviour by pointing out that even if you bravely smile and carry on, you are still in some sense *disposed* to more expressive demonstrations of pain that you are suppressing for one reason or another. It is almost impossible to suppress tendencies to pain behaviour entirely, and other parties are very good at noticing the difference between, for instance, a child who has not hurt itself, and one who has but who is being brave. It seems essential to pain that it disposes in this way. But even this much is sometimes challenged by cases of people with certain kinds of brain damage, who apparently sincerely say that some pain is still present, but that they don't mind it any more. We should notice, however, that it is quite hard to make sense of that. If you give yourself a nice sturdy example of pain—touch a hotplate, or swing your toe into the wall—it is very hard to imagine *that* very mental state without imagining it as incredibly unpleasant. And it is hard to imagine it without its tendency to cause typical manifestations in behaviour.

Contemporary thinkers tend not to pin too much faith on behaviourism of this kind. They prefer a slightly more elaborate doctrine known as functionalism. This too pays prime attention to the function of the mental state. But it identifies that function in a slightly more relaxed way. It allows for a network of physical relationships: not only dispositions to behaviour, but typical causes, and even effects on other mental states—providing those in turn become suitably expressed in physical dispositions. But the idea is essentially similar.

Pain is a mental event or state that lends itself fairly readily to the project of analysis, for at least it has a fairly distinctive, natural, expression in behaviour. Other states with the same kind of natural expression might include emotions (sadness, fear, anger, and joy all have typical manifestations in behaviour). But other mental states only relate to behaviour very indirectly: consider the taste of coffee, for example. To taste coffee gives us a distinctive experience. There is something that it is *like* for us to taste coffee (not for Zombies). But it doesn't typically make us do anything much. Contemporary thinkers like to put this by saying that there are *qualia* or raw feels or sensations associated with tasting coffee. And friends of qualia are often fairly glum about the prospects of reducing qualia to dispositions in behaviour. As far as that goes, they are back with Locke. As it happens, these qualia are superadded to various physical events—in my case, if not in yours—but it could have been otherwise. But then scepticism whether you are Zombies or Mutants again threatens.

A SCIENTIFIC MODEL

One distinction the contemporary debate is fond of making is important to notice. So far, we have presented Leibniz as opposing the element of brute happenstance in Locke, in the name of a rational quasi-mathematical relation between mind and body. It is possible to suggest that there is a middle route: one that opposes the happenstance, but does not go so far as a mathematical or rationally transparent relationship. This is usually put by saying that perhaps there is a *metaphysical* identity between mental and physical facts or events, but that it is not necessarily one that can be known a priori.

A common analogy is this. Classical physics identifies the temperature of a gas with the mean kinetic energies of the molecules that compose it. So in making hot gases God has only *one* thing to fix: fix the gas and the mean kinetic energy of its molecules, and this thereby fixes the temperature. There is no independent variation. There can't be Zombie or Mutant gases, in which the kinetic energy of the molecules either issues in no temperature at all, or issues in different temperatures from those associated with the same energy in other gases.

On the other hand it is not *simply* reason or thought or mathematics that enabled scientists to equate temperature with mean kinetic energy. The breakthrough was not a priori, armchair analysis of what is meant by temperature, but took experiment and observation, and general *theoretical* considerations. The result was not purely a priori, but at least mostly a posteriori. The relation is not one that could be worked out in advance just by mathematics or by 'clear and distinct ideas', like the fact that a circle on a tilted plane casts an ellipse.

In general, in science, when one theoretical term or property, like temperature, becomes identified with another (here mean kinetic energy of constituent molecules), the link is given by bridge principles that are part of the theories of the sciences in question. So, for example, the current identification of genes with bits of DNA happens because in classical biology genes are defined in terms of their function in making characteristics heritable, and now in molecular biology it turns out that bits of DNA are the things that have that function. Notice that analysis is not *entirely* absent. We have to know what genes are meant to do before the equation can be made. But the big discovery is the contingent, scientific discovery of what it is that does what they are defined as doing.

If we modelled our approach to the mind–brain problem on scientific reductions of the kind just described, we would find some physical state characteristic of people sharing some mental state. So, for instance, we might find that all and only people in pain share some brain state (often indicated vaguely by saying that their 'C-fibres are firing'). And then it would be proposed that this then *is* the state of being in pain, just as some bits of DNA are genes. Once again, there would be a complete reduction of the mental to the physical.

This would be what is called a psycho-physical identity theory.

Opponents sometimes say that you can only believe this theory at the cost of feigning permanent anaesthesia. The complaint is that everything distinctively mental has been left out. The correct rebuttal to this is to ask the challenger just what he thinks has been left out, and watch him squirm on the difficulties of dualism. But there are other difficulties in front of this kind of psycho-physical identity theory. One is that in the case of mental events, one's own consciousness rules, in the following sense. From the subject's perspective, anything that feels like pain is pain. It doesn't matter if it is C-fibres, or something quite different. If someone had a mini-transplant, in which organic C-fibres were replaced by something silicon, for example, then if the silicon brings about the same results, it is still pain. Our knowledge of our pain is not hostage to the question of whether we have C-fibres inside us, or any other particular kind of biological engineering. There is a first-person authority. Equally, although we might know whether marginal candidates for feeling pain, such as perhaps shrimp, do or do not have C-fibres, we might be uncomfortable in declaring them to suffer pain or not purely on that account. So the identity does not seem quite so straightforward as in other scientific cases (this could be challenged).

We would be pleased enough if we could come to see the relation between mental events and events in the brain or body as clearly as we can see the relation between temperature and mean kinetic energy in gases. Perhaps it would not matter much to us whether the result was achieved more by 'pure thought', or more by experiment. So we can appreciate Leibniz's objection to Locke without entirely sharing his rationalism. Still, when we try to think hard about the relationship between brain and body on the one hand and mind on the other, it usually seems to be our thinking rather than mere scientific ignorance that is letting us down. Recently many scientists have turned their attention to consciousness, and a variety of brain states have been identified as implicated in normal conscious functioning. For example, electromagnetic waves in the brain of a particular low frequency have been thought to be vital. But it is not clear that this kind of truth is adapted to solving the problem—to enabling us to side with Leibniz against Locke. From the Lockean point of view, all the scientist may have discovered is that *when* the brain is in some specific state, we get symptoms of consciousness. But *that* might just tell us what consciousness is annexed to, by happenstance. It does not make the combination intelligible. And it also presupposes a right to shove the Zombie and Mutant possibilities out of sight, for otherwise the scientist could never establish the correlation, except at best in his or her own case. But according to new mysterians, neither science nor philosophy will ever get us to a point where things are better. We will never be able to side wholeheartedly with Leibniz against Locke.

INVERTED SPECTRA: PRIVATE LANGUAGES

The case of colour often seems especially to open wide the possibility at least of Mutants—people physically identical who nevertheless perceive colours quite differently. There might even be Mutants whose colour spectra are completely inverted with respect to each other, so that the experience one gets from light at the red end of the spectrum is the very experience that the other gets from light at the blue end. And there would be nothing to tell them that this is so.

Cartesian dualism opens the possibility of Zombies and Mutants. But perhaps it also opens an even more frightening possibility. If we think in the dualist way, we are apt to feel secure that at least we know what our *own* experience is like. The minds of others may be a bit conjectural, but our own minds are well known to us. But is even this true? Consider now not the minds of others, but *your own past experience.* Are you sure that the world looks to you today the same colour as it looked yesterday? Are you in fact sure that it looked any colour yesterday—in other words, that you actually received the conscious experience that you remember yourself as having had?

By asking these questions you are applying the Zombie and Mutant possibilities to your own past. Now of course, at first sight the possibilities are even more outlandish and absurd than applied to other minds. And we are inclined to retort that of course we know perfectly well that colours looked much the same yesterday as they do today. We would surely notice it if we woke up and the sky now looked like grass did yesterday, and vice versa.

I agree of course that we *would* notice the change. But is this security guaranteed, given Cartesian dualism? It depends on what we think about memory and mental events. Why should we be sure that mental events—thought of as entirely distinct, remember, from anything physical—leave reliable traces in memory? I can *check* that my memory of the physical world is reliable enough. I remember putting the car in the garage, and lo and behold, when I go down, there it is. I remember the way to the kitchen, and lo and behold, get there without any effort or any mistake. But what would check that my memory of the mental world is accurate? In Locke's terms, why should it not be 'God's good pleasure' to annex certain mental modifications to me today, together with the delusive memory that similar ones were annexed to me yesterday? Wittgenstein said:

> *Always get rid of the idea of the private object in this way: assume that it constantly changes, but that you do not notice the change because your memory constantly deceives you.*

This is the heart of the 'anti-private-language' argument in his *Philosophical Investigations* (published posthumously in 1953), one of the most celebrated arguments of twentieth-century philosophy. Wittgenstein tried to show that there could be no significant *thought* about the nature of one's past (or future) mental life if that mental life is divorced from the physical world in the way that Cartesian dualism proposes. It becomes, as it were, too slippery or ghostly even to be an object of our own memories or intentions.

The Mutant and Zombie possibilities, applied to our own pasts, are certainly unnerving. But really they ought only to unnerve us about the dualist picture. Once more, can we recoil from Locke to some version of Leibniz? Leibniz, remember, wants there to be a 'rational' relationship between the physical and the mental, so that the mental event of seeing a colour is some kind of rational *expression* of what is going on physically, not an accidental annexation to it. How could this work in the case of colours? The Leibnizian idea is that if I and my twin (which now might be myself as I was yesterday) are functioning physically in the same way, then there is no possibility that our mental lives are different. How can we flesh out this suggestion? Here is a sketch of an answer.

Many of the physical changes underlying colour perception are fairly well understood. Colour perception is the result of the stimulation of the cones that pack the central part of the retina. The current best theory suggests that there are three different kinds of cone, L, M, and S (long, medium, and short). L cones 'spike' or send messages down the optic nerve more readily when light of longer wavelength hits them, M cones get excited more when light of medium wavelength does, and S cones when light of shorter wavelength does. The colour we perceive then depends in the first place on a comparison between the levels of excitation of these three kinds of cone. So, for instance, if S is much more excited than L this codes for blue, the colour at the short wavelength end of the spectrum. If L is much more excited than S, this codes for yellow. If L is more excited than M we get red, and if M is more excited than L, we get green. It is as if the channels are 'opponents' and the result depends on which of the opponents overcomes the other.

Now consider the fact that colours have a lot of interesting properties. Here are some: you cannot have a surface that is yellowy blue. You can't have one that is reddish green. You can on the other hand have surfaces that are bluish green, or yellowish red (orange). You can't have a bright brown. You cannot have a bright grey (it is difficult to imagine a grey flame or a brown flame). Yellow is a lighter colour than violet. You can have a transparent red or blue or green gem, but you cannot have a transparent white gem—the nearest would be a milky white, like an opal. You can have white light, but not black light.

All these might seem to be brute facts about the Cartesian realm of the mind, where colours are supposed to hold their residence. But we can begin to see them as expressions of various physical facts. We can't see a surface as yellowy blue, because yellow and blue are produced by mathematical opposites: we get yellow when $L > S$, and blue when $S > L$. Similarly for red and green. We cannot have bright brown, because brown is darkened yellow. A surface is seen as brown when it would be coded for yellow, except that there is only a low overall energy level compared with that of other sources of light in the context. Similarly for grey, which is darkened white. Yellow is lighter than violet because yellow light ($L > S$) is also nearer the frequency at which our visual systems are maximally responsive. By comparison both red at one end and blue at the other end of the visual spectrum are taking us towards the dark, where we cannot respond at all. You cannot have transparent white because something is only seen as white when it scatters light.

All this of course only scratches the surface of colour science. But it gives us a glimmering at least of the way in which things 'make sense'. With enough facts of this kind in front of us we might be less enchanted by the inverted spectrum possibility. Let us take first the simpler case of monochromatic (black-and-white) vision. Suppose it is suggested that someone might be a physical duplicate of me, but see as dark what I see as light, and vice versa. Is that possible? Our snap judgement might be that it is. Perhaps we imagine the world appearing to him as it appears in a photographic negative. But this does not really work. If I make a piece of grey glass lighter, I see better through it; if I make it darker, I see less well through it. Since he is a physical duplicate, this has to be true of my twin. But for him, when we clear the glass it 'seems' as though we added soot, since it becomes subjectively darker. And when we add soot it 'seems' as though it is becoming clearer. But then we have to imagine that for him, as a plate of glass becomes darker he sees through it better and better, and as it becomes lighter he sees through it worse and worse. And that just doesn't seem to make sense. It doesn't mark a coherent possibility.

Now consider someone who is physically identical with me, but supposedly sees yellow as I see blue, and vice versa. It is now not quite so easy to imagine him. He has to respond in the same way as I do, so he cannot go round saying that yellow is a dark colour, for example. That difference in response and behaviour would be a physical difference. So we have to ask *how* he sees blue as bright, and yellow as dark. If he really sees yellow as dark, as I see blue, how does he see brown? How does he see orange? Brown is darkened yellow, but for him yellow is already dark. So it is difficult to imagine how his physical discriminations could match mine, given this complete disparity in mental experience.

In short, the possibility becomes a good deal less clear, and we may feel our way to denying that it is a possibility at all. We would be engineering a conception of the mind that closes the gap between the physical and the mental, that is, between the fully functioning and responsive visual system in the brain and the apparently superadded 'subjective' qualia of colour experience. Such a piece of engineering would be a vindication of Leibniz's position. Subjective colour experience becomes not just a queer add-on, but the inevitable, rationally explicable, *expression* of the kinds of physical functioning of the creatures that we are. If the same can be done for all the elements of our consciousness, the problem is solved.

THOUGHT

We now turn to a slightly different aspect of consciousness. This chapter has concentrated upon sensations and qualia. But our consciousness is also largely made up of thoughts. Thoughts are strange things. They have 'representational' powers: a thought typically represents the world as being one way or another. A sensation, by contrast, seems to just sit there. It doesn't, on the face of it, point towards anything beyond itself, such as a fact or putative fact. (Some thinkers deny this. They think, for instance, that a sensation of pain is a perception of bodily injury, and that this perception represents the body as injured, just as the thought that tomorrow is Friday represents tomorrow as being Friday. I leave the reader to ponder how plausible this is.) The representative nature of thoughts, sometimes called their intentionality or directedness, is itself highly puzzling. If we imagine thoughts as kinds of 'thing' present in consciousness, the question becomes how a 'thing' can in and of itself point towards another thing (a fact or state of affairs). Certainly a signpost, for instance, can point towards a village. But that seems to be a matter of the way it is taken. A signpost doesn't in and of itself represent the way to the village. We have to learn how to take it. We could imagine a culture in which the same physical object, which is to us a signpost, had a quite different function: a display board, or a totem, or a piece of abstract art. We see this with animals: when you point at something, dogs typically pay attention only to the pointing finger, to their owners' irritation. Whereas it seems incoherent to imagine a creature with the same *thoughts* as us, but who hasn't learned to take those thoughts in the way that we do. It is the 'take' that *makes* the thought.

Probably the right reaction to this is to deny that thoughts are things at all. The mistake of supposing that to every noun there corresponds a 'thing' is sometimes called the mistake of *reification*. Thinkers frequently charge one another with mistaken reifications. It is people who think, and their doing so is not the matter of some kind of blob being present either in the brain or the mind. This is true even if the blob is thought of as a small sentence written in the brain. Thinking is a matter of taking the world to be one way or another, and so taking it is a matter of our dispositions rather than a matter of what things are hanging out inside us.

Perhaps it ought to be no more puzzling that we can think about absent states of affairs—distant states, and past and future states—than that we can pay attention to the world at all. Yet it is a feat that sets us apart from other animals. Animals can presumably perceive the world, but we are nervous about supposing that they can represent to themselves distant and past and future states of affairs. Yet we can certainly do so.

The most popular current approach to this is to concentrate upon the way in which we can attribute thoughts to the well-functioning person. It should be something about a person's behaviour that enables us to interpret him or her as thinking about yesterday, or concentrating upon the weather predicted for the weekend. Thoughts are expressed in both linguistic and non-linguistic behaviour, and perhaps we can hope for some kind of reduction: 'X thinks that p' if and only if X's plans or desires or behaviour are *somehow in line* with the world being such that p. The trick would be to fill out the 'somehow in line'. It is fair to say that nobody has successfully done that. But there are suggestions about how to go. We say that an intelligent system, such as a guided missile, thinks that there is a plane a mile away and two hundred feet up if its systems point it in a direction that is *appropriate* to there being a plane in that place—given its aim (or function) of bringing down planes. Similarly we might say of a person that she thinks the weather will be fine at the weekend if her behaviour is appropriate, given her aims (or functions), to that being the weather at the weekend. The difficulty would be to fill out this thought without relying in other ways on other mental states of the subject, and this is what nobody knows how to do.

I leave thinking aside for the moment. Instead, in the next two chapters I consider two more elements in our view of the world that also nourish Cartesian dualism. The first is a range of thoughts about our own freedom. The second is a range of thoughts about our own identity.

CHAPTER THREE

Free Will

Again, if movement always is connected,
New Motions coming in from old in order fixed,
If atoms never swerve and make beginning
Of motions that can break the bonds of fate
And foil the infinite chain of cause and effect
What is the origin of this free will
Possessed by living creatures throughout the earth?

Lucretius, *De Rerum Natura*

OR, IN A SLIGHTLY LESS elevated tone:

There was a young man who said, 'Damn,
It is borne upon me that I am
*   A creature that moves*
*   In predestinate grooves—*
Not even a bus, but a tram.'

The last chapter had us thinking about what the brain produces: elements of consciousness such as thoughts, or sensations, or qualia. But when we think about ourselves, we are conscious of other things as well. We don't only register the world, as we take it to be. We act in it. We concentrate on alternatives. We deliberate and do things. We take control. How should we think about that?

THE BONDS OF FATE

We usually regard ourselves as free agents. We live our lives within an open space of possibilities. We deliberate which ones to pursue, and having deliberated, we choose. I went to the mountains this year for a holiday, but I could have gone the seaside. It was my choice. I could not have gone to the Moon, because it was not feasible.

We seem to be conscious of our freedom. Consciousness of freedom seems closely allied to any kind of consciousness at all. When we thought of Zombies in the last chapter, we probably imagined jerky, robotic, Frankenstein creations, slaves to particular programs, acting inflexibly and unintelligently. But we are not like that, are we?

Sometimes we are proud of our freedom: we are not mere creatures of instinct and desire. We can pull ourselves together and fight to control our obsessions or addictions. We deserve praise when we succeed. If we fail, we may deserve and sometimes receive punishment. Freedom brings responsibility, and people who abuse it deserve blame and punishment. But nobody deserves punishment for failing to do something if they *could not do it.* It would be most unjust to punish me for not having gone to the Moon, or to punish a man in prison for not keeping an appointment outside the prison, for example. Here the obstacles are beyond the agent's control. That means, he or she is not to blame.

So our moral reactions as well as our ordinary thinking seem to presuppose that sometimes, even if we acted badly, we could have done otherwise.

But might this consciousness of freedom be an illusion? Could we ever really have acted otherwise than we did?

Lucretius and the young man at the beginning of the chapter can be given an argument:

> The past controls the present and future.
> You can't control the past.
> Also, you can't control the way the past controls the present and future.
> *So*, you can't control the present and future.

In fact, you can't control anything at all, past, present, or future.

The first premise of this argument is a thumbnail version of the doctrine known as determinism, which can be put by saying that every event is the upshot of antecedent causes. The state of the world at any moment is the result of its state immediately before, and evolves from that preceding state in accordance with unchanging laws of nature. The second premise looks certain. The third reminds us that we cannot control the laws of nature—the ways in which events give rise to one another. And the conclusion certainly looks to follow.

People who accept this argument are called *hard* determinists, or *incompatibilists*, since they think that freedom and determinism are incompatible.

Perhaps to restore human freedom we should deny determinism? We might be optimistic about doing this, because the best current science of nature, quantum physics, is standardly interpreted as postulating uncaused events. In the quantum world, there are microphysical events that 'just happen'. On these interpretations one system can be in *exactly* the same state as another—there are no 'hidden variables'—and yet in one system a quantum event occurs, and in the other it does not. Such events have no cause: they just happen, or do not happen. Quantum physics gives them a probability, but cannot determine, from the state of play at one moment, whether such an event will happen or not in the immediate future.

But this is not quite what we wanted: it is introducing an element of *randomness* into things, but not an element of control or responsibility. To see this, think of the full neurophysiological state of your brain and body. Events follow their causes. If sometimes little fits and starts occur at a micro level you can hardly be held responsible for any differences that do arise from the fits and starts. You can't control electron jumps. If they are genuinely indeterministic, *nothing* can control them. It is just as much bad luck if one jumps the wrong way, as if your good intentions were frustrated by outside accidents beyond your control. Putting the accident into your brain does not restore your responsibility.

If anything, physical indeterminism makes responsibility and the justice of blame even more elusive. This is sometimes called the dilemma of determinism. If determinism holds, we lose freedom and responsibility. If determinism does not hold, but some events

'just happen', and then, equally, we lose freedom and responsibility.
Chance is as relentless as necessity.

FIG TREES AND WATERFALLS

In the Gospel according to Mark, 11: 12–14, 20–1, there is a strange
story:

> *And on the morrow, when they were coming from Bethany, he
> was hungry.*
>
> *And seeing a fig tree far off, having leaves, he came, if haply
> he might find any thing thereon; and when he came to it he
> found nothing but leaves; for the time of figs was not yet.*
>
> *And Jesus answered and said unto it, No man eat fruit of
> thee hereafter for ever. And his disciples heard it . . .*
>
> *And in the morning, as they passed by, they saw the fig tree
> dried up from the roots.*
>
> *And Peter calling to remembrance, saith unto him, Master,
> behold, the fig tree that thou cursedst is withered away.*

Let us ignore the disturbing social, economic, and ecological problems with this story, and concentrate on the apparent injustice to
the fig tree. It is true that Jesus did not curse the fig tree for not
bearing, say, apples, or plums. It was figs he was after. And fig trees
do *sometimes* bear figs. But it still seems unfair on the fig tree. It is
as if Jesus is arguing 'You sometimes bear figs, so you could be bearing figs now'. To which is seems a completely adequate defence for
the fig tree to point out that it bears figs in the summer, but it is now
winter, or at any rate 'the time of figs was not yet'. It takes a certain

set of circumstances for a fig tree to bear figs: even the best tree does not do so out of season, any more than it bears plums.

The fig tree might not be aware of this. Perhaps if it was a thoughtful fig tree it would have felt bad because it was itself unaware of the precise causes necessary for it to bear figs: perhaps it only remembers that it sometimes does so, and then feels bad about not doing so on this occasion. But that is just ignorance. If the fig tree feels bad about not bearing figs in winter, then that is irrational: the time was not right, that is all.

You might think like our imagined fig tree: I just know that I am free. I stand here, able to raise my arm or not, just as I please. Suppose I do it—thus—then I have felt myself controlling the way events unfolded. My *consciousness* reveals my freedom to me.

But here is the German philosopher Schopenhauer (1788–1860):

> Let us imagine a man who, while standing on the street, would say to himself: 'It is six o'clock in the evening, the working day is over. Now I can go for a walk, or I can go to the club; I can also climb up the tower to see the sun set; I can go to the theater; I can visit this friend or that one; indeed, I also can run out of the gate, into the wide world, and never return. All of this is strictly up to me, in this I have complete freedom. But still I shall do none of these things now, but with just as free a will I shall go home to my wife.' This is exactly as if water spoke to itself: 'I can make high waves (yes! in the sea during a storm), I can rush down hill (yes! in the river bed), I can plunge down foaming and gushing (yes! in the waterfall), I can rise freely as a stream of water into the air (yes! in the fountain), I can, finally, boil away and disappear (yes! at certain temperature); but I am doing none of these things now,

*and am voluntarily remaining quiet and clear water in the re-
flecting pond.'*

In this parable, the water is not conscious of the causal setups necessary for it to boil, make waves, and so on. It only remembers that
it *sometimes* does these things. Hence, it thinks, it can do them. So
it attributes its calm to its own voluntary decision. But in this it is
mistaken: if it 'tries' to boil when the temperature is wrong, or
'tries' to make waves when there is no wind, it will soon discover
that these things do not depend on its own decision. To make the
same point, Wittgenstein imagines the leaf falling in the autumn
winds, and saying to itself, 'Now I'll go this way, now I'll go that.'

Schopenhauer denies that our own self-understanding, our
self-consciousness, displays our real freedom. We can interpret
him as criticizing this argument:

> I am not conscious of the causal background needed for me
> to do Y.
> I know I sometimes do Y.
> *So*, I am conscious that there is no causal background
> needed for me to do Y.

His point is that this argument is invalid. Being *unconscious of
something* cannot be parlayed into being *conscious of its absence.*
When I speak I am not conscious of the incredible causal structures that make it possible for me to speak: the musculature, the
coordination of muscle and breath control, the movement of the
tongue and palate, the configuring of my jaw. But all these things
are necessary, as I would quickly discover if just one of them went
wrong.

At this point one might start thinking something like this:

> Perhaps if we confine our thoughts to the physical world, we seem to have no option but determinism or random indeterminacies, and we lose sight of real freedom. But suppose there is another level. Behind or above the evolutions of brain and body, there is the Real Me, receiving information, and occasionally directing operations. There will be times when left to themselves the brain and body would move one way. But with direction from the Real Me, they will go the other way. I can take over, and interfere with the way things would otherwise have gone. This is where my freedom lies.

This conceptualizes the relationship between me on the one hand and my brain and body on the other in terms of a two-way interaction. The brain and body bring the Real Me messages, and this Real Me then issues them instructions. The Real Me sits in the control room, and the whole person behaves freely when it is in command. If it is not in command, the brain and body get on with their ('mindless') physical evolutions.

This is mind–body dualism again. The Real You dictates events. Messages come in, perhaps through the pineal gland. A breath of soul then fans neurones and synapses into action, and initiate new causal chains. There is a ghost in the machine, and the machine behaves freely when the ghost is in charge. Now, we have already seen something of the mystery of mind–brain interaction on this picture. But here we can raise a different objection. Dualism tries to understand human freedom by introducing an extra ingredient, the controlling soul. But how do we understand the freedom of the soul?

Look again at the dilemma of determinism. How does a ghost or soul inside the machine escape the same problem? Are there laws governing how ghost-stuff behaves, so that if a ghost is in one state at a particular time, there is a law determining what its next state will be? If not, then is ghost-stuff subject to random fits and starts? How does that help *me* to be free and responsible? Remember as well that there is no God-given correlation between an event being 'mental' and the event being under my free control: I cannot wish away pains, desires, obsessions, unwelcome thoughts, and confusions, just like that.

The dualist approach to free will makes a fundamental philosophical mistake. It sees a problem and tries to solve it by throwing another kind of 'thing' into the arena. But it forgets to ask how the new 'thing' escapes the problems that beset ordinary things. We meet this kind of mistake again in Chapter 5, on the philosophy of religion. In fact, if you think about it, you will find that you surreptitiously think of the freedom of any non-physical soul, any ghost in the machine, *on the model of human freedom.* That is, far from helping to understand human freedom, the idea depends upon it. For the ghost is really a kind of ethereal little human being, a 'homunculus' that takes in information, deliberates, wants various things, is swayed or influenced or guided by different pieces of information, and that in the light of all that does something. If we cannot understand how human beings are free, we cannot understand how such a homunculus can be free either.

And of course there is the whole problem of mind–brain

interaction, which is so intractable given Cartesian dualism. The physical system is a *closed* system. It takes a physical cause to produce a physical effect.

To try to reconcile freedom with a deterministic universe composed of small, hard, indivisible atoms in motion, the Greek philosopher Epicurus (341–270 BC) had already suggested that the spirit of a person could step in and make the atoms 'swerve' in direction. In fact, Lucretius, who is interpreting Epicurus in the passage at the beginning of the chapter, goes on to talk of a minute swerving of the atoms, and the way in which 'that [which] the minute swerving of the atoms causes is neither place nor time determinate'. Unfortunately, the laws of motion are not very hospitable to this 'swerve'. The laws that we actually find tell us that linear momentum, a joint function of motion *and* direction, is physically conserved. It would shatter the laws of motion just as badly if the Real Me could make the Moon change direction by just thinking, as if the Real Me could make it speed up or slow down.

As an aside, it is worth noticing, however, that the Greek and Roman atomists, including Epicurus and Lucretius, were better off in one respect than Descartes. For they thought, as he did not, that the spirit itself must be understood in *mechanical* terms. The mind or spirit, they held, was composed of particularly fine, small, and exceedingly mobile mechanical particles, so there is no reason in principle why these should not influence the directions and velocities of the larger particles of the body. Lucretius explains the way in which this subtle stuff is 'of seeds extremely small, through veins, flesh, sinews, woven'. The soul has to be made of thin stuff, for 'dreams of smoke and mist can move it'. Such dreams are presumably made of much smaller particles than even smoke and mist themselves. But Lucretius unfortunately fails to revisit the question of how the motions of even tiny particles can break the bonds of fate and foil the infinite chain of cause and effect. Ancient atomists liked to compare the action of the soul on the body with the action of the wind on a ship, but of course the wind is part of the infinite chain of cause and effect. It is not something standing outside it, and neither, on this model, is the soul.

PULLING YOURSELF TOGETHER

Is there any better way of breaking the argument for incompatibilism?

The argument for hard determinism does not talk of the *kinds* of causal influences in play as an agent performs a given action. Now sometimes the causal routes are totally independent of what we think. The causal route that leads from my being irreversibly under water to my drowning is one of them. The same outcome is inevitable for Einstein and for a donkey. But sometimes the causal routes only go via high-level neural processes. This is no more than to say that we often move as we do because our brains are functioning properly.

So let us try a primitive model. Think of the brain in 'software' terms, as having various 'modules'. One (a 'scanner') takes in information about a situation. Another (a 'tree producer') delivers options for behaviour in the light of what the scanner says. A third (an 'evaluator') ranks the options in the light of concerns that it has programmed into it. It may work by attaching emotional indicators such as fear or joy to the different paths. Finally a fourth (a 'producer') fixes on the option ranked best by the preceding processes, and outputs neural signals that move muscles and limbs. Here is a schematic diagram:

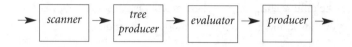

Remember that all this is supposed to be just a 'software' description of parts of the brain. Now suppose a decision is the upshot of these modules functioning. Suppose it is one of your decisions, and these parts function to produce it in the way that they normally do. If we call these modules, 'decision' modules, and if these modules are engaged in producing the output, then we can say that *you* chose the output. It was not forced on you, in the way that drowning is forced on the trapped swimmer.

Suppose the decision was to do something really bad. You come into my room, and chuck my peaceable old dog out of the window. I am outraged, and minded to blame you. Suppose you try to defend yourself by invoking the incompatibilist argument.

> Look, this action was the result of the way my scanner/producer system had been 'set'. Perhaps events in my childhood, quite outside my control, 'set it' so that making the environment dog-free has for me the highest priority. My tree producer told me it was an option, after my scanner had told me that there was a dog present and a window nearby. My evaluator immediately selected that option,

and my producer smoothly initiated the action of chucking the dog out of the window. Why blame me?

Surely I am not likely to be very impressed. I might reply something like this:

> I am not all that interested in how you came to be 'set' like you are. What bothers me is that this *is* your set. I don't care how it came to be your set, or what deterministic forces brought you to have these systems set that way. All I am concerned about is that now, at the end of the day, you are a nasty piece of work, and I am going to thump you. Maybe it was indeed bad luck your getting to be like you are. And now it is doubly bad luck, because you are going to get thumped for it.

At least I have the consolation that, following your own argument, you cannot blame me for thumping you! It's just the way I am set: I react badly to people who do this to my peaceable old dog.

Thumping you may have a point—in fact, several points. It might readjust your evaluator. Next time round, this module may rank throwing the dog out of the window below putting up with its presence. In a more complex picture, we could imagine this happening by means of a number of other mechanisms: perhaps it attaches a risk-of-being-thumped flag to the dog-throwing option. Or perhaps my anger shocks you into a more general re-evaluation of strategies of behaviour. And even if thumping you does not succeed in changing you, it sends a signal to other would-be dog-chuckers. It also relieves my feelings.

This is different from blaming someone for drowning, while not blaming him or her for being trapped in the water. The causal route there lies through basic animal physiology that cannot be altered by education or the attitudes of others. Praise and blame cannot 'reset' it. The causal route does not lie through modules that are *elastic*, or flexible, capable of being reset by anger or blame. But dog-throwers can be deterred and changed and warned away.

Schoolteachers sometimes say things like this: 'I don't mind a stupid pupil, but I do dislike a lazy one.' In the grip of the hard determinist argument, you might think that this is just prejudice: some people are born stupid and pitied for it; why should those born lazy not be similarly pitied for that? It is just tough luck, either way. But the schoolteacher's attitude will have a point if laziness responds to incentives in a way that stupidity does not. If respect for the teacher's opinion can make you work harder, whereas it cannot make you smarter, then there is one justification for the asymmetry. The teacher is in the business of resetting your evaluating module. It is an empirical fact, a fact to be learned from human experience, how far modules do get reset by interactions with others, including the unpleasant ones in which the others display their anger or contempt for us.

We have here the beginning—but only the beginning—of the programme of *compatibilism*, or the attempt to show that, properly understood, there is no inconsistency between acknowledging determinism and our practices of holding people responsible for their actions. Compatibilism is sometimes called 'soft' determinism, in opposition to 'hard' determinism. This is not a very good label for two reasons. First, it is not really a different kind of determinism. It accepts determinism in just the same sense as anybody else. There is no ghostly power stepping in to interfere with the natural causal order of events. Second, in moral or political terms, the 'soft' determinist may actually be pretty hard, in the sense of harsh. If you come to her with the heartrending excuse that your biology or your environment made you the way you are, she turns deaf, and vents her anger on you just the same. Not for her the facile equation between crime and illness: people can pull their socks up, and if it seems appropriate, she will use punishment or any other appropriate reaction to make you do so too.

Of course, a compatibilist can accept some kinds of excuse. If you were constrained in some situation so that no matter how well-functioning your 'modules', no good upshot was possible, then you are not to blame for events. This is the case of the drowning swimmer: no matter how good their character, there is nothing they can do about it. Equally, if an action is quite 'out of character', for instance, because you have had to take some medications whose result is to disorientate you or depress you, then perhaps you can be forgiven, when you are yourself again.

We might think at this point: well, the reaction to the villainous dog-thrower was natural enough. Perhaps it is even justifiable in terms of its *consequences*. Perhaps blame and associated reactions have a function, and we just need things with that function. But all the same, isn't there a hint of injustice? Because we have done nothing to show that the dog-chucker *could have done otherwise*. For on any occasion, the modules will be set one way or another, so the outcome is determined. Compatibilists, so far, seem to blame someone for events, when the person could not have done otherwise. To this they may reply by distinguishing different senses of 'could have done otherwise'. If the causal route to the agent's action lay through the decision modules, then she 'could have done otherwise' in some sense, and may be regarded as being free. To get at the right sense of 'could have done otherwise', we might offer what I shall call the *first compatibilist definition*:

> A subject acted freely if she could have done otherwise in the right sense. The subject could have done otherwise in this sense provided she *would* have done otherwise *if* she had chosen differently.

And, says the compatibilist, that is all that is needed to justify our reactions of holding people responsible, and perhaps reacting to them with blame and anger.

The ghostly response to determinism posited a kind of intervention from *outside* the realm of nature: a 'contra-causal' freedom, in which the ghost is distinct from the causal order of nature, yet mysteriously able to alter that order. We could call that conception, *interventionist* control. It is sometimes known in the literature as a *libertarian* conception of freedom, although this is confusing, since it has nothing to do with political or economic libertarianism, which is the ideology of free markets and minimal government. I shall stick with calling it interventionist control. Compatibilism on the other hand substitutes a view of you as entirely situated *inside* the causal order of nature. Your freedom lies in the way action flows out of your cognitive processes. So how does the compatibilist respond to the original argument about control? He might suggest that the argument is no better than this:

> The past controls the present and future.
> A thermostat cannot control the past.

A thermostat cannot control the way in which the past controls the present and future.
So, a thermostat cannot control the future.

There has to be something wrong with this, because a thermostat
can control the future, in respect of temperature. That is what thermostats do. A thermostat controls the temperature by being *part of
the way* in which the past controls the present and future. And according to compatibilism, that is how we control things. We are involved in the causal order. We are part of the way in which the past
controls the future. And therein lies our responsibility. We can call
this conception of control, *inside* control, control from inside nature. When we exercise inside control, the compatibilist holds, we
are responsible for various events. And if we exercise that control
badly, we may justly be held responsible for the upshot, and held to
blame if blame is an appropriate reaction.

But is this compatibilist freedom what we really wanted? We do
not attribute any freedom to the thermostat. And compatibilism
can seem more like a dismissal of the problem of freedom, rather
than a solution of it. This is how it seemed to the great Immanuel
Kant (1724–1804), who dismissed it as giving us only the 'freedom
of clockwork' and called it nothing better than a 'wretched subterfuge'.

PUPPETS AND MARTIANS

Here is another way of sharing Kant's worries. The modules and
complexities of information processing complicated the causal

picture. But do they alter it fundamentally? Imagine counsel for the fig tree, pointing out that it was winter rather than summer. This is a complete defence of the tree. Well, if I acted badly, then does not that show that it was winter too? The modules had been badly set, presumably by events belonging to causal chains that stretch back before my birth. It may be that if you are angry with me that will alter my decision-making system *for the future*, but it does not show that I could have acted differently *in the past*.

As we come to learn about causal regularities lying behind actions and other mental states, we are apt to switch into less moralistic modes. We might blame someone for being depressed all the time, until we learn a chemical story explaining it. We might be angry with someone for being unable to stir himself, until we learn that he has mononucleosis. But according to the determinist, there are *always* things like this to learn. Quite apart from increasing neurophysiological evidence, we may think of cases where we learn of 'brainwashing' or 'conditioning'. Parents may be inclined to blame their teenage daughter for spending time, energy, and income on valueless cosmetics, but a better reaction would be to understand the social and commercial pressures that paralyse her better judgement and bring this state of affairs about.

Things get worse for compatibilism if we indulge in a little science fiction. Imagine the invasion of the mini-Martians. These are incredibly small, organized, and mischievous beings: small enough to invade our brains and walk around in them. If they do so, they can set our modules pretty well at will. We become puppets in their hands. (If this kind of example sounds too far-fetched, reflect that there actually exists a parasite that lives by colonizing the brains of ants. Under its influence, the ant climbs blades of grass. This makes it more likely to be ingested by passing sheep, which the parasite then infects [the particular individual in the ant's brain itself perishes, but others hitch-hike]. For all one knows, the ant feels free as air as it climbs its blade of grass.) Of course, the mini-Martians might set us to do what we would have done anyhow. But they might throw the chemical switches so that we do quite terrible things. Then let us suppose that, fortunately, science invents a scan to detect whether the Martians have invaded us. Won't we be sympathetic to anyone who suffered this misfortune? Wouldn't we immediately recognize that he was not responsible for his wrongdoings?

But, says the incompatibilist, why does it make a difference if it was mini-Martians, or causal agencies of a more natural kind?

This kind of reply takes issue with the compatibilist version of 'could not have done otherwise'. It is all very well, it points out, to say that someone would have done otherwise if he or she had chosen differently. But suppose they were set so that they *could not* have chosen differently. Suppose at the time of acting, their choosing modules were locked into place by mini-Martians, or chemicals, or whatever. What then? The compatibilist we have so far shrugs the question off—he is not interested in how the subjects got to be as they are, only whether the outcome is good or bad. The objector finds it important, and at least some of our reactions, when we find more about causal routes, show that we agree with the objector.

OBSESSIONS AND TWINKIES

I think the best line for compatibilism, faced with this counter-attack, is to query the word 'set', when there is talk of the modules being set to produce some outcome. This in effect repeats a similar move to the one he made to distinguish decision-making from drowning. There, he introduced a degree of flexibility into the causal process, by highlighting modules that are capable of being tuned or set differently. When the objector claims that in that case the subject is a mere victim if the modules are 'set' wrong, the reply ought to be to introduce another level of flexibility. True, we can say, in the case of the brainwashed teenager, or the mini-Martians, the modules may really be set. We are imagining the modules badly *fixed* by chemical or other processes. But these cases are special, precisely because once they are in them subjects become inflexible: immune to argument, or to additions or changes in the decision-making scenario. But normally agents are not *so* set in their ways. Their freedom consists in the fact that they are responsive to new information, and new differences in the situation. They are not driven or bound to chuck dogs out of windows or to stand all day at the cosmetics counter.

We might pursue the idea with something like this, that I shall call the *revised compatibilist definition*:

> The subject acted freely if she could have done otherwise in the right sense. This means that she would have done otherwise if she had chosen differently *and*, under the impact of other thoughts or considerations, she *would* have chosen differently.

Of course, on an occasion, it may have been bad *luck* that the right thoughts did not arise. Well, says the compatibilist once more, that is indeed bad luck. But perhaps my anger and the fact that I am going to thump you will prevent it recurring.

Some philosophers (Baruch Spinoza [1632–77] is the most famous example) like to associate freedom with increased knowledge and understanding. We are free, they say, in so far as we understand things. This is in many ways an attractive idea: it ties freedom of the will to things like political freedoms: freedom of information and freedom of speech. We are only free in so far as we have opportunities open to us, and lack of information denies us opportunities. We could add this thought to the revised compatibilist definition, by specifying that the 'other thoughts or considerations', first, are accurate representations of the agent's situation and options, and second, are *available* to the agent. That is, it is not much use saying that under the impact of other thoughts or considerations she would have chosen differently, if those other thoughts and considerations were simply not in the landscape. Thus, suppose I set about to poison you and cunningly put arsenic in your coffee. You drink it. It is not much use saying that you were free not to do so. For although it is true that you would have avoided the coffee if you had chosen differently, and true that the thought or consideration that perhaps the coffee was laced with arsenic would have made you choose differently, nevertheless, since there was no reason for that thought to enter your mind, you were a victim rather than a free agent. We might incorporate that into a revised revised compatibilist definition:

The subject acted freely if she could have done otherwise in the right sense. This means that she would have done otherwise if she had chosen differently *and*, under the impact of other *true and available* thoughts or considerations, she *would* have chosen differently. True and available thoughts and considerations are those that represent her situation accurately, and are ones that she could reasonably be expected to have taken into account.

What of the person to whom the thoughts or considerations just didn't occur? Is she a victim rather than a responsible agent? This introduces a new twist to things.

So far we have talked as if 'free choice', either of some mysterious interventionist kind or of some substitute 'inside' or compatibilist kind, is necessary for responsibility. But is this right? I said above that it might be just bad luck that some crucial consideration does not occur to someone at a moment of decision. But sometimes we do not treat it as 'mere' bad luck. We say that the thought *should* have arisen. The agent is liable to censure if it didn't. Someone setting fire to buildings for fun cannot seriously plead that 'it never occurred to him' that someone might get hurt—not unless he is a child or mentally deficient. Even if it is true that it never occurred to him, so there was no free choice to put people at risk, he is still responsible. Recklessness and negligence are faults, and we can be held responsible for them, just as much as we are for more controlled decisions. Some philosophers have found it hard to accept that. Aristotle rather desperately held that negligent people have actually chosen to make themselves negligent, perhaps in early childhood, and that this is the only reason they can be held responsible.

There is actually a whole range of interesting thoughts that open up here. Some kinds of bad luck are really incidental: things that do not affect our relationship to the agent. But others in some way cast a reflection on the agent. Imagine a golfer. Suppose on day one he hits a fine ball, but, amazingly, a passing seagull gets in its way and spoils the shot. Then on day two he hits an equally fine ball, but a little breeze blows it off course and again spoils the shot. We might say each of these is bad luck. The first is pure bad luck. But the second is not quite so simple. It is bad luck, yes, but the kind of bad luck that a really good golfer is expected to foresee and play around. It should be within the player's purview. Whereas the seagull represents a pure act of God. Enough bad luck of the second kind, and we start to think less well of the golfer, and it is the same with agency. Hence the reply made by a pianist whose admirer gushed about how lucky he was to have so much talent: 'Yes, and the more I practice the luckier I get.'

The conceptual engineering we are doing at this point is supposed to tease out or make explicit real elements in our thinking. We want to highlight and try to encapsulate things like this: we do make a distinction between changing the past (cannot do) and acting differently than we do (sometimes can do); we do have discriminating practices of blame; we do make a distinction between being ill and being bad; we do allow some excuses and disallow others. The philosophical analysis is supposed to give us intellectual control of all this. It is supposed to exhibit it all, not just as an irrational jumble of disconnected habits, but as the application of a reasonable and defensible set of concepts and principles. It is because it is hard to do this that the philosophy is hard. The compatibilist account is a piece of engineering, either plotting our extant concepts, or designing improved ones. It has to answer to the ways we often think, or think when we are best in control of the problems that face us. Myself, I believe that the revised revised compatibilist definition does that pretty well. But others take Kant's objection more seriously. They think that our 'interpersonal reactions', which include the ways we hold each other and ourselves responsible for things, do depend upon some lingering affection for interventionist freedom. So if that is metaphysically bankrupt, our attitudes ought to change. The philosophical problem would be that interventionist control is untenable, and inside control inadequate.

Sometimes an analysis will settle hard cases. But sometimes it leaves grey areas, and this may not be a bad thing. Return to the teenage girl spending an incredible amount of time and money on cosmetics. Can she do otherwise? If we run the revised revised definition, we may find that the issue hinges now on what other thoughts and considerations are 'available' to her. In one sense, we might want to say, it is possible that she should start realizing that her popularity or attractiveness is not greatly improved by cosmetics (it would increase more if she got a decent mind, perhaps by reading a book like this). This may be a true and potentially available thought. But in another sense, perhaps it is not. Perhaps people subjected to the influences she is subjected to just cannot get themselves to believe this. The culture is awfully good at blinding teenagers to this truth. So it would not be reasonable to expect her to believe it. Myself, I would incline to this diagnosis, seeing her as a victim rather than an agent. But the point is that even if the revised revised analysis does not *settle* this issue, it certainly *pinpoints* it. And this is itself a step towards getting the issue of responsibility and freedom under control. But it must in fairness be added that there is still a road to travel. An incompatibilist, for instance, might insist that thoughts are only available if they are themselves the objects of free (interventionist) selection, and this would put us back to square one.

Contemporary culture is not very good on responsibility. Consider the notorious 'Twinkie defence'. One day in 1978, an ex-employee of the city of San Francisco, Dan White, entered the City Hall with a gun, evading metal detectors by going through a basement window. He went upstairs, and shot and killed Mayor George Moscone and a supervisor, Harvey Milk. In court a defence psychiatrist, Martin Blinder, testified that White had been depressed, which led to his eating too much, and in particular the high-sugar junk food known as Twinkies. According to Blinder, this further deepened his depression, since White was an ex-athlete and knew that Twinkies were not good for him. Blinder claimed that the emotional state White would have got into would have meant it was impossible to have acted with premeditation or real intent, both of which were necessary conditions for first-degree murder. The jury were impressed by the argument, and acquitted White of murder, finding him guilty instead of the lesser crime of 'voluntary manslaughter'.

California later revised its law to close the space for this kind of defence, and on the face of it the state was right to do so. White *obviously* acted with intention and premeditation, since that is why he procured a gun and went in through the basement. And we can see that the revised revised analysis is not at all hospitable to the Twinkie defence. A defendant would have to work awfully hard to show that enough sugar literally takes our behaviour out of the range of our decision-making modules and our thoughts. It does not seem to be true that with enough Twinkies inside us we become literally incapable of certain thoughts, so that we could not reasonably be expected to realize that murdering people is a bad idea, for example. Even a lot of sugar does not tend to do that. (But then, contemporary juries are not very good on causation either. In Michigan recently a man won a lawsuit for substantial damages because, he claimed, a rear-end collision in his car had made him a homosexual.)

Before leaving compatibilism, it is worth noticing a difficulty in front of all the definitions. Compatibilism tries to generate the right notion of control out of the reflection that under different circumstances the agent *would* have done otherwise. There are nasty cases that suggest that these notions do not fit together quite so tightly. These are called 'causal overdetermination' cases. In such a case something does control some outcome, although the outcome would have been the same anyway because of a 'fail-safe' mechanism. Thus, a thermostat might control the temperature even if, because of a fail-safe mechanism, the temperature *would* have been the same even *if* the thermostat had malfunctioned. If the thermostat had malfunctioned, something else would have clicked in to keep the temperature at its proper level. Similarly an agent might do something bad, be in control, be acting with intent and responsibility, even if *were* he to choose to do otherwise unknown mechanisms would click in to ensure that he does the bad thing anyhow. Imagine the mini-Martians sitting there not actually interfering with things, but ready to do so whenever the outcome looks set to be one that they don't want. These cases are surprisingly tricky to handle. But the compatibilist can reflect that they make it no harder to define the right sense of control for human beings than they do for thermostats. Since the problem must have a solution in the case of mechanical control, it must have one for people as well.

OBJECTIFYING PEOPLE

Is there anything else to worry about? One might think like this:

> The compatibilist vision describes the operation of organic beings with brains in terms of decision-making modules. But all this is just describing things in terms of what happens. It is not describing things in terms of agency, or of *my* doing things. It is therefore leaving out something essential to my humanity, and essential to my human regard for others, which is that we are not just passive patients and victims, but active agents.

This is how we regard ourselves, and regard other normal people, and normally it is how we want to be regarded.

The fear is that something essential to human living is being lost. It is essential to us that we think of ourselves as agents, not just as patients. And it is essential to us that other people so regard us. In a famous paper the philosopher Peter Strawson (1919–) contrasts an 'objective' or impersonal attitude to other people with a 'personal' or human attitude. On the objectifying track, other people are just there like blocks to our progress, needing to be 'managed or handled or cured or trained'. They are not the objects of personal attitudes. People are looked at as if they were mad, rather than intelligent agents who can be understood.

There is an interesting 'gestalt switch' in Strawson's picture. At first, it might seem that the moral attitudes associated with blame are hard and harsh, and we might think that it is an improvement if we can get past them to more liberal and understanding attitudes to such things as crime or 'deviant behaviour'. Treating people as patients rather than as criminals looks to be a step in a humane, decent direction. Strawson asks us to confront what is *lost* in this change. He suggests that a lot of what makes human relationships distinctively human is lost. Suppose, for instance, that I have behaved in a way that I want to explain. But I find other people listening to my story with a look in their eyes that suggests that this talk is just another symptom. It is just another sign that I need to be managed or handled or cured or trained. Then I have been dehumanized. I want my decision to be understood, not patronized. I want other people to 'hear my voice', which means appreciating my point of view, seeing how things appear to me, rather than wondering what causes a human organism to behave like this. This kind of objectification concerns us again in Chapter 8, when among other things we confront the therapy industry with it.

The right response to the highlighted complaint, taking account of Strawson's point, is this. The compatibilist is not intending to deny agency, but to give a particular *account* of it. The account is in terms of modular brain functions, in which data are taken in, and alternatives generated and ranked, until eventually an output comes 'on line' and initiates action. True, these events are all things that 'just happen' (passively, as it were) but, according to the compatibilist, they *are* the things that happen, and *all* that happens, when you, the person, do something. Describing you as doing something, and for a reason, is a description at the *personal* level of the upshot of these multiple micro-level happenings.

Some thinkers like to say that there are two perspectives on all of this. There is the deliberative, first-person stance you adopt when you yourself are making a choice. And there is an 'objective' or third-person stance, one that a scientist might take, seeing you as a complex, determined, neurophysiological system. The problem lies in reconciling the two stances.

If the problem is put this way, then the right solution is surely this. There would only be a difficulty about reconciliation if what is disclosed in the deliberative stance is incompatible with what is disclosed in the third-person stance. But the deliberative stance discloses nothing about causation. Thinking otherwise is making the mistake that Schopenhauer's water made: mistaking absence of awareness of the functioning of brain and body for awareness of the absence of such functioning. The first is universal, but the second is impossible, for without the functioning there could be no awareness.

So, since nothing is seen from within the deliberative stance that conflicts with the scientific world-view, perhaps there is no need to find the problem of reconciliation at all difficult. What we may be left with is just a moral problem: one of making sure that we approach one another not with the objectifying stance, but with full human understanding, enriched, rather than undermined, by knowledge of the conditions that bring about the decisions of other people.

FATE, ORACLES, AND DEATH

I knew an old man who had been an officer in the First World War. He told me that one of his problems had been to get men to wear their helmets when they were at risk from enemy fire. Their argument was in terms of a bullet 'having your number on it'. If a bullet had your number on it, then there was no point in taking precautions, for it was going to kill you. On the other hand, if no bullet had your number on it, then you were safe for another day, and did not need to wear the cumbersome and uncomfortable helmet.

The argument is sometimes called the 'lazy sophism'. If I am going to get cancer, I am going to get it, says the smoker. You cannot avoid your fate. And if determinism is true, isn't the future fixed already, by the indefinite chain of states of the world already passed? These give birth to the future: it unfolds inevitably from the womb of the past. And if the future is fixed shouldn't we just resign ourselves to our fates? Doesn't action become pointless? Is it not better to withdraw, and perhaps sit in an orange shawl saying 'Om' all day?

There are many stories reminding us that we cannot avoid our fates. Here is a version of the famous Islamic parable of Death in Samarkand:

The disciple of a Sufi of Baghdad was sitting in an inn one day

*when he heard two figures talking. He realized that one of
them was the Angel of Death.*

*'I have several calls to make in this city,' said the Angel to
his companion.*

*The terrified disciple concealed himself until the two had
left. To escape Death, he hired the fastest horse he could, and
rode day and night to the far distant desert city of Samarkand.*

*Meanwhile, Death met the disciple's teacher, and they
talked of this and that. 'And where is your disciple, so-and-
so?' asked Death*

*'I suppose he is at home, where he should be, studying,' said
the Sufi.*

*'That is surprising,' said Death, 'for here he is on my list.
And I have to collect him tomorrow, in Samarkand, of all
places.'*

The disciple seeks to evade his fate, but it overtakes him all the
same. The story of the futile flight resonates worldwide. In Sopho-
cles' tragedy *Oedipus Rex*, King Laius of Thebes was told that his
son would murder his father and marry his mother. When he fathers a son, Oedipus, Laius seeks to avoid his prophesied doom by
crippling the baby, and leaving it to die on a hillside. Oedipus is
saved by a shepherd and grows up in Corinth, believing himself to
be the son of the king of that city. He learns rumours of his destiny,
and consults the oracle at Delphi, who confirms it. So he flees in the
opposite direction from Corinth, where he takes his father to be.
And thus, at a place in the wilderness where three roads meet, he
encounters Laius. . . . The twofold attempts at thwarting destiny are
exactly what make the doom unfold.

My friend's soldiers thought that taking precautions was as

pointless as Oedipus's flight from his doom. But there is a crucial difference. Oedipus is supposed to know his fate, but seeks to avoid it in any case. On the other hand, the soldiers did not know whether they would die that day or not. This leaves them open to the proper reply, which is that whether a bullet has your number on it or not may very well depend on whether you choose to wear a helmet. A bullet that would *otherwise* have had your number on it may be kept unwritten-on by this simple precaution. And since you do not know whether any bullet has your number on it, and you would like none to have it, you had better take the precaution.

Doing nothing—failing to put on a helmet, putting on an orange shawl and saying 'Om'—represents a choice. To have your choosing modules set by the lazy sophism is to be disposed towards that kind of choice. The lazy sophism can be represented as this argument for a course of action:

> The future will be what it will be. Its events are already in time's womb.
> *So*, do nothing.

But why is it better to be impressed by this argument than by this one?

> The future will be what it will be. Its events are already in time's womb.
> *So*, get cracking.

The first might be a better argument if we knew that, as events unfold from time's womb, human actions make no difference. It would be as if we were watching a game, behind one-way glass walls, spectating events in which we can never participate, and whose players are deaf and blind to us. But it is not normally like that. Events do unfold from time's womb, but in quite predictable sequences. The event of someone eating an omelette is always preceded by the event of someone breaking an egg. The event of reaching the top of the mountain is always preceded by the event of starting out. Doing nothing is invariably followed by no omelette, or no summit. Which events unfold from time's womb depends on what we decide to do—this is what the *inside* control of a person or a thermostat means. Our choosing modules are implicated in the process, unlike those of mere spectators.

Is this response to the 'lazy sophism' final and conclusive?

I think it is, if the lazy sophism is taken as an argument for acting one way or another. There is no conceivable reason for preferring the 'do nothing' conclusion to the 'get cracking' conclusion. Putting it another way, in this practical sphere, accepting one argument is equivalent to admiring or desiring to be someone whose modules have a certain shape. The shape would be achieved by accepting this advice: on thinking about the future and the womb of time, do nothing. But why should one admire anyone who genuinely follows that advice? They are simply good-for-nothings: people who do not make omelettes and do not reach summits, nor even set out for them.

But perhaps the line of thought bears a different interpretation. Fatalism is usually thought of as *dissolving* choice rather than recommending one kind of choice over another. It is supposed to show that choice is an illusion.

But what, in turn, is that supposed to mean? We have already argued that one conception of choice is an illusion. This was interventionist choice, or the full-scale uncaused intervention of the Real Me into the physical and neurophysiological order of events. We have retreated into thinking of the flexible choosing modules that are implicated in our doings. How could thoughts about the passage of time show that their operations are unreal or illusory? It seems no more plausible than suggesting that because of the passage of time, the operations of computers, or thermostats or chainsaws are illusory.

When you don't know what will happen, and you think events will respond to your doings, you deliberate about what to do. We have seen that fatalism affords no argument for conducting that deliberation one way or another. And it affords no argument that the process itself is unreal, unless the process is construed in the outside way we have considered and rejected.

But suppose you don't know what is going to happen, but it is known, perhaps to God. Or just: it is knowable. We think, as we deliberate, that the future is open, but the past fixed. But suppose the future is as fixed as the past is. Thus we think like this:

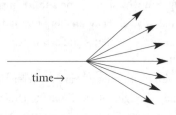

—where the arrows represent open possibilities, spreading out from now. But perhaps this way of thinking is illusory. Perhaps the truth is only seen from a 'God's eye view', or what has been called the 'view from nowhen'. From this perspective, time is laid out like a celluloid movie film; a frame of the film corresponds to the events at any one time. Given the way the world works, we can be aware only of past frames (sometimes people think that prophets can 'see' future frames). But there is no metaphysical asymmetry between past and future:

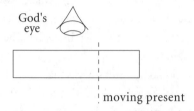

If that's the truth, we might think, surely it is as useless trying to influence the future as it would be to try to influence the past. If God has this view, he must be looking at our efforts, and laughing. This is the implication of the Sufi story. Death has already written his list. And this is why my friend's soldiers used the metaphor of a bullet 'having a number on it', which implies 'already having a number on it'—regardless, that is, of what we do.

But why is God or Death laughing? Suppose God has the timeless view. He still does not see omelettes at one date, without people breaking eggs at a slightly earlier date. He knows whether we will have an omelette in one frame of the film. But then he also knows whether we will set about preparing the omelette in a slightly earlier frame. There is no reason for him to know that the future will be what it is whatever we do, any more than he knows that the tree will blow down whatever the wind does. From the timeless vantage-point, all that is seen is the wind, and the destruction. God is *not*, as far as this goes, like a medical practitioner who knows that a cancer will kill us whatever we do. That would mean that there would be frames in which people behave in a whole variety of ways, but die from the cancer anyhow. The 'view from nowhen', from outside time, sees our doings, and their upshots, but it doesn't see upshots without doings. God sees us eating omelettes, because our choosing modules set us to break eggs. And he only sees us eating omelettes when he sees, in the previous time frame, us breaking eggs.

The implication of the Sufi story is that Death had the disciple on the list *before* the disciple decided to flee. So, it seems, it would have come for him wherever he had been—in Baghdad, or in Samarkand. This is why his flight was futile. But perhaps Death only had him on his list because of his flight—if he ran under a bus, having arrived in Samarkand, for example. Running then brought him to his fate, but this does not tell us whether the disciple behaved reasonably. If Death was having a field day in Baghdad, for instance because there was a plague there, then the flight might have been quite rational, although unlucky in the event. It *could* have been that Death did not have him on his list, just because of his flight.

What about the asymmetry between past and future? If they are symmetrical in God's eyes, why is it rational to try to change the future? How can it be any more rational than trying to change the past? Well, as I have said, even God does not see us setting about making omelettes, with a slightly *previous* event of eating one (unless he sees us greedily preparing and devouring second omelettes). So in fact, it is useless to try to influence the past. That however leaves open a huge and intractable philosophical problem. For is it just a matter of fact, a contingency that might have been otherwise, or might be otherwise in different regions of space and time, that we cannot influence the past? If it is only a matter of the patterns seen from the timeless point of view, it seems that it should be. Might the patterns be different elsewhere?

For the moment I leave this is an exercise (an extremely difficult one). But returning to fatalism, the truth, then, is that there is no general philosophical or rational justification for it. It corresponds to a mood, a state of mind in which we feel out of control, and feel that we are indeed just spectators of our own lives. This is not *always* unjustified. People are sometimes largely powerless, politically, or even psychologically (because we are not flexible, but are indeed brainwashed, or in the grip of strange obsessions that we cannot shake). When we are powerless, fatalism may be a natural frame of mind into which to relapse. If our best efforts come to nothing often enough, we need consolation, and thoughts of unfolding, infinite destiny, or *karma*, are sometimes consoling.

But not appropriate when we are acting. We cannot safely think, while driving a car, that it makes no difference whether we turn the wheel, or hit the brake. Our best efforts do not come to nothing.

FLEXIBILITY AND DIGNITY

The ideology of mind–body dualism runs very deep. By an ideology, I mean not a specific argument or set of arguments, but rather a framework of thought: a reference point or a guiding idea. Dualism is often supposed to make possible freedom, dignity, human experience itself. It underwrites the big words: the kinds of words that get on banners. In the last two chapters I have tried to disconnect these things from dualism. But people fear the alternative. Are we reducing people, in all their living colourful complexity, to drab monochrome machines, conditioned into being this way or that, or worse, passive vehicles for our selfish genes?

Absolutely not.

The problem here is that the alternatives are posed as if they exhaust the field: either a free spirit, blissfully floating apart from the natural order, or a determined machine like a bus, or even a tram. We shall meet this fallacy of misrepresenting the alternatives again in subsequent chapters. It is not the philosophy of compatibilism that denigrates human nature, but this way of putting the alternatives. This way of putting the matter supposes that nature is so awful that it takes a magical moment, a divine spark struck from the ghost in the machine, to make it sing. It is either clockwork (Zombies) or Ghosts. But that is the view that denigrates nature, including human nature. We must learn to think with Wittgenstein when he wrote:

> It is humiliating to have to appear like an empty tube, which is simply inflated by a mind.

The key word to catch hold of is 'flexibility' (remember those inflexible, programmed, Zombies again). And you cannot tell a priori how flexible human behaviour is. Our biology, let us say, gives us the modules. But then, how the modules turn out—how they are programmed if we like, differently in different environments—is another thing. By comparison, biology gives us the structures, whatever they may be, we need to learn language. We have them; no other animal has them to any remotely similar degree. But which language we then learn is not determined by biology, but by environment, as infants imitate the language of their mothers and their kin.

Similarly our awarenesses, our capacities to think of alternatives, our evaluations of them, and our eventual behavioural routines *might* have been highly inflexible. But the evidence suggests that they are the reverse. People can quite naturally grow up caring about a whole variety of things. It is quite difficult to detect any universal pattern at all: flexibility rules. Human beings can grow to make killing fields, and they can grow to make gardens.

Theorists and gurus like to make a pattern: people are all selfish; people are only influenced by class interests; people hate their parents; people can be conditioned; men are aggressive; women are gentle; people cannot help themselves, and so on. But this is not so much a matter of *following* the evidence, as of *imposing an interpretation* on it. Like all stereotypes, such interpretations can be dangerous, for people can be caused to conform to them, and often become worse as a result than they might have been otherwise. The job of conceptual engineering, here, is to supply a clearer outline of alternative structures of thought, and there are many.

CHAPTER FOUR

The Self

We have looked at consciousness of the contents of our own minds. And we have looked at agency and freedom—our activities in the world. But what about the self itself: the 'I' that I am? We saw that Descartes salvaged this alone out of the wreckage of universal doubt. Lichtenberg, we also saw, queried his right even to do that. Who was right and how are we to think about the self?

AN IMMORTAL SOUL?

Here are some actual things we think about ourselves:

■ LIST 1

I was once very small.

Barring accident or bad luck, I will become old.

When I get old, I will probably lose quite a lot of my memories. I will also change, for instance in wanting to do different things. My body will change too.

The organic material of my body (except my brain) changes roughly every seven years.

If my body suffered as a result of an accident, for example by losing some parts, I would have to cope with the result.

Now here are some possible things to think about ourselves. When I say that they are possible, I only mean that we seem to *understand* them, not necessarily that we believe them. The possibilities may strike us as quite *outlandish*, but that is not at present to the point:

■ LIST 2

I might have been born at another time and place.

I might survive my bodily death, and live another kind of life as a spirit.

I might have been blessed or cursed with a different body.

I might have been blessed or cursed with different mental capacities—a different mind.

I might have been blessed or cursed with both a different body and a different mind.

I might be the reincarnation of some historical personage.

I might have to live life again, e.g. as a dog, unless I behave well.

In fact, there are people who believe, or say that they believe, such things, and indeed whole religions may hold some. Christianity holds the second on this list to be actually true, and Hinduism holds the last. And even if we don't accept any, still, we seem to know what is meant.

The difference between these two lists is this. The first list is compatible with a straightforward view of what I am. I am a large, human animal. My biography is like that of other animals, beginning with a natural birth, including natural changes, and ending with a natural death. I am firmly located and bounded in space and time. I survive various natural changes, such as ageing. But that is all.

The second list suggests that I am something much more mysterious, something that is only contingently 'fastened to a dying animal'. According to the possibilities on the second list, I am something that can change shape and form, body and mind, and that could exist even without a body at all. The biography of the 'I' could span centuries, and it could span endless changes of character, rather like an actor.

As we saw in the first two chapters, Descartes thought we had a 'clear and distinct' perception that the self was distinct from the body. And the possibilities we contemplate, from the second list, may seem to support him. It is as if there is something—my soul, or self, or essence—that *does* endure through quite a lot of changes (list 1) and *could* endure through even more remarkable events (list 2). But what then is this self? Here is David Hume again:

> *For my part, when I enter most intimately into what I call my-self, I always stumble on some particular perception or other, of heat or cold, light or shade, love or hatred, pain or pleasure. I never can catch myself at any time without a perception, and never can observe any thing but the perception. When my per-*

*ceptions are removed for any time, as by sound sleep, so long
am I insensible of myself, and may truly be said not to exist.
And were all my perceptions removed by death, and could I
neither think, nor feel, nor see, nor love, nor hate, after the dis-
solution of my body, I should be entirely annihilated, nor do I
conceive what is further requisite to make me a perfect non-
entity.*

Hume is pointing out that the self is elusive. It is *unobservable*. If
you 'look inside your own mind' to try to catch it, you miss because
all you stumble upon are what he calls particular perceptions, or
experiences and emotions. You don't also get a glimpse of the 'I'
that is the subject of these experiences. Yet we all think we know
ourselves with a quite peculiar intimacy. As we saw, Descartes
thought that this self-knowledge survived even 'hyperbolic' doubt.

This nugget of the self has seemed to many philosophers to have
another remarkable property. It is *simple*. The self is not *composite*.
Here is one of Hume's contemporaries, the 'common-sense' Scottish philosopher, Thomas Reid (1710–96):

*A part of a person is a manifest absurdity. When a man loses
his estate, his health, his strength, he is still the same person,
and has lost nothing of his personality. If he has a leg or an
arm cut off, he is the same person he was before. The amputated member is no part of his person, otherwise it would have
a right to part of his estate, and be liable for a part of his en-
gagements. It would be entitled to a share of his merit and de-
merit, which is manifestly absurd. A person is something
indivisible ... My thoughts, and actions, and feelings, change
every moment; they have no continued, but a successive existence; but that self or I, to which they belong, is permanent,*

and has the same relation to all the succeeding thoughts, ac-
tions and feelings which I call mine.

This simple, enduring 'I' is the thing which Hume complained he could never stumble upon. Reid bangs the table, and announces its existence.

The simplicity of the soul conveniently opens the door to a traditional argument for its immortality.

> All change and decay is the coming together or falling apart of composite things. *So*, anything that is not composite cannot change and decay. The soul is not composite. *So*, the soul cannot change or decay.

As it stands, the first premise might not look all that compelling. It would require some kind of defence. The idea would be that in any natural (physical) change, we can detect something that is *conserved*. If you break a biscuit, the matter of the biscuit is conserved. It used to be thought that atoms are conserved, so that chemical change would be simply the rearrangement of atoms in a substance. Now we might think we have to dig deeper: perhaps it is energy that is conserved, or sub-atomic particles whose rearrangements are responsible for changes in composite stuff. In either event, it is only the compositions that change. The real 'stuff' (fundamental particles, energy) just keeps on.

If you could really defend the first premise as an a priori truth, and if you think Reid has given good grounds for the second premise (the soul is not composite), then the argument looks pretty good. Of course, it is equally an argument for the existence of my Self before my natural birth, which might be a bit deflating.

Might all these thoughts be illusions? Should we really accept that list 2 gives us even bare possibilities? Never mind, for the moment, whether these possibilities actually obtain, as various believers hold. Let us ask instead whether they are even coherent.

OAK TREES AND SHIPS

It is good to reflect how strange some of the beliefs on the second list are. They prise the self away from *everything* that seems to give it an identity, whether body, history, memory, or even mind. Does this make any sense? To approach this, let us turn our attention away from ourselves and think about the identity of other things. We can turn again to John Locke, who made an interesting observation about vegetables or plants:

> That being then one plant which has such an organization of parts in one coherent body partaking of one common life, it continues to be the same plant as long as it partakes of the same life, though that life be communicated to new particles of matter vitally united to the living plant, in a like continued organization conformable to that sort of plants.

Locke points out that we can have the same oak tree, for instance, through a period of time, although the constituent 'atoms', or cells or molecules, change. What is required is 'partaking of the same life', or in other words what we might think of as an organizational or functional unity. It does not matter whether the bits remain the same, so long as this unity of function is maintained. And so long as it is, we talk properly of the same oak tree. So we have the same oak tree as a sapling, and as a mature tree, after some branches have dropped off, and so on.

Locke can use this insight to explain why we identify the same human being through the normal changes of life. 'Same man or woman' is like 'same tree' or 'same monkey'. It accommodates growth and change, so long as there is continuity of function, or of organized life. So far then, so good. Locke has got a good hold on what enables us to reidentify the same human being (thought of as a large mammal: what you see when you look in a mirror) or same plant through time. Why should anything change when we come to the self?

If we look at the second list of things with which I began this chapter, we will see that if we confine attention to plants and animals, none of the thoughts there gets a foothold. They make no sense at all. We do not think of a particular oak tree, 'Hey, that tree might have been a maple,' unless this means that we could have planted a different tree, a maple, where we actually planted the oak. But then it would have been a *different* tree. It wouldn't have been that very oak dressed up, as it were, as a maple. Similarly, we do not imagine trees surviving organic death, so that the very same tree might come back, for instance, as a daffodil. So if there is nothing different to being the 'same self' than being the 'same human being', and if we settle the identity of human beings through time rather as we settle the identity of animals, then it looks as if none of the thoughts on list 2 should make any sense.

The same oak tree, at two different times, need not be the same aggregate of identical molecules, at the two different times. The same is true even of inorganic things. Consider the cloud that streams off the summit of Everest. To the mountaineer the same cloud may drift off the summit for hours or days. But it is changing its composition every second, as the wind tears water molecules through it at a hundred miles an hour. It is the same cloud for all that. We tolerate differences of constitution, at least up to a point. We think like this when we think of human groups, such as clubs or teams. We think of ourselves as supporting the 'same team' year in, year out, although the membership of the team (and possibly its management, and its ground) changes. The glorious history of the regiment would not be nearly so glorious if we could only identify the same regiment as far back as its present membership. We also think like this when it comes to inanimate things with a function. It is still the same computer, although I add to its memory, change the screen, update the system, and so on.

We are often quite careless about how much change to tolerate while still regarding it as the same 'thing': witness the joke about the Irish axe which has been in the family for several generations, although it has had three new heads and five new handles. Sometimes we get confused: an illustration is the case of the 'ship of Theseus'. Theseus goes on a long voyage, and in the course of it bits of his ship need replacing. In fact, by the end, he has tossed overboard used sails, spars, rigging, planks, and replaced them all. Does he come back in the same ship? We would probably say so. But suppose some entrepreneur goes round behind him, picking up the discarded bits, and reassembles them. Can't the entrepreneur claim to have the original ship? But surely we cannot have two different ships each of which is identical with the original?

SOULS AND ELASTIC BALLS

So perhaps to make sense of the thoughts in list 2 we would invoke an 'immaterial substance'—the mysterious, simple, soul of Me. It might even seem that these thoughts are sound enough to give some kind of argument for Cartesian dualism, it only being within that framework that they make any sense. But then Locke makes an extremely interesting move. We have seen that plants and animals survive change of material substance. So why shouldn't persons (me, you) survive change of soul substance?

> But the question is, whether if the same substance, which thinks, be changed, it can be the same person, or remaining the same, it can be different persons?
>
> And to this I answer first, this can be no question at all to those, who place thought in a purely material, animal, constitution, void of an immaterial substance. For, whether their supposition be true or no, 'tis plain they conceive personal identity preserved in something else than identity of substance; as animal identity is preserved in identity of life, and not of substance. And therefore those, who place thinking in an immaterial substance only, before they can come to deal with these men, must shew why personal identity cannot be preserved in the change of immaterial substances, or variety of particular immaterial substances, as well as animal identity is preserved in the change of material substances, or variety of particular bodies.

Locke's wonderful move is to point out that even if we are very worried by personal survival through time and change, invoking 'immaterial soul substances' *won't help*. Why not? Because just as we count plants through time regardless of change of material elements, so we count persons over time without any reference to 'immaterial substances'. There is a nice illustration of his point given by Kant. In this quotation from his masterpiece, the *Critique of Pure Reason*, 'representations' are things like experiences or thoughts—what Descartes would have lumped under 'cogitationes'—contents of the mind:

> *An elastic ball which impinges on another similar ball in a straight line communicates to the latter its whole motion and therefore its whole state (that is, if we take account only of the positions in space). If, then, in analogy with such bodies, we postulate substances such that the one communicates to the other representations together with the consciousness of them, we can conceive a whole series of substances of which the first transmits its state together with its consciousness to the second, the second its own state with that of the preceding substance to the third, and this in turn the states of all the preceding substances together with its own consciousness and with their consciousness to another. The last substance would then be conscious of all the states of the previously changed substances, as being its own states, because they would have been transferred to it together with the consciousness of them.*

The point is that we don't know anything about 'immaterial substances'. Perhaps our immaterial substance gets replaced every evening, like the change of disk drive in a computer that preserves all the software and files.

All this is quite enough to put grave doubts in front of the argument for immortality that we considered. As Kant continues:

> *For we are unable from our own consciousness to determine*

whether, as souls, we are permanent or not. Since we reckon as belonging to our identical self only that of which we are conscious, we must necessarily judge that we are one and the same throughout the whole time of which we are conscious. We cannot, however, claim that this judgment would be valid from the standpoint of an outside observer. For since the only permanent appearance which we encounter in the soul is the representation 'I' that accompanies and connects them all, we are unable to prove that this 'I', a mere thought, may not be in the same state of flux as the other thoughts which, by means of it, are linked up with one another.

We can summarize the negative point by saying that nothing in our inner musings about 'myself' licenses thinking in terms of a permanent inner substance, capable of surviving even the most remarkable changes and possibilities. But each of Locke and Kant has a more positive point to make.

THE BRAVE OFFICER

Locke says that it is 'the same consciousness that makes a man be himself to himself'—and neither the subject nor third parties looking on care whether that consciousness is 'carried' by enduring substances, or by a succession of different ones. He himself goes on to expand the emphasis on consciousness by claiming that a person A at a time is the same person as person B at an earlier time only in so far as A is conscious of B's experiences. In other words, A must remember thinking what B thought and remember sensing and feeling and acting as B sensed and felt and acted.

The suggestion has some consequences that we might quite like. It rules out, for instance, the possibility that I am Cleopatra, reincarnated, since I am not conscious of having done or felt anything that Cleopatra may have done or felt. The memory wipeout destroys personal identity. Similarly, I can be sure that I will not live another life as a dog. For no dog could remember doing things I did; if it did remember them (but think of the neural complexity required!) it would not be a dog, but at best a doggiform human being. But dogs are not doggiform human beings.

On the other hand, the suggestion has some consequences we might not like so much. It means that I cannot survive complete amnesia, for instance, since whatever person remains after such an event cannot be me. But it also has problems with partial amnesia. Suppose I commit a crime, but then, perhaps because of the untoward rush of blood or adrenalin, retain no memory of the time in question. Then it seems to follow from Locke's theory that I am not the person who committed the crime. I am the same human being, but not the same person. It seems that the one human being is inhabited by multiple successive personalities, as memories come and go.

Thomas Reid presented a version of this problem, as the 'brave officer objection':

> *Suppose a brave officer to have been flogged when a boy at school for robbing an orchard, to have taken a standard from the enemy in his first campaign, and to have been made a general in advanced life; suppose, also, which must be admitted to be possible, that, when he took the standard he was conscious of his having been flogged at school, and that, when made a*

general, he was conscious of his taking the standard, but had
absolutely lost the consciousness of his flogging. These things
being supposed, it follows, from Mr. Locke's doctrine, that he
who was flogged at school is the same person who took the
standard, and that he who took the standard is the same per-
son who was made a general. Whence it follows, if there be any
truth in logic, that the general is the same person with him
who was flogged at school. But the general's consciousness
does not reach so far back as his flogging; therefore, according
to Mr. Locke's doctrine, he is not the person who was flogged.
Therefore the general is, and at the same time is not, the same
person with him who was flogged at school.

In fact, Locke himself was perfectly aware of this problem. His
reply is simple:

But yet possibly it will still be objected, suppose I wholly lose
the memory of some parts of my life, beyond a possibility of re-
trieving them, so that perhaps I shall never be conscious of
them again; yet am I not the same person, that did those ac-
tions, had those thoughts, that I once was conscious of, though
I have now forgot them? To which I answer, that we must here
take notice what the word I is applied to, which in this case is
the man only. And the same man being presumed to be the
same person, I is easily here supposed to stand also for the
same person. But if it be possible for the same man to have dis-
tinct incommunicable consciousness at different times, it is
past doubt the same man would at different times make dif-
ferent persons.

A way of reconstructing his point is this. Either 'same person' just
goes along with 'same human being' or it does not. If it does, we all
agree that we have the one human being from infancy to death, re-

gardless of mental capacities. And none of the thoughts on list 2 make any sense. The reason for saying that 'same person' does not go with 'same human being', for Locke, is that we allow that if one man has 'distinct incommunicable consciousness' then we have different persons, successively inhabiting the one body (we might also think of multiple personality disorders). But in that case, it is surprising, but correct, to say that the senile general is not the schoolboy.

Locke's reason for his view is, in a way, the very thing Reid disliked. He thought that we primarily need a notion of the 'same person' through time in order to justify claims of *responsibility*. He thought that personal identity was a 'forensic' notion, meaning one whose home is in courts of law. We can see the point of his idea by considering cases where a doddering eighty-year-old is suddenly charged with crimes, say, from the war some sixty-five years ago when he was a naive conscripted teenager. Is this fair? Suppose he genuinely retains no memory of his crimes. Then to him, it is as if he is being condemned for deeds done by a completely different person. And this seems unjust: if the person has no consciousness, then he cannot 'repent' of his deeds just because they are not part of his own self-consciousness. They cannot weigh on his conscience.

Locke was aware, of course, that we do not conduct our own courts like that. Amnesia is not a valid excuse, after all. But he thought this just reflected our suspicions, since it is too easy to claim amnesia. In God's eyes, real amnesia really excuses. He would treat the genuinely amnesiac eighty-year-old as a different person from the one-time war criminal. This might sound attractive, but not quite so good in the case of the crime committed because of the rush of blood to the head, where we might say that it is neither here nor there that the agent has forgotten it. We might want to distinguish degrees of memory loss.

What of Reid's charge that Locke's theory contravenes logic itself, involving a contradiction? The contradiction is called 'failure of transitivity' of identity. Transitivity is the logical law that if $A = B$ and $B = C$, then $A = C$. Here the schoolboy = the officer, and the officer = the general, but for Locke it is not the case that the schoolboy = the general. This is what Reid calls a contradiction.

This certainly seems odd, but perhaps the oddity comes from abstracting out 'identity' when what we are really talking about is 'is the same person as'. Consider again any composite, such as a bicycle or a ship. Suppose age of ships matters, for instance to whichever tax bracket they get into. Perhaps antique ships over fifty years old are taxed less. When is the later ship, then, a genuine antique? (Here we can imagine Theseus and the entrepreneur who picked up the original pieces each trying to claim the tax break.) If these tiresome entrepreneurs became common, we might have to pass a law sorting out which is the original ship. A law might say something like:

> A ship must be registered every year, and to count as the same ship as on any particular previous year, a vessel must contain at least 55 per cent of the material making up the ship on the first day she was registered that previous year.

Then we can reproduce Reid's structure: you can easily verify that under this code $Argos_1$ might be the same ship as $Argos_2$, and $Argos_2$

the same ship as $Argos_3$, but $Argos_1$ not the same ship as $Argos_3$. But the law itself seems quite sensible, rather like laws which specify what something has to contain to count as butter or to count as corn-fed. And surely a sensible law cannot give rise to a *contradiction*?

Well, ships are composite things, made up of parts, and that seems to be what gives rise to the problem. So perhaps Reid's argument that you cannot have A = B, B = C, but not A = C, only goes through if each of A, B, C is simple, not composite. Now, as we saw, Reid himself held that the soul was simple, but Locke did not, so perhaps the argument does not count against him.

THE SELF AS BUNDLE

We saw Hume pointing out that when you reflect on the contents of your own mind, you find individual memories, thoughts, passions, experiences, but no *you*. Hume himself thought that if you did not (and could not) encounter something in experience, then you had no right to talk of it. Your mind could not embrace it, or even 'touch' it. Hence, consistently, he held that the self was nothing but an aggregate of its 'perceptions' or experiences, together with whatever connections there are between them. There was content, but no container. This is sometimes called a 'no ownership' theory of the self, or the 'bundle' theory of the self. For Hume, like Lichtenberg in the first chapter, we have 'it thinks', or rather, 'thoughts go on'. But we do not have an owner or possessor or 'I' doing the thinking.

The standard problem with this is that it requires that we can make good sense of the idea of an unowned experience. But it is objected that this is incoherent. It treats experiences as 'objects' or things in their own right: the kind of thing that might float around, unowned, waiting to be scooped into a bundle with some others, like sticks lying in a forest. But, the objection continues, this is a mistake, for experiences are *parasitic*, or *adjectival* on persons who have them. What does this mean?

Consider a dent in a car. We can talk about dents: this dent is worse than that one, or will be more costly to repair than the dent we suffered last year. But it is logically impossible that there could exist an 'unowned' dent, a dent without a surface that is dented. Dents are, as it were, the shadows of adjectives. In the beginning there is a surface, the surface is changed by becoming dented, and then we abstract out a noun, and talk about the dent. The noun 'dent' is logically downwind of the adjective, 'dented'. Similarly a grin is downwind of a face that is grinning, which is the joke behind Lewis Carroll's Cheshire cat, which disappeared leaving only its grin behind.

So the objection to Hume is that 'experiences' are in the same way parasitic on persons. You cannot imagine a pain, for instance, as a 'thing' floating around waiting to be caught up in a bundle of other experiences, so that it might be accidental whether it, that very same pain, attaches itself to one bundle or another. In the beginning there is the person, and the onset of a pain is just the event of a bit of the person beginning to hurt, just as the onset of a dent is a bit of a surface becoming dented.

Kant puts this point by talking of the 'I think' that accompanies all my representations. In other words, my experiences come billed as 'mine'. I do not first become acquainted with the experience, then look round for the owner, and then (provided, against Hume, that this last search is successful) announce that the experience is one of mine. Rather, for me to feel a pain is in and of itself to be aware that I am in pain.

But how is this possible, if Hume is right that we are never aware of a 'self'? It is all very well comparing pains to dents, and it is certainly true that when I am aware of a dent this is only because I am aware of a dented surface. But at least we are aware of surfaces, dented or not. Whereas if Hume is right we do not seem to be aware of our soul or self.

Perhaps the way forward has to be to deny that the 'self' is the kind of thing of which awareness is possible. Wittgenstein talks of cases where we describe ourselves as subjects of experience: 'I hear the rain' or 'I have a toothache'. He points out that in this kind of case 'there is no question of recognizing a person'. 'It is as impossible that in making the statement "I have a toothache" I should have mistaken another person for myself, as it is to moan with pain by mistake, having mistaken someone else for me.' You cannot *misidentify* the subject as yourself. Wittgenstein thinks this gives rise to an illusion:

> We feel then that in the cases in which 'I' is used as subject, we don't use it because we recognize a particular person by his bodily characteristics; and this creates the illusion that we use this word to refer to something bodiless, which, however, has its seat in our body. In fact this seems to be the real ego, the one of which it was said, 'Cogito ergo sum'. 'Is there then no mind,

but only a body?' Answer: the word 'mind' has meaning, i.e.,
it has a use in our language; but saying this doesn't yet say
what kind of use we make of it.

We should try thinking of self-consciousness some other way.
What way?

THE SELF AS AN ORGANIZING PRINCIPLE

Imagine the problem in terms of artificial intelligence. Imagine a
robot, equipped with a video camera, and able to motor around a
room in which various objects are arranged. Suppose our plan is to
get the robot to deliver an output describing the arrangement of
the objects in the room. What kind of thing would we need to do?
If the robot simply directs its camera at an object, pixels fire up. It
has the kind of 'inner glow' that people sometimes link to consciousness. But if that is all it has, there is only what Kant called a
'rhapsody of perceptions', or what the pioneering American psychologist William James (1842–1910) later called a 'blooming
buzzing confusion'. In other words, the robot still has to organize
its data, in order to interpret the scene. Suppose the screen shows a
round shape. Is it near to a small round object, or far away from a
large round object? Is it looking slantways at an elliptical object? To
solve these problems the robot might move, and obtain a new picture. But it then has to 'synthesize' the various pictures together, to
build up a three-dimensional representation of the room. What

abilities would be involved in this synthesis? How is it to unify the different pictures obtained at different times?

The minimal ingredients would seem to be these. It needs some way of telling whether it is itself moving. In particular it needs some ability to distinguish whether it is moving, and getting new views of stationary objects, or whether it is still, and the objects around it are moving. To do this, it needs a memory of what the scene was like, to compare to what it is now like. It needs to be able to represent the *order* of different appearances, and then it needs some way of integrating the past scenes and the present scene. In other words, to solve for the position of objects in space, it has to solve for *its own point of view* and for elapsed *time* during which it can log *its* own movements.

What this suggests is that a minimal self-consciousness is a *structural* requirement on any kind of interpretation of experience. If the programmer can solve this problem for the robot, it cannot be by giving it just another ingredient on the screen (as if the camera always caught a glimpse of one of its wheels, down at the bottom of the screen). That would just be more 'input'. It wouldn't be part of the programming needed to turn input into a description of the room and of the robot's place in it.

In fact the robot need never catch any glimpse of itself. The camera can be rigidly pointed at the scene in front of it. This is why Hume would have been no nearer catching himself even if whenever he turned his eye inward he caught a continuing element of experience, like a background drone. What the robot does need instead is a way of tracking its own route through the space, and the time order of the appearances it gets. It is a requirement of the solution that it has an 'egocentric' point of view, or in other words presents the space as centred upon 'itself'. Given that it can now interpret a scene as containing a table three feet away, it can *also* say 'the table is three feet from *me*'—yet it need have no acquaintance with its bodily shape, or long-term history. And it most certainly needs no acquaintance with an internal ego or immortal soul.

If the room is chaotic enough, the problem might become insoluble. For example, if we unkindly put the robot into a kind of Keystone Cops environment, in which objects come and go at random or with amazing rapidity, then it will be stuck with an insoluble problem: just random pixels firing, but too little continuity from one moment to the next for any program to get a grip.

So thinking in terms of an 'I' now looks like a formal or structural requirement on interpreting experience in the way we do—as experience of a three-dimensional world of continuing objects, amongst which we move. The 'I' is the point of view from which interpretation starts. It is not something else given in experience, because nothing given in experience could solve the formal problem for which an 'I' is needed. But a point of view is always needed: to represent a scene to yourself is to represent yourself as experiencing it one way or another.

DELUSIONS OF IMAGINATION

The line of thought I have just introduced is due to Immanuel Kant. It is one of the great moves in philosophy, exploding in all kinds of directions, some of which we return to later. But for our purposes its present interest is that it suggests a diagnosis of the thoughts in list 2, at the beginning of this chapter.

These thoughts arise because I seem able to imagine myself in different shoes, including the shoes of historical characters, dogs, or angels. And I then think, I must have transported the mysterious self, my very soul, into the imagined scene. And the soul becomes something very strange, because part of my imagining may be to imagine myself at a different time, with a different body, or different mental properties, with different experiences, and so on. In other words, I abstract out from everything that gives me my identity as a human being, but still suppose that there is something, the essence of Me, left. Hence, Descartes's 'real distinction'.

But suppose instead I am not transporting *anything* in my imagination. All I am doing is representing to myself what *it would be like* to see the world from a different point of view, at a different time, or whatever. If there is no essence of Me transported to the different scenes, then the fact that I can imagine them gives no evidence that 'I' might have experienced them, or might survive to experience them. By way of illustration, consider the first on the list: I might survive bodily death. What imaginings lie behind this? Well, perhaps I can imagine looking at the funeral, with my coffin, and the family mourning. Perhaps I am skulking at the back of the church. Perhaps I am miffed that the congregation does not seem all that upset. Perhaps I would like to tell them that it is not so bad after all. Perhaps being dead I have X-ray vision, so I give myself a glimpse of my body lying inside. All very sad. How old I look. But wait! Here are the pearly gates and there is grandmother waiting to greet me . . .

In imagining all this, I rehearse for myself the experience of looking at my coffin and so on. And this I can surely do: I can understand what it would be like to see it, after all (not unlike seeing other coffins). I can understand what it would be like to glimpse inside it—a gruesome sight. But, and this is the crucial point, these exercises of understanding do not transport a 'me' who is doing the seeing, whilst the human being Simon Blackburn is dead. It is I here and now who am doing the imagining, but there *is no I* who is being imagined doing the viewing. The only relic of me in the scenario is the dead body.

The point can be put like this. Kant's line of thought suggests that there is an equivalence between 'I can imagine seeing X' and 'I can imagine myself seeing X'. But because this is a purely formal equivalence there is no substantive self, no soul of Me, involved in either imagining. Hence, it is wrong to take such imaginings as supporting any 'real distinction' between you as subject, as self or soul, and the animal that in fact you are. So the imaginings of X do not support the possibility that your biography *might* outrun the biography of that animal, just because X is something that the animal will not see.

Similarly, suppose I do what I might call 'imagining me being Genghis Khan'. I picture riders and battlefields. I am short, and crafty, and a wonderful horseman. God, the steppes are cold. All this politics sometimes gets me down. 'Another helping of fermented mare's milk,' I call. Whoops, I am supposed to speak Mongolian, and not English.

Here it should be more obvious that there is no soul of Me transported into the Genghis figure. In fact, in so far as there is anything of *me* left in the imagining, such as the lapse into English, the imagining is a failure. It is exactly as if an actor takes on a historical character, but brings to it anachronisms—Henry VIII looks at his watch or talks about what is on at the cinema.

What I really do is to visualize battlefields, the cold steppes, and so on, as if I were seeing them, and doing warrior-like things, like commanding events and jumping on horses. I might be more or less successful at doing this: some people are better at imagining the world from different points of view, just as some people are better actors than others. If my Genghis Khan is still speaking English, I haven't got very far.

Does this prove that all the thoughts on list 2 are illusions? It undermines the support that simple imaginings provide for them. If they have some other support, well and good. But it is healthy to reflect how much the list depends on first-person imaginings. If I try to suppose that *you* were once Genghis Khan, not much seems to happen. *You*, slaughtering people from a horse? Unaware of supermarkets, motor cars, and aeroplanes? *You* with a different gender, age, mind (for it is very unlikely that you think as Genghis did)? All I succeed in doing if I try to think through this possibility is to substitute thinking of Genghis Khan for thinking of you. It is like replacing thinking of the oak tree with thinking of a daffodil, which is certainly not thinking that the oak tree might have been a daffodil. I do not manage to think any kind of identity.

In short, I have to think of you just as a large human animal with a personality. Other human animals with other personalities are not you, and you could not have been one of them. How much of your personality could you lose and still be you? Well, that may be a bit like the problem of the ships. Perhaps we allow quite a lot, but eventually we say things like 'Well, he's not the person he used to be'. On the view suggested by Locke and Kant, this may literally be true.

SCRAMBLING THE SOUL

There is a curious difference between the past and the future, when we think of our own selves.

Suppose we lived in a world in which human bodies and brains were easier to aggregate and disaggregate than they are. We could take them apart and reassemble them as we can with computers or automobiles. Suppose that these operations are called scrambling operations. We can crank up the psychologies of people again after these operations, rather like copying the software and files on a computer. Or, we can change the dispositions, by changing the software or files, retaining some old and adding some new. Scrambling operations are regarded as beneficial and healthy.

Suppose in such a world *you* were told that tomorrow you would go into a scrambling operation. And you are given a glimpse of who will emerge. Person A has a lot of your stuff in him, and a lot of your qualities: he or she remembers things as you now do, looks much as you do, and so on. Anyhow, person A is going to be sent to the Arctic (perhaps you are army personnel). Person B is also a good match with you, again incorporating lots of your actual physical stuff—brain and cells—in him, and having a lot of your qualities (software and files). Person B is going to the tropics.

From *our* standpoint this is a bit like the ship of Theseus. We need not make a big issue of whether *you* become person A or *you* become person B. We might find ourselves regarding one of the new people, or even both of them, as *you*—or we might find ourselves regarding them as newborns. An analogy used by the contemporary philosopher David Lewis is with a road that splits. We do not think it is a big metaphysical issue whether we say that just one branch is the old Turnpike Way, or whether both are, or whether neither is.

But from *your* standpoint, it might seem the truth is crucial. Either you will spend next year in the cold, or in the heat, or you will not survive at all. There are just three crisp options. You can't wrap your mind around vagueness and indeterminacy: 'It will be a bit as if you are in the tropics and a bit as if you are in the Arctic' makes no sense. There is nobody *at the later time* for whom there is some kind of mixture of tropic and Arctic, heat and cold. A is cold, and B is hot. There is nobody for whom it is half-and-half. Equally, 'It will be a bit as if you don't exist and a bit as if you do' is just as bad. Either you will be in the one place sweating it out, or in the other place freezing, or you will have joined your ancestors. 'You will be there as both of them' just sounds like cant, as if someone consoled me for never having seen Venice by saying 'You will be there as your son goes'. Blow that. (As Woody Allen said of a similar consolation: 'I don't want to achieve immortality through my work. I want to achieve immortality through not dying.')

The queer thing is that we lose this sense of crispness when we think of the past. Suppose in this world you learn that you now are the result of a scrambling operation that involved two persons, C and D, who each contributed this and that to the person who you are. That is interesting, but it does not give you the same wrenching, urgent need to know. If you learn that C spent Christmas 1990 on a ship and D spent it up a mountain, but you can't remember either, you need not obsess over the question 'Where was *I* on Christmas Day 1990?' If the scrambling gave you vague awareness of *both* experiences that is fine too: you are someone for whom it is a bit as if you climbed a mountain that day, and a bit as if you went sailing.

It is chilling to realize that at *the later time* there need be nobody who is upset about identity. Person A in the Arctic has a partial continuity with you now, and so does person B in the tropics. Each of them can look back with nostalgia on some of your doings. And if they like they can wish for more or less of your parts or your psychological traits and memories, just as we can look back with nostalgia on our earlier selves, and wish to be more or less like them. We can grieve over lost powers and memories, or rejoice over gained knowledge and maturity, according to taste.

Some people think there are definite solutions when we look to the future. They might pin their faith on their identity surviving so long as the actual brain that they currently have survives, in working order. Locke, of course, denied this, since continuity of a functioning brain by no means guarantees continuity of consciousness: the brain might be 'reprogrammed', or reconfigured so that memory and personality all change entirely. And in any event, we might imagine that some scrambling operations pick and choose where bits of the brain go. Other people might pin their faith on a Lockean continuity of 'software' rather than hardware. But they face the difficulty that in a scrambling world we might be able to copy the software at will, creating many future people with identical 'memories' and personality traits.

In short, there seems to be no metaphysical *match* between the simplicity we imagine when we look to the future, and the complexities and vagueness that scrambling can bring about.

Some thinkers get impatient with this kind of scenario. They say that our notions of identity are tailored to the real world, where, perhaps fortunately, 'scrambling' operations are impossible. They say we should let identity look after itself in these bizarre, invented cases. My own opinion is that this is wrong. I agree with these thinkers that we should lose interest in questions of identity when bizarre possibilities are introduced. But I do not think we should lose interest in this feature of our thinking about ourselves: that the options in front of us seem to have a crisp determinate nature *whatever* the vaguenesses that beset our animal features and parts. I suspect it is a feature that fuels many peoples' thoughts about problems of life and death. It motivates hopes, and faiths. It motivates some people to get their brains put into frozen suspension, in the hope that one day *they* will unfreeze and begin a new life, when technology permits. It motivates Reid's belief that the soul is simple. A simple soul, that could not be divided, is just what is needed to preserve the three crisp options. It goes one place or another.

Perhaps however our attachment to the crisp options rests on illusion: the same kind of illusion as the imaginings we considered in the last section. There we insisted that no 'I' was transferred into the imagined scenarios. Here we would have to insist that no definite 'I' is to be introduced into these future scenarios. Once the facts about which current living human animal is going to be present go vague and indeterminate, then facts about *who now* is going to be present then go vague and indeterminate as well. Our propensity to think otherwise is an illusion. It might help to dispel the illusion to remember the reason why Hume could not find his 'self', and why the Kantian explanation of the need to think in terms of a self at all gives us a purely structural motivation. A nugget or atom of me, however simple, cannot do what we need the self for.

But I think I can promise the reader that the idea of those three crisp options is very hard to suppress. Thinking can help, but it is hard for it to destroy the illusions of the self.

So the 'real distinction' Descartes thought he had proved— Cartesian dualism—does not die easily. The reader is free to try to protect it against the line of thought of this chapter and the preceding two. For what it is worth, Kant himself tried to leave room for the immortality of the soul. His rather feeble reason is that we need to suppose that goodness brings happiness, and since it does not do so always or even reliably in this life, there had better be another life in which it does. Then people get their just deserts. Most philosophers think that this is not Kant at his best. But the religious dimension certainly affects the thinking of many people on this matter. So we shall turn to look more directly at that.

CHAPTER FIVE

God

FOR SOME PEOPLE, thinking about the soul is next door to think-ing about religion. And thinking about religion is for them one of the most important of life's occupations. For others it is almost a complete waste of time. In this chapter I introduce some of the ar-guments that surround this area. The arguments, at least, are not a waste of time, for they introduce important principles of thought.

BELIEFS AND OTHER THINGS

Beliefs are supposed to be true. 'I believe that p' and 'I believe that it is true that p' come to the same thing. You cannot say, 'I believe that fairies exist, but I don't think it is true that fairies exist.' And re-ligious people apparently believe various things, which other peo-ple do not believe.

But it is not actually obvious that religion is a matter of truth, or that religious states of mind are to be assessed in terms of truth and falsity. For perhaps religion is not a matter of beliefs, and these states of mind are not beliefs. Accepting a religion may be more like enjoying a poem, or following the football. It might be a matter of immersion in a set of practices. Perhaps the practices have only an emotional point, or a social point. Perhaps religious rituals only serve necessary psychological and social ends. The rituals of birth, coming of age, or funerals do this. It is silly to ask whether a marriage ceremony is true or false. People do not go to a funeral service to hear something true, but to mourn, or to begin to stop mourning, or to meditate on departed life. It can be as inappropriate to ask whether what is said is true as to ask whether Keats's ode to a Grecian urn is true. The poem is successful or not in quite a different dimension, and so is Chartres cathedral, or a statue of the Buddha. They may be magnificent, and moving, and awe-inspiring, but not because they make statements that are true or false.

Some think that this is all there is to it. So if someone says 'God exists', it is not like saying 'Abominable snowmen exist' (where it is an empirical question whether they do) or 'Prime numbers between 20 and 30 exist' (a mathematical question). It is more like expressing joy, or expressing fear (or, more sinister, expressing hatred against outsiders or infidels). Because of this, what is said is immune from criticism as true or false. At best, we might scrutinize the states of mind involved, and try to see whether they are admirable or not.

But this way of understanding religion has not been common. While admitting the emotional and social side, people have taken themselves to be making definite claims about the world—literally true claims, for which there is argument, and evidence. On this view, religious belief is like other belief: an attempt to depict what the world is like, what things it contains, and what explains the events in it. On this view, a funeral service is not true or false, but some of the things said in it are, such as that we will rise again from the dead. On this view, people sincerely saying that they will be resurrected are not choosing a metaphorical, or poetical, or emotionally resonant way of saying something else, or of putting a certain colour on the ordinary world. They are announcing something they expect, as literally as they might expect to take a journey, or expect the appearance of a friend.

In this chapter, I shall discuss religious beliefs in terms of argument, reason, and evidence. We suppose them to be intended as true, and therefore to answer to our best ways of getting at the truth. It is only when they are taken in this sense that they have interested most philosophers, although some moral philosophers, notably Friedrich Nietzsche, have railed against the moral attitudes and emotions (humility, self-abasement, and compassion) that they think certain religions encourage.

To jump the gun a little, I am going to present a fair number of reasons against supposing that anything recognizable as religious belief is true. Some readers may feel threatened by this. They can take some comfort from the tradition in theology that the more unlikely a belief is to be true, the more meritorious is the act of faith required to believe it. But at the end of the chapter, the restless spirit of reflection will cause us to look at that view as well. I start, however, by considering the classical philosophical arguments for the existence of God: the ontological argument, the cosmological argument, the design argument, and arguments from revelation and miracles. We end by thinking more about the nature of faith, belief, and commitment.

ANSELM'S ARGUMENT: DREAMBOATS AND TURKEYS

There is a story of a guru who attracted a large audience to a stadium with the promise of a definitive proof of the existence of God. When all were assembled, he dramatically revealed the *Oxford English Dictionary*, and showed that it contained the word 'God'. Since the word was there, with a definition, there had to be something answering to it. I do not know how the audience felt, or whether any of them managed to reflect that the dictionary also mentions Santa Claus and fairies, although admittedly qualifying them as mythical or imaginary. But it is interesting to think how there can be meaningful words with nothing answering to them.

The reason is that you can define a concept, but it is quite another question whether anything answers to the concept you define. You can define what you want from a partner, if you are minded to advertise in the dating columns:

> Thoughtful person in search of fun-loving, vegetarian, banjo-playing soccer fan, must be non-smoker.

This defines your dream partner—let us call him or her Dreamboat. But there may unfortunately not be any fun-loving, vegetarian, non-smoking, banjo-playing soccer fans. You can decide what you want to put into the description, but the world decides whether anybody meets it. Dreamboat may not exist.

The description is perfectly intelligible. It defines a condition that in principle someone could meet. It is just that as it happens, nobody does meet it. One way of putting this is to say that the terms have a *sense*, but no *reference*. You know what you mean, but you don't know whether there is anything that answers to it. You cannot argue from the sense to the reference, because whether there is a reference is a question of how the world is, not to be settled in the study, or by consulting a dictionary.

It might irk you to realize that there might be nobody to answer to your description. But you might hit on a plan to get round the problem. Why not add a postscript, specifying that the dream person should exist? So now you advertise:

> Thoughtful person in search of fun-loving, vegetarian, etc.
> *who exists.*

And now, you might think to yourself, I have solved my problem by definition.

Well, it is certainly true that nobody is going to call you to explain that they meet all the conditions except the last one. But then, anybody who called you after the original advertisement also existed: 'I call, therefore I am' is just as good an inference as 'I think, therefore I am'. And your adding the clause cannot have altered one jot the chance of someone meeting the other conditions—the ones you started with. So you have wasted your money on the last two words. Putting 'who exists' is not further specifying the dream partner, and nor is it improving your chances that he or she in fact exists. Philosophers sometimes express this by saying that 'existence is not a predicate', meaning that adding 'and exists' is not like adding 'and likes Guinness'. You are in charge of sense: you can add what you like to the job description. But the world is in charge of reference: it says if anything exists meeting your conditions.

With this properly understood, we can now turn to the arguments. We have already met one argument for the existence of God, in Chapter 1: Descartes's 'trademark' argument. It did not seem all that strong, and in fact at a later point in his book, *Meditation* V, Descartes supplemented it with another. The second was a version of a much older argument, the *ontological* argument of St Anselm (1033–1109). Anselm defines God as a being 'than which nothing greater can be conceived'. And he addresses himself to 'the fool' (from Psalm 14) who has said in his heart that there is no God:

> But when this same fool hears me say 'something than which nothing greater can be thought,' he surely understands what he hears, and what he understands exists in his understanding; even if he does not understand that it exists (in reality) . . . So even the fool must admit that something than which nothing greater can be thought exists at least in his understanding, since he understands this when he hears it, and whatever is understood, exists in the understanding. And surely that than which a greater cannot be thought cannot exist only in the understanding. For if it exists only in the understanding, it can be thought to exist in reality as well, which is greater . . . [T]herefore, there is no doubt that something than which a greater cannot be thought exists both in the understanding and in reality.

The notable thing about this argument is that it is purely a priori.

It purports to prove God's existence simply from considering the concept or definition of God. It is like the specimen proof in mathematics, that deduces from the concept of a circle that chords dropped from a point to opposite ends of a diameter meet at right angles. The argument requires no empirical premises—no measuring, or results from experience.

Anselm's argument could be presented in two stages:

> The concept of God is understood. Whatever is understood, exists in the understanding. *So* God exists in the understanding.

And then:

> *Suppose* God only exists in the understanding, and not in reality. Then a greater being than God can be conceived: one that exists in reality. *But* God is defined as that than which nothing greater can be conceived. *So* no greater being can be conceived, by definition. But now we have a contradiction. *So* our original supposition was false.

This is an argument form I describe more fully in the next chapter, called *reductio ad absurdum*. Anselm has us make the original atheistic assumption, but only en route to showing that it is false, for it implies a contradiction.

Descartes's version of the argument trades on 'perfection' rather than greatness, but the structure is similar. God is defined as perfect, but it would be an imperfection in something with God's other qualities not to exist: 'existence is a perfection'. So existence belongs to God's essence, and God cannot be conceived as not existing.

A monk named Gaunilo attacked the argument in Anselm's own time. Gaunilo pointed out that if the argument were good, it could be used to prove all sorts of conclusions that are too good to be true: for instance, that there exists a perfect island than which none greater can be conceived. Staying with Dreamboat, we can work it through like this. Suppose you carefully added to Dreamboat's specifications that he or she must be not only a great lover, but also as great a lover as can be imagined. Then you can argue in a parallel fashion:

> The concept of Dreamboat is understood. Whatever is understood, exists in the understanding. *So* Dreamboat exists in the understanding.

And then:

> *Suppose* Dreamboat only exists in the understanding, and not in reality. Then a greater lover than Dreamboat can be conceived: one that exists in reality. *But* Dreamboat is defined as that lover than which no greater can be conceived. *So* no greater lover than Dreamboat can be conceived, by definition. But now we have a contradiction. *So* our original supposition was false.

Dreamboat exists in reality. Wonderful! But do not rejoice too quickly. You might also unfortunately prove by the same means that you have as dangerous a rival as can be imagined, for Dreamboat's affections. The crucial premise will be that real rivals are more dangerous than merely imagined ones—which they surely are. And the ontological argument looks set to prove the existence of the Devil—defined as that than which nothing worse can be conceived. For if something is to be that than which nothing worse can be conceived, it had better not exist only in the imagination, for then something worse can be conceived, namely a being that is that bad but also really exists (notice that existence in a devil is an *imperfection:* it makes him worse).

Most philosophers have recognized there is something fishy about the ontological argument—as fishy as trying to make sure that Dreamboat exists by writing the right job description. But they have not always agreed on just what the mistake must be. Part of the problem is the move of treating 'existence as a predicate'. That problem is resolved by the theory we meet in the next chapter, called quantification theory. But it is hard to be sure that this move introduces the fatal flaw.

In my own view, the crucial problem lies in an ambiguity lurking in the comparison of 'reality' and 'conception'. In the argument, things 'in reality' are compared with things 'in conception' (i.e. according to a definition, or in imagination or dreams), for such properties as greatness, or perfection. This sounds simple, as if we are comparing things in two different geographical regions, and we know that those in one region are greater or lesser than those in the other. It would be like asking whether chickens in Germany are heavier than chickens in France. But in fact it is not at all like that. Consider this sentence:

Real turkeys are heavier than imagined turkeys.

There seems to be a sense in which it is true. In that sense, imagined turkeys weigh nothing (after all, you cannot make even a small meal from one). But there is also a sense in which it is false, because you can imagine a turkey heavier than any real one—a five-hundred-pound turkey the size of a small barn, for example. In the ontological argument, 'God' in imagination is compared with God in reality, like the imagined turkey compared to the real turkey, and found to weigh less. In the argument above, Dreamboat in reality is compared to imagined Dreamboat, and thought to be better: for surely even quite mediocre real lovers are greater lovers than imaginary ones! And this is supposed to contradict the definition. But that kind of comparison does not in fact show *anything* contradicting the definition.

It is as if a schoolteacher required you to imagine a turkey heavier than any actual turkey. You do so: you imagine a five-hundred-pound turkey. But the teacher then complains that since imagined turkeys always weigh less than real turkeys, you have failed to imagine what she asked for. Your imagined turkey weighs nothing (you can't eat it) and so you have 'contradicted the definition' and you get no marks. Here you would be right to feel aggrieved. It is not you who went wrong, but the teacher.

This suggests that we must not think of 'imagined turkeys' or 'turkeys in the understanding' as kinds of turkey that can, in principle, be weighed against real ones but are always found to weigh less. Yet the ontological argument requires just this kind of comparison. It is here that it fails. For even if God only exists in imagination, like Dreamboat or the five-hundred-pound turkey, it does not follow that a greater being can be described or imagined. After all, the description had the superlatives put into it. But unhappily for Anselm's proof, that does not settle the question whether anything answers to it.

ELEPHANTS AND TORTOISES

The ontological argument has always seemed fishy. St Thomas Aquinas (*c.* 1225–74), the greatest medieval theologian and philosopher, did not accept it. He preferred to argue that God is needed in order to *explain* the world or cosmos as we apprehend it. This argument, the *cosmological* argument, has a much stronger appeal to the imagination. There are various versions of it. They all require identifying a way in which things in the physical universe, things as we know them by touch and sight and the other senses, are *dependent* beings. And it is then argued that dependent beings eventually presuppose a being that is *not* itself dependent upon anything, as their explanation. One version of this, and perhaps the easiest to understand, is the *first cause* argument. Here is the character Demea, from Hume's *Dialogues Concerning Natural Religion* (these *Dialogues*, first published a year after Hume's death in 1776, are the classic philosophical analysis of traditional theological arguments, and I shall quote from them extensively in what follows):

> *Whatever exists must have a cause or reason of its existence, it being absolutely impossible for any thing to produce itself or be the cause of its own existence. In mounting up, therefore, from effects to causes, we must either go on in tracing an infinite succession, without any ultimate cause at all, or must at last have recourse to some ultimate cause, that is necessarily existent: Now, that the first supposition is absurd, may be thus proved. In the infinite chain or succession of causes and effects, each single effect is determined to exist by the power and efficacy of that cause which immediately preceded; but the whole eternal chain or succession, taken together, is not determined*

or caused by any thing: And yet it is evident that it requires a
cause or reason, as much as any particular object which be-
gins to exist in time. The question is still reasonable why this
particular succession of causes existed from eternity, and not
any other succession, or no succession at all. If there be no nec-
essarily existent being, any supposition which can be formed
is equally possible; nor is there any more absurdity in noth-
ing's having existed from eternity, than there is in that succes-
sion of causes which constitutes the universe. What was it,
then, which determined something to exist rather than noth-
ing, and bestowed being on a particular possibility, exclusive
of the rest? External causes, there are supposed to be none.
Chance is a word without a meaning. Was it nothing? But
that can never produce any thing. We must, therefore, have re-
course to a necessarily existent Being, who carries the reason
of his existence in himself; and who cannot be supposed not to
exist, without an express contradiction. There is, conse-
quently, such a Being—that is, there is a Deity.

The argument is powerfully presented, but is it valid?

Russell is supposed to have remarked that the first cause argument was bad, but uniquely, awfully bad, in that the conclusion not
only failed to follow from the premises, but also actually contradicted them. His idea was that the argument starts off from the
premise 'everything has a [distinct, previous] cause', but ends with
the conclusion that there must be something that has *no* distinct,
previous cause, but 'carries the *reason* of his existence in himself'.
Then the conclusion denies what the premise asserts.

Russell's dismissal is a little glib. For the point of the argument,
from the theological perspective, is that although everything material or physical has a distinct previous cause, this very fact drives us

to postulate something else, that has none. In the theological jargon, this would be a thing that is 'necessary' or 'causa sui': a thing that is its own cause. And since this is not true of the ordinary things that surround us, we need to postulate something extraordinary, a Deity, as the bearer of this extraordinary self-sufficiency.

In Hume's *Dialogues* the problem with this is quickly exposed.

> *It is pretended that the Deity is a necessarily existent being; and this necessity of his existence is attempted to be explained by asserting, that if we knew his whole essence or nature, we should perceive it to be as impossible for him not to exist, as for twice two not to be four. But it is evident that this can never happen, while our faculties remain the same as at present. It will still be possible for us, at any time, to conceive the nonexistence of what we formerly conceived to exist; nor can the mind ever lie under a necessity of supposing any object to remain always in being; in the same manner as we lie under a necessity of always conceiving twice two to be four. The words, therefore, 'necessary existence', have no meaning; or, which is the same thing, none that is consistent.*

Hume's spokesman at this point, the character called Cleanthes, goes on to say that for all we know, the material world or universe as a whole itself might be the necessarily existent being, in spite of the way in which parts of it depend upon other parts. For it must be 'unknown, inconceivable qualities' that make anything a 'necessary existent'. And for all we know, such unknown inconceivable qualities may attach to the ordinary physical universe, rather to any immaterial thing or person or deity lying behind it.

It is important to remember here that as far as everyday experience goes, minds are just as much in need of explanation, just as much dependent beings, as physical objects. Postulating a mind that is somehow immune from dependency on anything else whatsoever is jumping away from experience just as violently as postulating a physical thing that is so.

The first cause argument speaks to worries that are natural, and indeed according to some philosophers, notably Kant, inevitable. When we think back to the 'big bang' our next question is why that event, then? We are not happy with the answer 'no reason', because we are not happy with events 'just happening': the drive to explanation grips us. So we postulate something else, another cause lying behind this one. But the drive now threatens to go on forever. If we have cited God at this point, we either have to ask what caused God, or cut off the regress by arbitrary fiat. But if we exercise an arbitrary right to stop the regress at that point, we might as well have stopped it with the physical cosmos. In other words, we are in the position of the Indian philosopher, who asked what the world rested on replied 'an elephant', and asked what the elephant rested on, replied 'a tortoise', and asked what the tortoise rested on, begged to change the subject.

There are versions of the cosmological argument that are not concerned with the first cause, in time. Rather, they consider the ongoing order of the universe: the uniformity of nature. It can seem an amazing fact that laws of nature keep on holding, that the frame of nature does not fall apart. One can think that these facts must be 'dependent' and require a necessary sustaining cause (like Atlas propping up the world). But once more, there is either a regress, or a simple fiat that something has 'unknown inconceivable properties' that make it self-sufficient. This would be something whose ongoing uniformity requires no explanation outside itself. And that might as well be the world as a whole as anything else. But we return to the uniformity of nature in the next two chapters.

THE WISE ARCHITECT

The same Cleanthes who is given the job of refuting the cosmological argument is the spokesman for a different attempt to prove the existence of a deity: the argument to *design*—the view that heaven and earth declare the glory of the creator. This argument was the showpiece of eighteenth-century theology, and still exerts a powerful influence. I shall follow the classic discussion given in Hume's *Dialogues*. Cleanthes presents the argument:

> Look round the world: Contemplate the whole and every part of it: You will find it to be nothing but one great machine, subdivided into an infinite number of lesser machines, which again admit of subdivisions to a degree beyond what human senses and faculties can trace and explain. All these various machines, and even their most minute parts, are adjusted to each other with an accuracy which ravishes into admiration all men who have ever contemplated them. The curious adapting of means to ends, throughout all nature, resembles exactly, though it much exceeds, the productions of human contrivance; of human design, thought, wisdom, and intelligence. Since, therefore, the effects resemble each other, we are led to infer, by all the rules of analogy, that the causes also resemble; and that the Author of Nature is somewhat similar to

the mind of man, though possessed of much larger faculties, proportioned to the grandeur of the work which he has executed. By this argument a posteriori, *and by this argument alone, do we prove at once the existence of a Deity, and his similarity to human mind and intelligence.*

There are two important points about this argument. First, it is an argument by *analogy*. The world resembles the objects of human design. Therefore, just as it would be reasonable, coming across a watch, to postulate a human designer, so it is reasonable, coming across the entire frame of nature, to postulate a godly designer. Second, the argument is 'a posteriori'. That is, it argues from experience, or from what we know of the world as we find it. It is here that the evidence for design shines out.

After Darwinism had begun to offer a natural explanation of the way in which complex biological systems become adjusted to one another, the argument began to lose some of its lustre. But in fact Hume (and Kant) makes the right points without relying on any alternative explanation of such things as biological adaptation. And that is just as well, for the argument is not essentially about biology, which give us just one kind of instance of the adjustments of nature. Cosmology affords others. (For instance, on one current authoritative estimate, the chances of the various cosmological constants being adjusted so that organized life became possible anywhere in the universe, are 1 in 10 to the 10^{125}—an unimaginable number—against. So perhaps it took a wise architect to adjust them.)

So how does Hume, in the persona of Philo, his spokesman in the *Dialogues*, attempt to rebut the argument to a designer? Philo points out that the argument takes one of the operations we encounter in nature, the operation of thought, as a 'rule for the whole'.

> But, allowing that we were to take the operations of one part of nature upon another for the foundation of our judgment concerning the origin of the whole (which never can be admitted), yet why select so minute, so weak, so bounded a principle as the reason and design of animals is found to be upon this planet? What peculiar privilege has this little agitation of the brain which we call 'thought', that we must thus make it the model of the whole universe? Our partiality in our own favour does indeed present it on all occasions; but sound philosophy ought carefully to guard against so natural an illusion.

Argument by analogy requires certain conditions in order to be reliable. First, the bases for the analogy should be extremely similar. Second, we should have experience covering the likely explanations. That is, we should know as much as possible about the kind of cause that produces this kind of effect. For example, a hole in a tree is quite similar to a hole in a human body. But to suppose 'by analogy' that since the human is apt to die from the one, the tree is apt to die from the other, is to stretch our reasonings too far. We need more observation, more refined understanding of the way things fall out before we would be wise to make any such inference. It is this second kind of experience that is sadly lacking in theology, for we have no inkling of the kinds of 'thing' that cause entire physical universes to come into existence.

Furthermore, resemblances are quite easy to come by, and Philo has a great deal of fun inventing them. First, even if the universe resembles a clock, still more it resembles a vegetable:

> The world plainly resembles more an animal or a vegetable, than it does a watch or a knitting-loom. Its cause, therefore, it is more probable, resembles the cause of the former. The cause of the former is generation or vegetation. The cause, therefore, of the world, we may infer to be something similar or analogous to generation or vegetation.

Of course, a theist is going to urge that this gets us nowhere, for it would only take us back to another vegetable-like cause, whose origin we would then ask about. But the same is true if we are taken back to something resembling a mind. If Cleanthes, defending the argument, stops the regress there, he cannot blame Philo, opposing the argument, for stopping the regress with a vegetable. As Philo says:

> If I rest my system of cosmogony on the former, preferably to the latter, it is at my choice. The matter seems entirely arbitrary. And when Cleanthes asks me what is the cause of my great vegetative or generative faculty, I am equally entitled to ask him the cause of his great reasoning principle. These questions we have agreed to forbear on both sides; and it is chiefly his interest on the present occasion to stick to this agreement. Judging by our limited and imperfect experience, generation has some privileges above reason: for we see every day the latter arise from the former, never the former from the latter.

This final point is quite devastating. Cleanthes prides himself on the 'scientific' nature of his reasoning: an argument by analogy, from experience. But then experience shows us how fragile, and dependent upon other things, the existence of intelligence is. In our experience minds require brains which are fragile, dependent, late, and unusual arrivals in nature. 'Generation', that is, animal or vegetable growth from previous animal or vegetable life, is by contrast common, and as far as we ever observe, necessary for the existence of intelligence. So, arguing from experience, it is much less likely that there is a self-sustaining mind than some other physical cause responsible for the whole show.

Since Philo's point here seems unanswerable, it is good to speculate a little about the allure of the argument to design. Why do not people appreciate Philo's counter? I suspect the root cause is the same as that responsible for some of the problems of free will. We think that it is more satisfactory to halt the regress with 'intelligence' rather than 'generation', because we think that in our own experience we have an example of an *uncaused* mental event, say, my deciding to initiate an action, giving rise to a physical event. So we take that as a model for the arbitrary creation of a universe by an intelligent deity. While we think like this we forget Schopenhauer's point (see Chapter 3): sometimes when we act we are not conscious of causation, but it does not follow, and is not true, that we are conscious of the absence of causation. This interaction between the design argument and the interventionist conception of free will has an interesting moral aspect. Arguably, the two images of God as supernatural, and of our 'selves' as equally outside nature, feed off each other. And each leads people to deny the sovereignty of nature. It leads people to see the world as something that 'we' have dominion over, just as God does. Whereas the truth is that the world is something of which we are a very, very small part.

I said that resemblances are cheap, and Philo has a field day with another kind. Suppose we waived all these objections, and allowed Cleanthes a 'designer'. What then? Designs are sometimes the product of one mind. But more often, and in the case of very great designs, like ships, they are the product of many minds acting together. Some are the product of better designers than others:

> In a word, Cleanthes, a man who follows your hypothesis is able, perhaps, to assert or conjecture that the universe sometime arose from something like design: But beyond that position he cannot ascertain one single circumstance, and is left afterwards to fix every point of his theology by the utmost license of fancy and hypothesis. This world, for aught he knows, is very faulty and imperfect, compared to a superior standard; and was only the first rude essay of some infant deity, who afterwards abandoned it, ashamed of his lame performance: It is the work only of some dependent, inferior deity; and is the object of derision to his superiors: It is the production of old age and dotage in some superannuated deity; and ever since his death, has run on at adventures, from the first impulse and active force which it received from him . . . And I cannot, for my part, think that so wild and unsettled a system of theology is, in any respect, preferable to none at all.

And this takes us inevitably to:

THE PROBLEM OF EVIL

Most systems of religion want more from their gods than the very abstract qualities of 'necessary existence'. They want love and concern. A god that created the world and then walked off the site leaving it to its own devices is not a fit object of worship, nor a source of moral authority. So the traditional attributes of God include moral perfection. God is to be all-powerful, of course, all-knowing, but also all-caring. But then there arises the classic argument against the existence of God: the problem that, in the world that he (or she, or they) created, this care seems sadly lacking. As Philo says:

> His power, we allow, is infinite; whatever he wills is executed: But neither man nor any other animal is happy; therefore, he does not will their happiness. His wisdom is infinite; he is never mistaken in choosing the means to any end; But the course of Nature tends not to human or animal felicity: Therefore, it is not established for that purpose. Through the whole compass of human knowledge there are no inferences more certain and infallible than these. In what respect, then, do his benevolence and mercy resemble the benevolence and mercy of men?
>
> Epicurus' old questions are yet unanswered.
>
> Is he willing to prevent evil, but not able? then is he impotent. Is he able, but not willing? then is he malevolent. Is he both able and willing? whence then is evil?

Cleanthes' problem is that the world as we have it is at best mixed, in terms of the happiness of its creatures. Life is tough, and for many it is short, brutal, filled with want and pain. The well-being of many creatures depends on the disease and death of others. But it is absurd to argue from a mixed creation to a perfect creator. Even a moderately good parent does not wilfully choose to put his or her children into a brutal environment if at no cost they could choose a better one. The very analogies that Cleanthes prizes speak against him here.

Suppose you found yourself at school or university in a dormitory. Things are not too good. The roof leaks, there are rats about, the food is almost inedible, some students in fact starve to death. There is a closed door, behind which is the management, but the management never comes out. You get to speculate what the management must be like. Can you infer from the dormitory as you find it that the management, first, knows exactly what conditions are like, second, cares intensely for your welfare, and third, possesses unlimited resources for fixing things? The inference is crazy. You would be almost certain to infer that either the management doesn't know, doesn't care, or cannot do anything about it. Nor does it make things any better if occasionally you come across a student who declaims that he has become privy to the mind of the management, and is assured that the management indeed knows, cares, and has resources and ability to do what it wants. The overwhelming inference is not that the management is like that, but that this student is deluded. Perhaps his very deprivations have deluded him. Nobody ever inferred from the multiple infirmities of Windows that Bill Gates was infinitely benevolent, omniscient, and able to fix everything.

Similar remarks apply to the belief that this world is a 'vale of tears', which is a kind of proving ground for that which is to come. The inhabitants of my dormitory might believe this: the management is looking to see how they behave in order to sort them into better or worse—indeed, perfect or hellish—dormitories next year. This might at a stretch be true. But they have no shadow of a reason to believe that it is true, based on what they have got. All they have to go on is what they see of the management. And if he, she, they, or it does not establish good conditions here, why suppose that they do so anywhere else? It would be like supposing that since it is warm here, there must be a dormitory somewhere else where it is perfectly hot, and another where it is perfectly cold. The inference is crazy.

Cleanthes is especially vulnerable to this, because he attempted a reasonable inference, based on analogy, from the way of the world to the nature of the creator. But even putting aside the other difficulties with the design argument, from a mixed and spotty world he is bound to be left with at best a mixed and spotty creator. Or:

> The true conclusion is that the original source of all things . . .
> has no more regard to good above ill than to heat above cold,
> or to drought above moisture, or to light above heavy.

Demea—the character who sympathized with the ontological and cosmological argument—has a different problem. He is not attempting to reason from the way of the world to his deity, so he is not vulnerable in the same way at this point. The difference is that since Cleanthes is arguing from the world as we have it, to the nature of God, he needs to show that the world is *what you would expect* from the assumption of an all-knowing, all-powerful, all-caring God. He needs that the world *fits* the idea of such a being. Demea can admit it is not quite what you would have expected, but claims only that it is *compatible* with his deity. It does not *refute* the idea of such a being.

Still, he has to face 'Epicurus' old questions'. The strategy he follows has become ever more popular in the succeeding centuries. It is to take refuge in the mysterious and incomprehensible nature of the divine mind. Demea is opposed to impious attempts to understand God's goodness on the model of human goodness, or God's intentions or perceptions or understanding on the model of human intentions or perceptions or understanding.

The problem then becomes one of explaining how it should have any consequences whether we believe in an incomprehensible God. As Wittgenstein was to say later, in a different connection:

> *a nothing will serve just as well as a something about which nothing could be said.*

Even Hume, the 'great infidel', is quite happy with leaving mysteries. At the end of the *Dialogues*, Philo, the sceptic, is perfectly prepared to allow one:

> *If the whole of Natural Theology, as some people seem to maintain, resolves itself into one simple, though somewhat ambiguous, at least undefined, proposition,* That the cause or causes of order in the universe probably bear some remote analogy to human intelligence: *If this proposition be not capable of extension, variation, or more particular explication: If it affords no inference that affects human life, or can be the source of any action or forbearance: And if the analogy, imperfect as it is, can be carried no further than to the human intelligence, and cannot be transferred, with any appearance of probability, to the other qualities of the mind: If this really be the case, what can the most inquisitive, contemplative, and religious man do more than give a plain, philosophical assent to the proposition, as often as it occurs, and believe that the ar-*

guments on which it is established exceed the objections which lie against it? Some astonishment, indeed, will naturally arise from the greatness of the object: Some melancholy from its obscurity: Some contempt of human reason that it can give no solution more satisfactory with regard to so extraordinary and magnificent a question.

Demea's problem is going to be that having got himself to an utterly mysterious deity, he cannot reap any consequences. You can check into the Mysterious Mist, if you so wish, but you cannot check out carrying any more than you took in with you. Religious belief, reduced to its respectable core, turns out to be completely inert. It has no consequences.

This is surprising to people—so surprising that many commentators have puzzled at length over whether Hume was really a theist or an atheist. Many people think that the difference between being a theist, believing, and an atheist, unbelieving, is incredibly important. But if nothing does as well as something about which nothing can be said, it vanishes. If all we can reasonably believe is that the cause of the universe probably bears some remote inconceivable analogy to the other operations of nature, then we are given no *usable* comprehension, no real understanding, that we can bring back from these misty regions. We might say, following Wittgenstein's remark, that Hume here 'deconstructs' the apparent difference between theism and atheism.

In particular, if 'God's goodness' is not to be understood in the same terms as what we think of as good (so that, for instance, it might be 'good' of God in this different sense to unleash bubonic plague on defenceless infants) then it has no implications for how

I am to live my life. It gives me no way of deciding whether to prefer pleasure to pain, or turning the other cheek to taking an eye for an eye, any more than it tells me to prefer heat to cold. But religion is supposed to do these things. It is important, because people take it to make a difference to how we act. Yet now we find that if we follow the traditional range of arguments, it makes no difference whatsoever.

Theodicy is the branch of theology that attempts to cope with the problem of evil. One move is to point out that some values seem to presuppose pains. We can cheer up people in the mixed and spotty dormitory, by extolling the virtues of patience or fortitude—goods that require deprivation and difficulty to flourish. The difficulty with this is that we ourselves think that things are going better when the situations requiring those virtues lose some of their edge. The imperfections of Windows have no doubt led to virtues of patience or fortitude, but even Microsoft have never used that to defend the perfection of the product, and indeed that is why they continue to try to improve it.

Again, people sometimes defend belief in a genuinely good deity, good in a sense we can understand, against the problem by what is known as the 'free will defence'. The idea is that God created a good universe, and out of his goodness created us with free will. But by misusing the freedom thus granted, we ourselves brought evil into an otherwise perfect world. The myth of the Fall and the expulsion from the Garden of Eden embody the idea.

There are many objections to this defence. First, it seems to depend upon a conception of free will that seems to be incoherent: the interventionist conception according to which something that is not part of the natural order (the Real Me) occasionally interferes in the natural order. For without this, if free will is understood in a compatibilist way, my decision-making is done with a natural endowment which is ultimately, for the theist, due to God. If God had not wanted Stalin to slaughter millions, he should not have created the nature that eventually gave rise to the decision-making modules of such a person.

Second, it is just not true that all, or even many, of the ills that afflict human beings are due to human decisions at all. They are due to disease, pain, want, and accident. They afflict the animal creation as well as human beings, and did so long before there were human beings.

Third, even if the metaphysics of free will were accepted, a good God might be expected to protect some of the weaker from the misuses of free will of the stronger. A parent might recognize the value of letting children make their own choices, and give them some liberty. But if some of the older children show alarming tendencies to murder and mutilate the younger, the parent would be wise to put them under supervision, or to protect the younger by diverting the older from their plans. Unhappily, God does not do this in the world as we have it. There are no natural playpens, in which the weak are segregated from the strong. We have to try to create our own safe areas.

My own view about this is that religious traditions are at their best when they back away from the classical virtues of God. God is elevated in some traditions to being above good and virtue, or in Hume's down-to-earth phrase, has no more regard to good above ill than heat above cold. In other traditions, he is by no means omnipotent, but subject to forces not of his own making. Each of these at least affords some kind of theodicy. But if we really were concerned to puzzle out the nature of God's mind from the nature of his creation, we might look seriously at the idea that he (she, they, it) is a God with a twisted sense of humour. After all, as the Jewish joke goes, he led the chosen people round the desert for forty years just to drop them on the only part of the Middle East that has no oil.

MIRACLES AND TESTIMONY

Perhaps the core arguments we have looked at fail. But many people suppose that religious faith is well supported by the occurrence of miraculous events. A prophet may establish divine credentials by foreseeing the future, or by miraculous healing, or appearance after death, or other such signs.

Most of us are not directly privileged to see such events. Rather, we take our belief from other reports of them: testimony. We read of them in the Bible, or the Koran, or the *Lives of the Saints*, or even the *National Enquirer*. We don't personally watch, for instance, an amputated limb growing back to normal, but we may have heard that somewhere over the hills there is an absolutely unshakeable confirmed sighting of such a thing. People may not personally have been abducted by aliens, but they may believe wholeheartedly other people who tell them that they have, or that their brothers or cousins have. Even if we have not recently sighted the long-buried Elvis, we may read and believe that some people have.

Hume asked the telling question: when is it reasonable to believe such testimony?

Suppose we leave on one side the 'miraculous' element—the question of whether any such event is due to invisible powers, or divine intervention. Still, any candidate for a miracle has to be not only surprising, but totally surprising, the kind of thing that, in the normal course of events, just never happens (we are not talking here about the sense in which the whole creation is miraculous, since that would take us back to the cosmological argument). To establish divine credentials, it is not enough for someone to be the hero of unusual events. He needs really incredible events: people elevating themselves in the air, lead floating, water turning into wine, the dead coming back to life. The challenge to the putative miracle-worker is: go on, amaze me. So when is it reasonable to believe testimony for such outlandish, totally out-of-the-ordinary events?

Hume begins by making a straightforward enough claim about human sayings. It is, we believe, a fact that they are mostly true. Hume claims that if we infer from a premise of the kind 'This person is telling me that p' to a conclusion 'So, p is probably true', we are doing the same kind of thing as if we infer from one event, say 'The baseball is flying into the window', to another, 'The window will break.' These inferences are *empirical* (a posteriori) and are founded on the way we experience the world to behave. The truthfulness of human testimony is a matter of fact, and founded on experience. And when things go wrong, we do not in fact rely on it. There can be a 'contrariety of evidence', or in other words, some things pointing one way, and others a different way:

> *This contrariety of evidence, in the present case, may be derived from several different causes; from the opposition of contrary testimony; from the character or number of the witnesses; from the manner of their delivering their testimony; or from the union of all these circumstances. We entertain a suspicion concerning any matter of fact, when the witnesses contradict each other; when they are but few, or of a doubtful character; when they have an interest in what they affirm; when they deliver their testimony with hesitation, or on the contrary, with too violent asseverations. There are many other particulars of the same kind, which may diminish or destroy the force of any argument, derived from human testimony.*

In other words, experience itself shows us when not to be too gullible. But now suppose that what is testified to is absolutely amazing, approaching the miraculous. Then:

> *The very same principle of experience, which gives us a certain degree of assurance in the testimony of witnesses, gives us also, in this case, another degree of assurance against the fact, which they endeavour to establish; from which contradiction there necessarily arises a counterpoise, and mutual destruction of belief and authority.*

Before pausing to analyse the line of thought, we should see where it leads. Hume draws a famous conclusion:

> *The plain consequence is (and it is a general maxim worthy of our attention), 'That no testimony is sufficient to establish a miracle, unless the testimony be of such a kind, that its falsehood would be more miraculous, than the fact, which it endeavours to establish; and even in that case there is a mutual destruction of arguments, and the superior only gives us an*

> *assurance suitable to that degree of force, which remains, after deducting the inferior.' When any one tells me, that he saw a dead man restored to life, I immediately consider with myself, whether it be more probable, that this person should either deceive or be deceived, or that the fact, which he relates, should really have happened. I weigh the one miracle against the other; and according to the superiority, which I discover, I pronounce my decision, and always reject the greater miracle. If the falsehood of his testimony would be more miraculous, than the event which he relates; then, and not till then, can he pretend to command my belief or opinion.*

The argument can be analysed in a number of ways. It can usefully be thought of like this:

Suppose somebody tells me of a highly surprising or improbable event, *m*. In fact, let *m* be an event about as improbable as you can imagine. So my evidence for *m* is that 'this person is saying that *m* happened'. I now have a choice between two views of the matter:

(a) This person is saying that *m* happened. But *m* did not.
(b) This person is saying that *m* happened. And *m* did.

Now *each* of (a) and (b) contains *one* surprising element. View (a) contains the surprise: this person spoke falsely. View (b) contains the surprise of *m* occurring. So I have to balance which is more surprising or improbable, and then reject 'the greater miracle'.

The problem, as Hume gleefully points out, is that it is quite common for testimony to be false. There are the obvious cases of deliberate lies. There are cases of delusions. There are notorious lapses of memory. Where there is a transmission of information, errors get introduced: mistranslations, misunderstandings, people taking things intended metaphorically for literal truth, and so on. So (a) does not involve the same kind of improbability as (b). View (b) involves the miracle: an event about as improbable as can be imagined. View (a) only involves the kind of thing that we know happens anyhow: people get things wrong. Therefore the hurdle that 'no testimony is sufficient to establish a miracle, unless the testimony be of such a kind, that its falsehood would be more miraculous, than the fact, which it endeavours to establish' is an incredibly difficult hurdle for any piece of testimony to cross. And even then, all we are left with is a kind of confusion: not knowing what to believe, so that the wise course is to suspend judgement.

In fact, Hume goes on to argue that no evidence being used to establish a system of religion ever comes at all close to crossing the hurdle. He makes a number of points: reports of miracles tend to come from remote and barbarous times and places; from persons whose passions are inflamed; from persons who have an interest in selling a story:

> The wise lend a very academic faith to every report which favours the passion of the reporter; whether it magnifies his country, his family, or himself, or in any other way strikes in with his natural inclinations and propensities. But what greater temptation than to appear a missionary, a prophet, an ambassador from heaven? Who would not encounter many dangers and difficulties, in order to attain so sublime a character? Or if, by the help of vanity and a heated imagination, a man has first made a convert of himself, and entered seriously into the delusion; who ever scruples to make use of pious frauds, in support of so holy and meritorious a cause?

He points out the way people love such reports:

> *The passion of surprise and wonder, arising from miracles,*
> *being an agreeable emotion, gives a sensible tendency towards*
> *the belief of those events, from which it is derived. And this*
> *goes so far, that even those who cannot enjoy this pleasure im-*
> *mediately, nor can believe those miraculous events, of which*
> *they are informed, yet love to partake of the satisfaction at*
> *second-hand or by rebound, and place a pride and delight in*
> *exciting the admiration of others.*
>
> *With what greediness are the miraculous accounts of trav-*
> *ellers received, their descriptions of sea and land monsters,*
> *their relations of wonderful adventures, strange men, and un-*
> *couth manners? But if the spirit of religion join itself to the*
> *love of wonder, there is an end of common sense; and human*
> *testimony, in these circumstances, loses all pretensions to au-*
> *thority.*

And he makes a more subtle point, concerning the relation between different religions, each of which has its budget of miracles:

> *[L]et us consider, that, in matters of religion, whatever is dif-*
> *ferent is contrary; and that it is impossible the religions of an-*
> *cient Rome, of Turkey, of Siam, and of China should, all of*
> *them, be established on any solid foundation. Every miracle,*
> *therefore, pretended to have been wrought in any of these re-*
> *ligions (and all of them abound in miracles), as its direct scope*
> *is to establish the particular system to which it is attributed; so*
> *has it the same force, though more indirectly, to overthrow*
> *every other system. In destroying a rival system, it likewise*
> *destroys the credit of those miracles, on which that system was*
> *established; so that all the prodigies of different religions are to*

be regarded as contrary facts, and the evidences of these prodi-
gies, whether weak or strong, as opposite to each other.

This would also be Hume's answer to the protest that so many people cannot be wrong. Whichever way the cake is cut, a huge number of people have to be wrong.

Hume's argument here is wonderfully *economical.* A less subtle
philosopher might have tried to show a metaphysical conclusion,
such as the absolute impossibility of miracles. Hume neither needs
such a conclusion, nor tries to argue for it. He allows the metaphysical possibility of an intervening deity. There *might* be a deity
who *might* on occasion let someone walk on water, or feed five
thousand people on a few loaves and fishes. Still, experience is our
only guide as to whether such events occur. If we are to believe that
they do because of testimony, then the testimony has to be good:
very good, and, in fact, miraculously good. But we never find testimony of the right kind.

People new to Hume's argument sometimes suspect that it is
unduly *cynical,* expressing some kind of mistrustful, suspicious attitude to the reports of other people. I do not think this is true, or
at least, that the suspicion is worse than is warranted by people's
tendencies. After all, you have to be extremely innocent to deny, for
instance, that it is wise to be suspicious of reports that flatter the
passions of the reporter. Here is a quotation from the British news-
paper the *Independent,* commenting on a report by the Royal College of Psychiatrists:

According to the Royal College of Psychiatrists, one in six of us
are neurotic. They must think that 100 per cent of us are

> *gullible as well. Bring out a report—the politically correct*
> *way to advertise your service. What next? The Institute of*
> *Builders says seven in ten houses need to be rebuilt, or the As-*
> *sociation of Garage Mechanics that thirteen out of twenty*
> *cars need servicing?*

In fact, the discussion in the second part of Hume's great essay is an ancestor of a whole academic study. Psychologists now investigate common cognitive malfunctions: failures of perception, of memory, the influences of other people, the infectious qualities of confidence, and the love of the marvellous, as influences that interfere with people's capacities to tell truth from falsehood. We are mostly quite good instruments for registering truth and dismissing falsehood. But we are not as good as we like to believe, and we are often not very good at all.

Hume's argument can elegantly be put in terms of Bayes's theorem, which I explain in the next chapter. The reader may want to return to this way of putting it after absorbing the explanation there. In Bayes's terms, we let h be the hypothesis that a miracle occurred, and e be the fact that some person or persons *say* that it occurred. Then the prior probability that the miracle occurred is very, very small. The 'base rate' is near zero. That is because miracles are the kind of thing that either never happen, or almost never happen. When I leave for the office in the morning, my wife might warn me against the cold, or the traffic, or my colleagues. But she doesn't warn me against flying elephants, being taken into sexual slavery by Martians, or conversations with the living Elvis. But now consider the fact that someone or some text is saying that the miracle occurred. Well, this is unhappily very much the kind of thing that happens. The antecedent probability of such evidence coming into being is never so very small, because there are lots of other, natural, hypotheses that explain it. These are the common human frailties: deception, delusion, inflamed passions, mistakes, and so on. Even the defenders of one favoured set of miracles have to believe in these frailties, in order to rule out the impostors. The Roman church has a whole department devoted to unmasking fake miracles. Christians had better not believe that Muhammad took his night flight from Mecca to Jerusalem since his credentials as a miracle-worker contradict those of Jesus. But this means that the prior probability of e is relatively high. There are many ways in which 'false positives' are generated. Bayes, as we shall see, requires us to compare these prior probabilities in order to assess how probable the hypothesis is, given the evidence. The ideal would be a hypothesis that is not all that improbable, and evidence that cannot easily arise except if the hypothesis is true. But in this kind of case the prior probabilities are exactly the wrong way round. The hypothesis is immensely improbable, and the evidence can easily arise for other reasons. So the Bayesian calculation always comes down against the truth of the testimony, and in favour of the uniformity of nature.

This is not to say that reports of things hitherto quite outside our experience have to be false. Science proceeds by finding such things. But we reason rightly when we maintain a sceptical attitude, until such time as the new phenomena are repeated and established, becoming part of the uniformities of nature.

Once we think of the theology of miracles, things become even worse. For a deity that sets the laws of nature into motion and never relents at least has a certain dignity. One that occasionally allows hiccups and intermissions, glorified conjuring tricks, is less impressive. Why just those miracles, just then? It is not what you would have expected. A little miracle or two snuffing out the Hitlers and Stalins would seem far more useful than one that changes water to wine at one particular wedding feast. It is no doubt very good of God to let St Giuseppe levitate in front of pictures of him, but other things being equal, one would have preferred, say, the miraculous quarantine or destruction of the Aids virus. It is what one might have expected antecedently, knowing that the world was under the regime of a good God. But the world as we know it does not confirm it. We soon see how this piece of reasoning too can be analysed in a Bayesian way. Here the weak card is the degree of fit between the evidence and the hypothesis, the second of the three crucial figures in Bayes's theorem.

INFINI——RIEN

None of the metaphysical arguments we have considered do much to confirm the hypothesis that the universe is the creation of a traditional God. And Hume's analysis of testimony from miracles destroys their value as evidence. Faced with these blanks, religious faith may try to find other arguments.

An interesting and ingenious one is due to the French mathematician and theologian, Blaise Pascal (1632–62), and is known as Pascal's wager. Unlike the arguments we have been considering, it is not presented as an argument for the *truth* of religious belief, but for the *utility* of believing in some version of a monotheistic, Judaic, Christian, or Islamic, God.

The argument is this. First, Pascal confesses to metaphysical ignorance:

> Let us now speak according to natural lights.
>
> If there is a God, he is infinitely incomprehensible, since, having neither parts, nor limits, He has no affinity to us. We are therefore incapable of knowing either what He is, or if He is ... Who then will blame the Christians for not being able to give a reason for their belief, since they profess a religion for which they cannot give a reason?

It is not too clear why this excuse is offered for the Christians, as opposed to those of other faiths, as well as believers in fairies, ghosts, the living Elvis, and L. Ron Hubbard. Still, suppose the choice is between religious belief and a life of religious doubt or denial:

> You must wager. It is not optional. Which will you choose then? ... Let us weigh the gain and the loss in wagering that God is. Let us estimate these two chances. If you gain, you gain all; if you lose, you lose nothing. Wager, then, without hesitation that He is.

With great clarity Pascal realizes that this is rather an odd reason for choosing a belief. But he also says, perceptively, that

> your inability to believe is the result of your passions, since reason brings you to this, and yet you cannot believe ... Learn of those who have been bound like you, and who now stake all their possessions ... Follow the way by which they began; by acting as if they believe, taking the holy water, having masses

*said, etc. Even this will naturally make you believe, and
deaden your acuteness.*

After you have 'stupefied' yourself, you have become a believer.
And then you will reap the rewards of belief: infinite rewards, if the
kind of God you believe in exists. And if it does not? Well, you have
lost very little, in comparison with infinity: only what Pascal calls
the 'poisonous pleasures' of things like playing golf on Sundays instead of going to mass.

The standard way to present this argument is in terms of a two-
by-two box of the options:

	God exists	God does not
I believe in him	+infinity!	0
I do not believe in him	– infinity!	0

The zeros on the right correspond to the thought that not much
goes better or worse in this life, whether or not we believe. This life
is of vanishingly little account compared to what is promised to believers. The plus-infinity figure corresponds to infinite bliss. The
minus-infinity figure in the bottom left corresponds to the traditional jealous God, who sends to Hell those who do not believe in
him, and of course encourages his followers to give them a hard
time here, as well. But the minus-infinity figure can be soft-
pedalled. Even if we put 0 in the bottom left-hand box, the wager
looks good. It would be good even if God does not punish disbelief,
because there is still that terrific payoff of '+infinity' cranking up
the choice. In decision-theory terms, the option of belief 'domi-
nates', because it can win, and cannot lose. So—go for it!

Unfortunately the lethal problem with this argument is simple, once it is pointed out.

Pascal starts from a position of metaphysical ignorance. We just know nothing about the realm beyond experience. But the set-up of the wager presumes that we *do* know something. We are supposed to know the rewards and penalties attached to belief in a Christian God. This is a God who will be pleasured and reward us for our attendance at mass, and will either be indifferent or, in the minus-infiinity option, seriously discombobulated by our non-attendance. But this is a case of false options. For consider that if we are really ignorant metaphysically, then it is at least as likely that the options pan out like this:

> There is indeed a very powerful, very benevolent deity. He
> (or she or they or it) has determined as follows. The good
> human beings are those who follow the natural light of rea-
> son, which is given to them to control their beliefs. These
> good humans follow the arguments, and hence avoid reli-
> gious convictions. These ones with the strength of mind
> not to believe in such things go to Heaven. The rest go to
> Hell.

This is not such a familiar deity as the traditional jealous God, who cares above all that people believe in him. (Why is God so jealous? Alas, might his jealousy be a projection of human sectarian ambitions and emotions? Either you are with us or against us! The French sceptic Voltaire said that God created mankind in his image, and mankind returned the compliment.) But the problem for Pascal is that if we really know nothing, then we do not know whether the scenario just described is any less likely than the Christian one he presented. In fact, for my money, a God that punishes belief is just as likely, and a lot more reasonable, than one that punishes disbelief.

And of course, we could add the Humean point that whilst for Pascal it was a simple two-way question of mass versus disbelief, in the wider world it is also a question of the Koran versus mass, or L. Ron Hubbard versus the Swami Maharishi, or the Aquarian Concepts Community Divine New Order Government versus the First Internet Church of All. The wager has to be silent about those choices.

EMOTION AND THE WILL TO BELIEVE

We can now briefly consider the 'fideistic' line, that although the arguments are negligible, nevertheless people at least have a right to believe what they wish, and there may be some merit in blind faith, like the merit attaching to the mother who refuses to acknowledge her son's guilt in spite of damning evidence.

Philosophers professionally wedded to truth and reason are not apt to commend this attitude. The faith that defies reason might be called a blessing by others who share it, but credulity and superstition by those who don't, and distressingly apt to bring in its wake fanaticism and zealotry. Chapter 2 of the famous essay *On Liberty* by John Stuart Mill (1806–73) talks memorably of the atmosphere of 'mental slavery' that sets in with the absence of the questing critical intellect. Even the truth, Mill says, when held as a prejudice

independent of and proof against argument, 'is but one superstition the more, accidentally clinging to the words which enunciate
a truth'. One classic discussion (by the late-nineteenth-century
English writer W. K. Clifford) compares beliefs held on insufficient
evidence to stolen pleasures. An apt quotation is from Samuel Taylor Coleridge:

> He who begins by loving Christianity better than truth, will
> proceed by loving his own sect or Church better than Chris-
> tianity, and end in loving himself better than all.

But although these views are attractive, it is actually quite hard
to show that the habit of blind faith is necessarily so very bad. If,
having got to Hume's inert proposition, we then invest it with
hopes, fears, resolutions, and the embellishments of our own particular creeds, where is the harm in that? Is not simple piety a Good
Thing?

Some people certainly think random belief is a good thing. I
have in front of me the advertisement for a company calling itself
'your metaphysical superstore'. It specializes in New Age books and
music, flower essence, essential oils and aromatherapy, magnetic
therapy, light balance therapy, astrology and numerology, tarot
and rune cards readings, crystals and gemstones, and at the end,
like a rueful note of something approaching sanity, healing herbs.
Why should thinkers mock the simple pieties of the people?

Of course, there are simple pieties that do not get this general
protection. If I check into the Mysterious Mist and come back convinced that God's message to me is to kill young women, or people
with the wrong-coloured skins, or people who go to the wrong

church, or people who have sex the wrong way, that is not so good. So we have to use our human values, our own sense of good or bad, or right or wrong, to distinguish an admirable return from the mountain from a lunatic one.

We seem to be irretrievably in the domain of ethics here. And it would be impossible in a brief compass to assess the harms and benefits of religious belief, just as it is hard (although not impossible) to estimate the benefit or damage done by belief in magnetic therapy or Feng Shui or whatever. It clearly fills some function, answering to some human desires and needs. Some of the needs may be a common part of the human lot: I have already mentioned the need for ceremonies at crucial parts of life, or the need for poetry, symbol, myth, and music to express emotions and social relationships that we need to express. This is good. Unfortunately some of the desires may be a little less admirable: the desire to separatism, to schism, to imposing our way of life on others, to finding moral justifications for colonialism, or tribal or cultural imperialism, and all made guilt-free because done in the name of the Lord. For every peaceful benevolent mystic, there is an army chaplain, convincing the troops that God is on their side. Myself, I have never seen a bumper sticker saying 'Hate if you Love Jesus', but I sometimes wonder why not. It would be a good slogan for the religious Right.

It is, perhaps, surprising to find the issue here turning into a kind of practical or moral issue. It might seem to be a purely intellectual case of Reason (good) versus Faith (bad, or at least suspect). But Hume himself is responsible for clouding the picture. For reasons we are about to meet, there seems to be quite a lot of brute trust or faith in many everyday elements of common sense. We already met in Chapter 1 our 'fingers-crossed' faith in the external world or past time. And in the next two chapters we come across other places where Hume was the first to see that everyday confidence seems more a matter of faith than reason.

Obviously the attitude one takes to the 'fideism' that simply lets particular religious beliefs walk free from reason may depend heavily on what has recently been happening when they do so. Hume was born less than twenty years after the last legal religious executions in Britain, and himself suffered from the enthusiastic hostility of believers. If in our time and place all we see are church picnics and charities, we will not be so worried. But enough people come down the mountain carrying their own practical certainties to suggest that we ought to be.

Maybe some day something will be found that answers to the needs without pandering to the bad desires, but human history suggests that it would be unwise to bank on it.

CHAPTER SIX

Reasoning

THIS CHAPTER GIVES US an acquaintance with some basic categories to use when we think about reasoning. We want our reasonings to be good. We want to follow reliable methods for sifting truth from falsehood, and forming beliefs about our world. But which are these reliable methods, and what are their credentials? In this chapter we take a very brief glance at formal logic, and then we come upon the problems of inductive reasoning, and some of the elements of scientific reasoning.

A LITTLE LOGIC

The working parts of an argument are, first, its *premises*. These are the starting point, or what is accepted or assumed, so far as the argument is concerned. An argument can have one premise, or several. From the premises an argument derives a *conclusion*. If we are reflecting on the argument, perhaps because we are reluctant to accept the conclusion, we have two options. First, we might reject one or more of the premises. But second, we might reject the way the conclusion is drawn from the premises. The first reaction is that one of the premises is *untrue*. The second is that the reasoning is *invalid*. Of course, an argument may be subject to both criticisms: its premises are untrue, and the reasoning from them is invalid. But the two criticisms are distinct (and the two words, untrue and invalid, are well kept for the distinction).

In everyday life, arguments are criticized on other grounds again. The premises may not be very sensible. It is silly to make an intricate argument from the premise that I will win next week's lottery, if it hasn't a dog's chance of happening. It is often inappropriate to help ourselves to premises that are themselves controversial. It is tactless and tasteless in some circumstances to argue some things. But 'logical' is not a synonym for 'sensible'. Logic is interested in whether arguments are valid, not in whether it is sensible to put them forward. Conversely, many people called 'illogical' may actually be propounding valid arguments, but be dotty in other ways.

Logic has only one concern. It is concerned whether there is *no way* that the premises could be true without the conclusion being true.

It was Aristotle (384–322 BC) who first tried to give a systematic taxonomy of valid and invalid arguments. Aristotle realized that any kind of theory would need to classify arguments by the patterns of reasoning they exhibit, or what is called their *form*. One of the most famous forms of argument, for instance, rejoicing in the title 'modus ponendo ponens', or modus ponens for short, just goes:

p;
If p then q;
So, q.

Here p and q stand for any piece of information, or proposition, that you like. The form of the argument would remain the same whether you were talking of cows or philosophers. Logic then studies forms of information, not particular examples of it. Particular arguments are instances of the forms, but the logician is interested in the form or structure, just as a mathematician is interested in numerical forms and structure, but not interested in whether you are counting bananas or profits.

We want our reasonings to be valid. We said what this means: we want there to be *no way* that our conclusion could be false, if our premises are true. So we need to study whether there is 'any way' that one set of things, the premises, can be true without another thing, the conclusion, also being true. To investigate this we need to produce a science of the *ways* things can be true. For some very simple ways of building up information, we can do this.

TRUTH-TABLES

The classical assumptions are first that every proposition (p, q ...) has just one of two *truth*-values. It must be either true or false, and it cannot be both. ('But suppose I don't grant that?' Patience.) The

second assumption is that the terms the logic is dealing with—
centrally, 'and', 'not', 'or', and 'If . . . then . . .'—can be characterized
in terms of what they do to truth-values. ('But suppose I don't
grant that?' Patience, again.)

Thus, consider 'not-p'. Not-p, which is often written $\neg p$, is the
denial or negation of p: it is what you say when you disagree with p.
Whatever it is talking about, p, according to our first assumption,
is either true (T), or false (F). It is not both. What does 'not' do? It
simply reverses truth-value. If p is true, then $\neg p$ is false. If p is false,
then $\neg p$ is true. That is what 'not' does. We can summarize the result as a *truth-table*:

p	$\neg p$
T	F
F	T

The table gives the result, in terms of truth or falsity, for each assignment of truth-value to the components (such an assignment is
called an *interpretation*). A similar table can be written for 'and',
only here there are more combinations to consider. We suppose
that 'and' conjoins two propositions, each of which can be true or
false. So there are four situations or interpretations to consider:

p	q	$p \,\&\, q$
T	T	T
T	F	F
F	T	F
F	F	F

We are here given the truth-value for the overall combination, the conjunction, as a function of the combination of truth-values of the components: the four different interpretations of the formula.

The fact that we can give these tables is summed up by saying that conjunction, and negation, are *truth-functional,* or that they are truth-functional operators. Elementary propositional logic studies the truth-functions. Besides 'not' and 'and', they include 'or' (*p* or *q*, regarded as true except when both *p* and *q* are false); and a version of 'If *p* then *q*', regarded as true except in the case where *p* is true yet *q* false. If we write this latter as '$p \rightarrow q$', its truth-table is:

p	q	$p \rightarrow q$
T	T	T
T	F	F
F	T	T
F	F	T

These are also called Boolean operators. People familiar with databases and spreadsheets will know about Boolean searches, which implement exactly the same idea. A search for widgets over five years old held in the warehouse in York returns a hit when it finds a widget meeting *both* conditions. A search for customers *not* paid up on 1 December returns just the reverse hits from a search for customers paid up on 1 December. A search for customers who *either* bought a washing machine *or* a lawnmower turns up those who bought one and those who bought the other.

We can now see a rationale for some rules of inference. Consider the rule that from '*p* & *q*' we can derive *p* (or equally *q*). You cannot thereby get from truth to falsity, because the only interpretation (the top line) that has '*p* & *q*' true also has each ingredient true. So this is a good rule. We can also see why modus ponendo ponens, introduced above, is a good rule. It has two premises, 'p', and 'If p then q'. Can we find an interpretation (a 'way') in which both these are true without q being true? No. Because given that p is true, the only interpretation of $p \rightarrow q$ that allows it to be true also displays q as true.

There are some interesting animals in this jungle. One is that of a contradiction. Consider this formula:

$$p \ \& \ \neg p.$$

This expresses a contradiction—the ultimate no-no. And we now have a precise sense in which it is a no-no. For it is easy to show from the two tables we have, that *whatever* the truth-value of p, the truth-value of this formula comes out as F. There is *no way* it could be true. Because when one of the conjuncts is true the other is false: there is always a false element. And the truth-table for conjunction shows that in that case the overall formula is false.

Now suppose we complicate things by negating it:

$$\neg(p \ \& \ \neg p).$$

The brackets here show that the outside $\neg$ negates the whole thing. They act like the brackets in $3 \times (4 + 2)$, which show that the result is to be 18, rather than what we would get if we had $(3 \times 4) + 2$, which is 14. This bracketing is extremely important in logic, as it is in arithmetic: many fallacies in formal and informal reasoning can be avoided by knowing where the brackets fall. This is called knowing the *scope* of operation of the negations and conjunctions and the rest. In this example the outside negation has the whole of the rest of the formula to operate upon. A quite different reading would be given by $\neg p \ \& \ \neg p$, which simply conjoins $\neg p$ to itself, and, incidentally, is false in the case in which p is true (saying something false twice does not make it any better). One of the terrific virtues of formal logic is that it sensitizes people to scope *ambiguities*, which arise when it is not clear where the brackets lie, or in other words what is governing what. Without knowing this, you do not know *in what ways* your premises and your conclusions might be true, and hence whether there is *any way* your premises might be true without your conclusion being so.

This new formula, $\neg(p \ \& \ \neg p)$, reverses the truth-value of the old contradiction. So it is true, whatever the truth-values of its components. It is called a *tautology*. This is an important notion. In propositional logic if we have premises blah-blah-blah and conclusion yadda-yadda, we want it to be true that 'If blah-blah-blah then yadda-yadda' is a tautology. There is no interpretation (no way of assigning truth-values) that is to make the premises true, while the conclusion is false. When this is so, the argument is valid in exactly the sense we have been talking about.

One way of discovering whether an argument is valid is common enough to deserve a name. You can find whether 'If blah-blah-blah then yadda-yadda' is valid by adding 'not yadda-yadda' to 'blah-blah-blah' and seeing if you can get out a contradiction. If you can, the argument was valid. This corresponds directly to there being no way that the premises could be true and the conclusion false. There is no interpretation or no model for that state of affairs. Contradiction bars the way. This is called 'assuming towards a contradiction' or 'assuming towards a reductio', from the Latin name for this kind of procedure: the *reductio ad absurdum*, or reduction to absurdity. Anselm's ontological argument in Chapter 5 had that form.

In mathematics we can have not only $2 + 2$, but also $3 \times (2 + 2)$ and $((2 + 3) \times (2 + 2)) - 5$, and so on forever, and so it is with information. In so far as complex bits of information are produced by applying and reapplying truth-functional combinations, we can keep perfect control of the interpretations under which we have truth and falsity.

NOTHING TO BE AFRAID OF

So logic studies the structure of information. Its aim is to exhibit that structure, and thereby also exhibit what follows from what: what is sufficient to prove p and what follows from p, for p of any complexity. The connection between structure and proof is just this: the structure shows us if there is *no way* that the premises can be true without the conclusion being true. Because to understand the structure of information is to understand the ways it can be true.

So far, we have looked at complexity of information arising because propositions are negated or conjoined, or connected by implication. But we have not broken inside propositions. As far as the analysis so far goes, 'Some persons are philosophers' and 'All persons are philosophers' will come out looking alike. Each is just an example of a proposition, p. But we cannot get inside the proposition, and understand how these mean different things.

The breakthrough that cracked this problem created modern logic. It was made by the German mathematician and logician Gottlob Frege (1848–1925), in his seminal *Begriffschrift* ('concept writing') of 1879. Consider this argument: every inquiry stops somewhere, so there is somewhere every inquiry stops (it is sometimes supposed that the foundationalists we met in Chapter 1 advanced something like this). Something must be wrong, for a parallel would be: everyone has a mother, so there is someone who is everyone's mother. Or, everyone ties his own laces, so someone ties everyone's laces. Until Frege, people could see that there was something wrong, but, lacking any understanding of how this kind of information is built, they could not say what it was.

The key to understanding Frege's achievement is to think in terms of two quite different kinds of information. The first is very familiar. It corresponds to attaching a term to a name or other expression that refers to a particular person or thing: Bill is rich, Tony grins, this is an orange. Here we have a subject term (the names 'Bill' and 'Tony', and the demonstrative 'this'), and things are said of what they pick out: 'is rich', 'grins', or 'is an orange'. These terms stand for conditions that things might meet. They are called 'predicates': the rich things satisfy the predicate 'is rich', and other things do not. This is the basic subject–predicate form of information.

Now we can do something surprising. Suppose we delete the term that stands for the subject. We are left with only a gappy sentence, or predicate: 'is rich', and so on. We can better signal the gap by the expression called a variable, usually written $x, y, z \ldots$, as in algebra. So we have 'x is rich'. This is no longer a sentence carrying a piece of information, because nobody is being said to be rich. It is a sentence with a hole in it: a predicate, or an open sentence, in logicians' jargon.

Now, here comes the magic. Suppose I ask you to take an open sentence into a particular domain, such as a classroom, or New York City, and come back giving me some information. You *could* just reconstruct a piece of information like the one we started with, naming some particular individual, and saying that he or she is rich. But you don't have to do this. You can do a fundamentally different kind of thing. You can come back and tell me about the *quantity* of times the predicate is satisfied. And you can tell me this without telling me who satisfies it. It is as if you use the open sentence by pointing the 'x' in it at all the different people in the domain in turn, and note how often you get a hit. Suppose we symbolize the predicate by ϕ (the Greek letter 'phi'). Then you ask: 'Is *this* ϕ, is *this* ϕ?' of each of the members of the domain in succession. Then you can tell me what happened.

Perhaps the simplest kind of thing you could tell me is that at least once, somewhere, you got a hit. This is equivalent to 'Something is ϕ'. Or you might tell me that somewhere you got a miss: 'Something is not-ϕ.' Contrast this last with getting a hit nowhere: 'Nothing is ϕ.' Or it might be that everywhere you got a hit: 'Everything is ϕ.'

'Something is ϕ' is given by a new piece of symbolism: the *existential quantifier*. It is written as $(\exists x)\phi x$ (the fact that the variable comes after the predicate in 'ϕx' whereas in English predicates usually finish sentences and things like names start them is irrelevant). If you never get a hit, you can enter $\neg(\exists x)\phi x$: nothing is ϕ. If, somewhere, you get a result that is not a hit, you have the very different

$(\exists x)\neg(\phi x)$. If you nowhere get a result other than a hit, you have $\neg(\exists x)\neg\phi x$. This says that nowhere is there anything that is not ϕ. Or, in other words, as far as this domain goes, everything is ϕ. This last kind of information is sufficiently important to have its own symbol, the *universal quantifier*, written as $(\forall x)\phi x$: 'Everything is ϕ.'

Leibniz thought that if we had a sufficiently logical notation, dispute and confusion would cease, and men would sit together and resolve their disputes by calculation. The invention of the quantifier did not bring about this utopia, but it does an astonishing amount towards it. Its full power is exhibited when we get multiple quantifications. This is information built with more than one quantifier in play. When we have more than one quantifier, we use different variables $(x, y, z\ldots)$ to indicate the different gaps to which they correspond. To illustrate the idea, we can see how easily it dissects the invalid argument: everybody has a mother, so someone is everyone's mother. If we write 'x is the mother of y' as 'xMy' we symbolize the first by $(\forall y)(\exists x)\ xMy$. The second is $(\exists x)(\forall y)\ xMy$. How are these different?

Start with a sentence claiming motherhood between two different people: Beth is the mother of Albert. Knock out reference to Beth, and we have the open sentence xMa (where 'a' abbreviates Albert) We know that this predicate is satisfied (it is satisfied by Beth), so we know $(\exists x)\ xMa$. Somebody is Albert's mother. Now knock out reference to Albert: $(\exists x)\ xMy$. We have a gappy, or open, sentence again, with y marking the gap. It corresponds to the predicate 'having someone as a mother'. We can take this into the domain and point the variable y at each in turn: does *this* person have a mother, does *this* . . .? If we get the answer 'yes' on each occasion (which we do), we can universally quantify $(\forall y)(\exists x)\ x\text{M}y$. Everyone has a mother.

Now look at the second formula. To get this, we similarly start with Beth (b) being the mother of Albert. But now we knock out reference to Albert first: b$\text{M}y$. We take this round the domain. *If* we could (as in the real world we cannot) write $(\forall y)$ b$\text{M}y$, this would be because Beth is the mother of everyone (whoever you point the variable y at, it turns out that Beth is their mother!). What has just been supposed of Beth, might be supposed true of someone (if not Beth): in that case you can knock out reference to Beth, take the predicate 'being mother of everyone', or in other words $(\forall y)\ x\text{M}y$, round the domain, and find eventually someone giving the answer yes. In that case you would be able to write $(\exists x)(\forall y)\ x\text{M}y$. But the point to notice is that this is an *entirely* different procedure. It gives an entirely different kind of information (false of the domain of human beings). And the quantificational structure shows the difference on its face, because the stringing out of the quantifiers shows how the information is built.

In the real world, nobody is the mother of everybody. Before we understood quantification, that might have sounded weird, as if the human race sprung out of Nothing. This might have seemed a creepy metaphysical thesis. But now it is tamed. It just means that $\neg(\exists x)(\forall y)\ x\text{M}y$. And this is a simple truth. At least, unless you use the relation 'mother' to include more remote kinds of ancestry, in which case you might want to claim that there is someone, biological Eve, the first female *homo sapiens*, who is the mother of everyone. But I would regard that as an illegitimate or metaphorical usage. My grandmother is not literally my mother.

We can give more precise information about the quantity of times some condition is met in a domain. We might say that there is *exactly* one thing satisfying the condition. This means that any time you get a hit, if you go on pointing the variable at the rest of the things in the domain, whenever you get a hit it turns out to be the same one. There are no two distinct hits. This is the core of Russell's famous theory of definite descriptions. For it to be true that the unique king of France has a beard, there would need to be someone who rules France and no other person who rules France, and it should be true of whoever does rule France that he has a beard. Otherwise, the claim is false.

Quantificational structure is just one thing, but a very important thing to be aware of. Ordinary language is good at generating ambiguities that it easily resolves. 'All the nice girls love a sailor' said the song. There is some lucky sailor they all love? They all have one, but perhaps a different sailor that they love? Take any sailor, then all the nice girls love him (or her)? Very different things, true in very different circumstances. A related ambiguity is responsible for some thirty thousand deaths a year in the United States. 'A well-regulated militia being necessary to the security of a free state, the right of the people to keep and bear arms shall not be infringed.' Each person? Or the people as a collective, as in 'The team can have a bus'? If the founding fathers had been able to think in terms of quantificational structure, a lot of blood might not have been spilt.

LANGUAGE AND LOGIC

The logician studies the forms of information that we have just described, and of course such other complex forms as come to light. But there is another side to the work of the philosopher, which is to decide when information couched in the idioms of ordinary speech indeed displays one or another of these forms. This proves a surprisingly fraught business.

Consider, for instance, the difference between 'She was poor and she was honest', and 'She was poor but she was honest'. The first clearly illustrates the form 'p & q'. But what about the second? It certainly *suggests* something else, along the lines that it is surprising or noteworthy that someone poor should be honest. But does it actually *say* that? A simpler suggestion might be that it strictly says only what the first says, but says it in a way to insinuate or suggest that the combination is surprising or noteworthy. Perhaps only the simpler information is strictly given, but it is given in a way that carries its own suggestions (which may, as in this example, be seriously unpleasant). So philosophers of language are led to distinguish what is strictly said or asserted—the information carried by the utterance, called its *truth-condition*—from what is suggested or implied, not as a strict logical consequence, but by the way things are put, called the *implicature*.

Language is such a flexible and subtle instrument, that there is almost no limit to the way nuances in the presentation of information affect the implicatures. A famous example is the way in which simply not saying something can have weighty overtones:

'What do you think of the new professor of logic?'
'They tell me he is famous for his tomatoes.'

Here what is strictly said has little or no bearing on whether the new professor is competent. But the fact that this response is *all* that is given shows unmistakably that the respondent thinks the professor is no good. Choice of terminology can have its own implicatures: consider the difference between

John is Fred's brother.
Fred has a male sibling, John.

Here, the second way of putting what is in fact the same information suggests some kind of significance—sinister psychoanalytic overtones, perhaps. Order of telling also carries implicatures about the order of events. It would be misleading, although what is said is strictly true, to report the life of a child who learned to read and then wrote poetry, by saying that she wrote poetry and learned to read.

The way in which implicatures are generated is part of the study of language called *pragmatics*, whereas the structure of information is the business of *semantics*.

Consider the dreaded lawyer's question, used to discompose married male witnesses: 'Have you stopped beating your wife—yes or no?' The witness cannot answer 'Yes', without admitting that he once did; he cannot answer 'No', without giving the strongest impression that he still does. So he is embarrassed, and the trick works. How can we do better? Well, suppose we analyse 'X stopped doing Y' as a conjunction: 'X once did Y & X does not now do Y.' This explains why saying 'Yes' to the lawyer is bad: it follows that you once did beat your wife. Saying 'No', on the other hand, is interesting. If we look at the truth-table for conjunction we see that a conjunction can be false in *three* different ways: p true, q false; p false, q true; and both false. And each of these three ways are ways in which the negation of a conjunction can be *true* (negation reverses truth-value). Now in the lawyer case it is vital to the innocent husband to establish that his is the *middle* case: false that he once did it, and true that he does not now do it. The trouble is that the one word 'no' is insufficient to establish which way it is, and the risk is that the jury thinks he hasn't stopped because he continues (true that he once did, true that he does it now, so false that he stopped).

The innocent witness needs enough words to specify which combination describes him. So he cannot stick with the one-word answer 'No' (true thought it is). The right thing for the witness to say is (in one breath) 'No I haven't stopped because I never started', or words to that effect. If we handle the lawyer's question this way, we can say that it 'presupposes' that the witness once beat his wife, but only in the pragmatic sense, that anyone asking that question would normally be taking this for granted. Uncovering the hidden presuppositions behind questions and opinions is an important part of thinking.

Some presuppositions even raise questions about the assumption we made when interpreting 'and', 'not', 'or', and especially 'If . . . then' as truth-functions, adequately described by the tables. They sometimes *seem* to do more complex things. For instance, consider a party to which Fred is invited, but to which he in fact does not go. Suppose two assassins are trying to establish Fred's whereabouts. One says, 'If Fred goes to the party, he will go by taxi.' The other says, 'If Fred goes to the party, he will go by elephant.' Intuitively, at most one of these is true—in the West, probably the first. But if we look at 'Fred goes to the party → . . .' we will see that *both* of them are true. Because it is false that Fred goes to the party, and the table for → gives the outcome true, whatever the truth-value of the other proposition. Philosophers used to argue a great deal about whether this shows that the English conditional 'If . . . then' means the same as the truth-function →. Nowadays there is often a slightly more relaxed attitude, it being conceded that at any rate → gives the core of the notion, and the rest can be handled either semantically or pragmatically.

Before we leave this brief sketch of formal logic, we might pause to consider one kind of reaction it sometimes provokes. People sometimes think that logic is *coercive* ('masculine') or that it implies favouring some kind of 'linear thinking' as opposed to 'lateral thinking'. Both these charges are totally mistaken. Formal logic is too modest to deserve them.

First, what could be meant by the charge of coercion? Formal logic enables you to determine whether a set of propositions implies a contradiction. It also interprets contradictions as false. Most of us will want to avoid holding sets of propositions that imply things that are false, because we care that our beliefs are true. If someone is not like that, then we may indeed be minded to moralize against them. But we are not wearing the hats of formal logicians as we do so. The work of the formal logician was finished with the result.

Perhaps someone might feel coerced by the assumption mentioned right at the outset—that every proposition is true or false, and no proposition is both. Perhaps we ought to try more complex assumptions: for instance, we might welcome vague propositions that are true to a degree, or propositions that are neither true nor false but have some third status. That is fine too: these are respectable ideas, and there are alternative logics that develop them. But it is fair to warn that, for various reasons, they become awkward and uncomfortable. It is usually wise to be grateful for the simple 'two-valued' assumption.

A third source of the feeling of coercion introduces wider issues. If someone voices a number of views, or comes up with a piece of reasoning, it can be crass and coercive to insist on seeing them as of such-and-such a form and therefore contradictory, or therefore invalid. This may well be insensitive to the other factors we have mentioned already: presuppositions, suppressed premises, and so on. But this was not the fault of the logic, but of the uncharitable way of taking what was said. By itself logic is indifferent, even to sayings that look as if they embody direct contradictions. In the short story 'The Lady with the Pet Dog' by Chekhov, Anna Sergeyevna tells her husband that she is going to Moscow every so often to visit a doctor, 'and her husband believed her and did not believe her'. Formal logic does not tell us to jump up and down on Chekhov for this blatant contradiction. We know that Chekhov is suggesting something else, which is that her husband half-believes her, or alternates between confidence and mistrust. It is the flat contradiction that prompts us to look for other interpretations.

What of the charge that formal logic privileges 'linear' thinking? This too is nonsense. Formal logic does not direct the course of anyone's thoughts, any more than mathematics tells you what to count or measure. It is gloriously indifferent between propositions that arrive through speculation, imagination, sheer fancy, sober science, or anything else. All it tells you is whether there is a way in which all the propositions in a set, however arrived at, can be true together. But that can be a pearl beyond price.

PLAUSIBLE REASONINGS

Formal logic is great at enabling us to avoid contradiction. Similarly, it is great for telling us what we can derive from sets of premises. But you have to have the premises. Yet we reason not only to deduce things from given information, but to expand our beliefs, or what we take to be information. So many of our most interesting reasonings, in everyday life, are not supposed to be valid by the standards we have been describing. They are supposed to be *plausible* or *reasonable*, rather than watertight. There *are* ways in which such an argument could have true premises but a false conclusion, but they are not likely to occur.

Nevertheless, we can go a little further in applying some of the ideas we have met, even to plausible reasonings. Why is it silly, for instance, to be confident that my bet at roulette will be a winner? Because my only information is that I have placed my bet on x, and *most ways* that the wheel might end up do not present x as the winner. What we are dealing with is a space of possibilities, and if we could show that *most* possibilities left open by our evidence are ones in which the conclusion is also true, then we have something corresponding to plausible reasoning. In the roulette case, most possibilities left open by our evidence are ones in which the conclusion that x is the winner is false.

Roulette and other games of chance are precisely little fields designed so that we know the possibilities and can measure probabilities. There are fifty-two outcomes possible when we turn up a card, and if we do it from a freshly and fairly shuffled pack, each possibility has an equal chance. Probabilistic reasoning can then go forward: we can solve, for instance, for whether *most* draws of seven cards involve two court cards, or whatever. Such probabilistic reasoning is precisely a matter of measuring the range of possibilities left open by the specification, and seeing in what proportion of them some outcome is found.

What underlies our assignments of probabilities in the real world? Suppose we think of our position like this. As we go through life, we experience the way things fall out. Within our experience, various generalizations seem to hold: grass is green, the sky blue. Water refreshes; chocolate nourishes. So we take this experience as a guide to how things are across wider expanses of space and time. I have no direct experience of chocolate nourishing in the eighteenth century, but I suppose it did so; I have no direct experience of it nourishing people tomorrow, but I suppose it will continue to do so. Our beliefs and our confidence extend beyond the limited circle of events that fall within our immediate field of view.

Hume puts the problem this way:

> As to past Experience, *it can be allowed to give* direct *and* certain *information of those precise objects only, and that precise period of time, which fell under its cognizance: but why this*

> *experience should be extended to future times, and to other*
> *objects, which for aught we know, may be only in appearance*
> *similar; this is the main question on which I would insist . . .*
> *At least, it must be acknowledged, that there is here a conse-*
> *quence drawn by the mind; that there is a certain step taken;*
> *a process of thought, and an inference, which wants to be ex-*
> *plained. These two propositions are far from being the same,* I
> *have found that such an object has always been attended*
> *with such an effect, and* I *foresee, that other objects, which*
> *are, in appearance, similar, will be attended with similar ef-*
> *fects. I shall allow, if you please, that the one proposition may*
> *justly be inferred from the other: I know in fact, that it always*
> *is inferred. But if you insist, that the inference is made by a*
> *chain of reasoning, I desire you to produce that reasoning.*

Experience stretches no further than limited portions of space and time. In particular, all our experience belongs to the past and present. If we make inferences to the future, then these are inferences, and Hume wants to know the 'chain of reasoning' that they employ.

The inference from what is true of one limited region of space and time to a conclusion true of different parts of space and time is called inductive inference. What Hume is bothered about has become known as the problem of induction.

THE LOTTERY FOR THE
GOLDEN HARP

Here is a science fiction. You are disembodied spirits, inhabiting a kind of Heaven. I am God. I tell you that I am about to embody you, to give you lives to lead in a physical universe that I have prepared for you: Earth. At the end of your period in this universe, you will return to Heaven. Unlike normal human life, you will all live the same period: nine acts, let us say.

To make things interesting, I am going to offer you a kind of lottery. Each of you will get a ticket. The tickets correspond to the colour of the clear midday sky for each of the nine acts. I covenant with you, as gods do, that I won't change the colour at any time other than the beginning of an act. Just one of you is going to have a ticket that corresponds to the actual colour of the sky in every act. I also tell you that this person, the winner, will get the Golden Harp when you come back to Heaven. This is a very valuable prize. Heaven is good, but Heaven with the Golden Harp is even better. So a ticket might look like this:

	1	2	3	4	5	6	7	8	9
red									
orange					✗				
yellow				✗		✗			
green		✗	✗				✗		
blue	✗							✗	
violet									✗
Time	1	2	3	4	5	6	7	8	9

This ticket corresponds to the sky starting blue, going green, then yellow and orange, before darkening back to blue and even violet. Call the person with this ticket, Wavy.

Some of you (six of you) get straight tickets:

red									
orange									
yellow									
green									
blue	✗	✗	✗	✗	✗	✗	✗	✗	✗
violet									
Time	1	2	3	4	5	6	7	8	9

Call this ticket, Straightie.

If there is going to be just one ticket for each of you, there need to be 6^9 of you, which is a very large number indeed, to have a ticket corresponding to each possible distribution of the colours. And correspondingly, your chance of being the winner is only $1/6^9$, which is a very small number.

Hume insists that we cannot know anything right from the beginning in this situation. We cannot have a priori knowledge which ticket will win. Antecedently, while we are still excitedly discussing tickets, there is no reason to prefer one to another. For all we know God may favour waves, or straight lines. Or he may favour Kinkie:

red									
orange									
yellow						✗	✗	✗	✗
green									
blue	✗	✗	✗	✗	✗				
violet									
Time	1	2	3	4	5	6	7	8	9

The clear midday sky starts off blue for the first five acts, and then turns yellow, and stays like that for the rest. So in heaven, before we get any experience of the world God is about to put us into, no ticket has any better chance than any other.

Well, now we go to Earth.

Immediately, 5/6 of us can throw our tickets away. Any ticket not showing blue in the first square is a loser. And similarly, on the first day of each subsequent act, 5/6 of the survivors can throw their tickets away, until at the beginning of the ninth act, only six remain. And a day after that, there is a single winner.

Now let us draw the curtain back towards the end of the fifth act. Each of Straightie and Kinkie has been doing well. They have seen their competitors fall away, on five previous occasions. In fact, the number of survivors in the lottery has dropped from 6^9 down to 6^4, and their chances of being the winner have risen accordingly.

But suppose they get into an argument with each other. Suppose Straightie urges Kinkie that his ticket is far the more likely winner, so that he will swap it with Kinkie but only for a terrific price. We would probably side with Straightie. But suppose that Kinkie resists, urging that there is no reason in what has happened so far to bet on Straightie rather than on him. What can they say to each other?

Each can point to their track record of success. But it is the same track record for each of them. They each have their five hits. And there is nothing else to go on. After all, neither of them can peer into the future. Like us, they are stuck in time, and cannot peek out of it.

What Straightie would like is an argument in favour of the *uni-*

formity of nature. In other words, an argument saying that since God has started off with a blue sky, and stuck with it so far, probably he is going to go on sticking with it. But Kinkie can point out that God has started off with an as-per-Kinkie sky, and by equal reasoning urge that he is probably going to stick with that.

Straightie wants the argument that Hume says he cannot find. But, as I said, in our bones we all side with Straightie. What's wrong with arguing that since nature has been uniform so far, it will probably go on being uniform?

> *It is impossible, therefore, that any arguments from experience can prove this resemblance of the past to the future; since all these arguments are founded on the supposition of that resemblance.*

Of course, Hume knows that we all learn from experience, and that we all rely upon the uniformity of nature. He thinks we share this natural propensity with animals. It is just that this is all it is: an exercise of nature. It is a custom or habit, but it has no special claim in reason. When we reason inductively there is a way in which our premises can be true and our conclusion false. Nature can change. In fact, there are many ways, since nature can change in many ways. There is no contradiction in imagining this. And now, it seems, we cannot even argue that such changes are *improbable.* We only think that because they have not occurred within our experience. But taking our experience to be representative, in this regard as in any other, presupposes the uniformity of nature. It seems that we engineer a bridge between past and future, but cannot argue that the bridge is reliable.

CHANCY STUFF

Here is a problem quite a long way from the problem of induction, but that introduces an incredibly useful tool for thinking about many things. It is a problem most people get wrong.

Suppose you decide to check yourself out for some disease. Suppose that this disease is quite rare in the population: only about one in a thousand people suffer from it. But you go to your doctor, who says he has a good test for it. The test is in fact *over 99 per cent reliable*! Faced with this, you take the test. Then—horrors!—you test positive. You have tested positive, and the test is better than 99 per cent reliable. How bad is your situation, or in other words, what is the chance you have the disease?

Most people say, it's terrible: you are virtually certain to have the disease.

But suppose, being a thinker, you ask the doctor a bit more about this 99 per cent reliability. Suppose you get this information:

(1) If you have the disease, the test will say you have it.
(2) The test sometimes, but very rarely, gives 'false positives'. In only a very few cases—around 1 per cent—does it say that someone has the disease when they do not.

These two together make up the better than 99 per cent reliability. You might think that you are still virtually certain to have the disease. But in fact this is entirely wrong. Given the facts, your chance of having the disease is a little less than 10 per cent.

Why? Well, suppose 1,000 people take the test. Given the general incidence of the disease (the 'base rate'), one of them might be expected to have it. The test will say he has it. It will also say that 1 per cent of the rest of those tested, i.e. roughly ten people, have it. So eleven people might be expected to test positive, of whom only one will have the disease. It is true the news was bad—you have gone from a 1 in 1,000 chance of disease to a 1 in 11 chance—but it is still far more probable that you are healthy than not. Getting this answer wrong is called the fallacy of ignoring the base rate.

How should we think accurately about chances in a circumstance like this?

We should start with a formula for the probability of one thing given another. Suppose we ask what the probability is of (a) some random person in a class wearing Levi jeans. Perhaps 20 per cent. And what is the probability of (b) some random person wearing a Levi jacket? Perhaps 20 per cent also. So what is the probability of a random person both wearing the jeans, and the jacket? You might think 20/100 × 20/100 = 4 per cent. But that would be wrong. For the two events are not necessarily independent. That means, the chance of someone wearing the jacket is very likely different if they are wearing the jeans. Perhaps nearly everyone who wears those jeans wears those jackets and vice versa. In that case the probability of (a) and (b) both being true of a random person would itself be 20 per cent. Or perhaps the fashion gurus say that you must *never* wear both. In that case the chance of (a) and (b) both being true might be zero.

To get this right we need an expression for the probability of someone wearing the jacket *given* that he is wearing the jeans. The probability of (a) given (b) is written Prob (a/b). The probability of (b) given (a) is Prob (b/a). Then the right figure is this:

Prob $(a \& b) = $ Prob $(a) \times$ Prob (b/a),

or equally:

Prob $(a \& b) = $ Prob $(b) \times$ Prob (a/b).

The first equation says that the probability of wearing jeans and jacket = the probability of wearing the jeans × the probability of wearing the jacket *given that* you are wearing the jeans. This last is called a 'conditional probability'. The second says it is also equal to the probability of wearing the jacket × the probability of wearing the jeans *given* that you are wearing the jacket. These have to be identical, by symmetry (since $a \& b$ is the same proposition as $b \& a$).

An English clergyman called Thomas Bayes (1702–61) looked hard at this result. Since each of them is equal to Prob $(a \& b)$, each of these is equal to each other:

Prob $(a) \times$ Prob (b/a) $=$ Prob $(b) \times$ Prob (a/b)

So we can write down an expression for the probability of b given a:

$$\text{Prob } (b/a) \ = \ \frac{\text{Prob } (b) \times \text{Prob } (a/b)}{\text{Prob } (a)}.$$

This rather frightening-looking equation is a simple version of what is known as Bayes's theorem.

The application of the result comes like this. Suppose now that we have some hypothesis, and a piece of evidence for it. We are interested in the probability of the hypothesis h, given the evidence e. We can write this as Prob (h/e). This is called the *posterior* probability of the hypothesis—its probability after the evidence comes in. Then the theorem tells us that:

$$\text{Prob} \, (h/e) \; = \; \frac{\text{Prob} \, (h) \times \text{Prob} \, (e/h)}{\text{Prob} \, (e)} \, .$$

This directs us to three different things on which the posterior probability depends.

Prob (h). This is known as the prior or antecedent probability of h.

Prob (e/h). This is the probability of evidence e, given h. It is a measure of the *fit* between the hypothesis and the evidence.

Prob (e). This is the prior or antecedent probability of the evidence itself.

Intuitively it can be thought of like this. There are three factors. First, how likely is the hypothesis from the word go? Second, how well does the evidence accord with the hypothesis? Third, how likely is the evidence from the word go?

It is often useful to treat this last figure in terms of the *different ways* the evidence might have come about. It is a figure that gets larger the greater the number of quite probable alternative explanations of the evidence. And when it gets larger, the probability of the given hypothesis on the evidence gets smaller. It has too many competitors. So in practice the figure on the bottom measures how many other ways there are in which that evidence could be explained, and how likely they are. We recognize the importance of this intuitively. When the call-girl Mandy Rice-Davies was told that some member of the aristocracy denied having had an affair with her, she replied, 'Well, he would, wouldn't he?' She was in effect reminding people that the antecedent probability of this particular piece of testimony was high *regardless* of which hypothesis is true, and this undermined its value as evidence. You could guess in advance that whatever their relations, the aristocrat would have said what he did. So his saying what he did was worthless as evidence.

The ideal would be: the hypothesis is antecedently quite likely. The evidence is just what you would expect, given the hypothesis. And there are not many or any other *probable* ways the evidence could have come about.

In the case of the disease, Bayes's theorem puts the base rate up front: it is the antecedent probability that you have the disease, of 1 in 1,000. The next figure, the fit between the test result and the hypothesis that you have the disease, is excellent: 1, in fact, since the test always says you have it if you do. But on the bottom line we have the number of ways that evidence could have come about. Informally, there is the 1 in 1,000 chance of a true result *plus* the 10 in 1,000 chance of a false positive. It is this that results in your overall chance, given the evidence, being (approximately) 1 in 11.

There is a nice way now of representing the impasse between Straightie and Kinkie in the lottery for the Golden Harp. Suppose S in the entire ninefold pattern—blue each time—on Straightie's ticket. And suppose E is the part of it that is within our experience: the five results of blue each time so far. Then

$$\text{Prob}\,(S/E) \;=\; \frac{\text{Prob}\,(S) \times \text{Prob}\,(E/S)}{\text{Prob}\,(E)}.$$

The antecedent or prior probability of S was $1/6^9$. The second figure is good, however. If S indeed describes the way events fall out, then the evidence E, i.e. the first five readings, is just what would be expected. Their probability is in fact 1, given S. And the prior probability of E? That is just five readings of blue, which, given that blue is one of six competing possibilities, is $1/6^5$. Calculating out, we get that Prob (S/E) is $1/6^4$, which is just what we got intuitively before.

The trouble is that exactly the same formula gives exactly the same result for Kinkie's ticket, K. You can easily see that the evidence has probability 1, given K, and the prior probability of the evidence is the same in either event.

Notice that the problem is not one of 'proving' that S will win, or that K will not win. It is just one of finding *some good reason* to expect S rather than K. It is a question of comparing probabilities. Hume's position is that even this cannot be done in S's favour. Reason remains entirely silent between them. And following Bayes's analysis, he looks to be right. The debate between Straightie and Kinkie is as stalemated as ever. In fact, if there was no reason for preferring the ticket S to the ticket K in Heaven, a priori, then there is no reason for preferring it after the evidence has come in. Or so it seems.

We could now revisit a number of areas: the Zombie possibility, the design argument, the likelihood of a good God creating or allowing evil, and especially the discussion of miracles, using Bayes's theorem. It is a tool of immense importance. The fallacies it guards against—ignoring the base rate, ignoring the chance of false positives—are dangerous, and crop up everywhere that people try to think.

Of course, very often it is difficult or impossible to quantify the 'prior' probabilities with any accuracy. It is important to realize that this need not matter as much as it might seem. Two factors alleviate the problem. First, even if we assign a range to each figure, it may be that *all* ways of calculating the upshot give a sufficiently similar result. And second, it may be that in the face of enough evidence, difference of prior opinion gets swamped. Investigators starting with very different antecedent attitudes to Prob (*h*) might end up assigning similarly high values to Prob (*h/e*), when (*e*) becomes impressive enough.

For interest, it is worth mentioning that there are quite orthodox methods of statistical inference that try to bypass Bayesian ideas. Much scientific research contents itself with ascertaining that some result would only occur by chance some small percentage of the time (less that 5 per cent, or less than 1 per cent, for example). But it *then* infers that probably the result is not due to chance—that is, there is a significant causal factor or correlation of some kind involved. This prevalent reasoning is actually highly doubtful, and Bayes shows why. If the antecedent probability that a result is due to anything else than chance is very, very low, then even enormously improbable results will not overturn it. If I put my hand in a shaken bag, throw seven Scrabble letters face down on a table, shuffle them into a line, and turn them up, the actual result (PQAERTU, say) will be very improbable indeed. I might do the same thing for a hundred years and not repeat it. But it was chance, for all that. In this setup *any* result is going to be very improbable, and we should not be able to infer back to say that anything other than chance is responsible for it. That is the very kind of reasoning that fuels lunatic attempts to prove that the pattern of occurrence of vowels in Shakespeare's plays is best explained by the hypothesis that he was writing the Name of the Beast 666 times, or whatever. In short, it is not just the fact that a result is improbable that should prompt us to look for some special explanation. We need some additional reason to think that the improbable result is not just due to chance anyway. Chance is just as good at throwing up improbabilities as design.

EXPLANATIONS AND PARADIGMS

Induction is the process of taking things within our experience to be representative of the world outside our experience. It is a process of projection or extrapolation. But it is only part of a wider process of trying to increase our understanding of things. In the final section of this chapter, I want to introduce some of the reasonings that this involves.

Suppose we have a complex system. We have various features, which seem to interact. We can find the ways in which they seem to interact, by noticing changes and variations. We might be able to plot these against each other, and find reliable relationships. Boyle's law, that the pressure of a given mass of gas is inversely proportional to its volume, at a given temperature, is an example. This is a purely *empirical* law. It is found to hold within experience, and we take it to hold across the wider world. Some disciplines would be mightily pleased if they could get that far. Economics, for instance, wants to find the *right* features of an economic system, and to be able to plot the relationships between them *reliably*. And this proves very hard. It takes art and craft, and most attempts crash in flames. We are apt to forget that the same was true of physical science. For example, it took a century of effort for scientists to learn to identify the energy of a mechanical system as its salient feature, whose conservation enabled them to predict its behaviour. This is a historical fact that science teachers should be made to write out a hundred times, when they upbraid children as 'dumb' because they do not cotton onto the idea immediately.

If an economist has a story about the right variables and the relationships between them, it can be called a model of the economy. But even if we had such a thing, we might still feel we did not understand what was going on. Isaac Newton (1642–1727) had a law plotting the gravitational attraction between bodies as a function of their masses and the distance between them: the famous inverse square law. But both he and his contemporaries felt that this gave them no real understanding of *why* gravity operated as it does. As with Boyle's law, we can say that while it is all we have got, we know something about the system. But we do not really understand *why* it is behaving as it does. Why should pressure vary inversely with volume? If it always does, why does it always do so? And why should constancy of temperature be important?

These questions were answered by providing a model in a more robust sense. The kinetic theory of gases sees gases as volumes of molecules in motion. Pressure is the result of the impact of these molecules on the walls of the container. The molecules speed up with increased temperature. Once a gas is seen like this, we have a *mechanism*, and given suitable assumptions, the empirical laws such as Boyle's law can be derived from the nature of the mechanism.

Finding a mechanism does not bypass the problem of induction. The continued uniform behaviour of items in a mechanism is a projection or extrapolation from what we have found so far, just as much as anything else. But it reduces the number of independent assumptions we need to make. A few stable features of things, and reliable interactions between them, might explain others. If we take the stable features for granted, we can explain the others in terms of them. These represent the *explanatory* and *simplifying* ideals of science.

But what kinds of thing count as satisfactory 'mechanisms'? Things whose behaviour we understand 'clearly and distinctly'? Or something else? The answer to this question opens one of the most exciting chapters of modern thought. Nearly everyone is inclined to think that there are some kinds of systems that we understand better than we understand others. To most people, some kinds of causation, like shunting, seem especially intelligible, whereas others, like action at a distance, or the effects of body on mind, seem very mysterious. In fact until Hume, almost everyone—both philosophers and natural scientists like Newton—thought this. They thought we had a priori knowledge of what *does* cause what, and still more, of what could *not* cause what. We have already seen this. Even Newton thought that it was clear that gravitational attraction could not be a case of action at a distance. He thought that any idiot could see that if the Sun exerts an attraction on the Earth this must be because of a chain of some kind between them. Causation had to be a matter of pushes and pulls:

> *That gravity should be innate, inherent and essential to mat-*
> *ter, so that one body may act upon another at a distance*
> *through a* vacuum, *without the mediation of anything else,*
> *by and through which their action and force may be conveyed*
> *from one to another, is to me so great an absurdity that I be-*
> *lieve no man who has in philosophical matters a competent*
> *faculty of thinking, can ever fall into it.*

Surely it 'stands to reason' or is 'clear and distinct' or 'a priori' that
a body cannot act somewhere where it is not! We still reason like
this when, for instance, we attempt to show by pure reason that the
Universe must be the creation of a god. We are supposing that we
know what kind of thing *must* cause some effect, and what could
not cause it.

Hume blows this rationalism right out of the water:

> *I shall venture to affirm, as a general proposition, which ad-*
> *mits of no exception, that the knowledge of this relation is not,*
> *in any instance, attained by reasonings a priori; but arises en-*
> *tirely from experience, when we find, that any particular ob-*
> *jects are constantly conjoined with each other. Let an object be*
> *presented to a man of ever so strong natural reason and abil-*
> *ities; if that object be entirely new to him, he will not be able,*
> *by the most accurate examination of its sensible qualities, to*
> *discover any of its causes or effects. Adam, though his rational*
> *faculties be supposed, at the very first, entirely perfect, could*
> *not have inferred from the fluidity, and transparency of water,*
> *that it would suffocate him, or from the light and warmth of*
> *fire, that it would consume him.*

As a good psychologist should, he gives an explanation of the
prejudice that we can argue a priori about cause and effect:

We fancy, that were we brought, on a sudden into this world,
we could at first have inferred, that one Billiard-ball would
communicate motion to another upon impulse; and that we
needed not to have waited for the event, in order to pronounce
with certainty concerning it. Such is the influence of custom,
that, where it is strongest, it not only covers our natural igno-
rance, but even conceals itself, and seems not to take place,
merely because it is found in the highest degree.

Hume knew that philosophers and scientists hankered after an
ideal of 'insight' into the laws of nature: something like a geometry
or algebra enabling them to see why events fall out in patterns that
are necessary, mathematically certain. They wanted a Cartesian
'clear and distinct' perception of why things have to be the way they
are. But Hume believes that this goal is an illusion. Nothing the scientist does would accomplish it.

It is good to remember here that when Newton published *Principia Mathematica* in 1687, revealing the laws of motion, there were
scientists of his time who were disappointed. They wanted an insight into what gravitational attraction *is*, but Newton only told
them what it *does*. Newton tells you how bodies accelerate towards
each other, and that is all. Hume argues that the kind of thing Newton did was the *only kind of thing* science can ever do. He holds that
anything else represents an incoherent ideal. In the following quotation 'philosophers' are scientists, and 'philosophy of the natural
kind' means what would now be called natural science, and especially physics and chemistry:

Hence we may discover the reason why no philosopher, who
is rational and modest, has ever pretended to assign the

ultimate cause of any natural operation, or to show distinctly the action of that power, which produces any single effect in the universe. It is confessed, that the utmost effort of human reason is to reduce the principles, productive of natural phenomena, to a greater simplicity, and to resolve the many particular effects into a few general causes, by means of reasonings from analogy, experience, and observation. But as to the causes of these general causes, we should in vain attempt their discovery; nor shall we ever be able to satisfy ourselves, by any particular explication of them. These ultimate springs and principles are totally shut up from human curiosity and enquiry. Elasticity, gravity, cohesion of parts, communication of motion by impulse; these are probably the ultimate causes and principles which we shall ever discover in nature; and we may esteem ourselves sufficiently happy, if, by accurate enquiry and reasoning, we can trace up the particular phenomena to, or near to, these general principles. The most perfect philosophy of the natural kind only staves off our ignorance a little longer.

What we have here is a splendid rejection of the rationalist ideal. In its place we seem to be left only with *more or less familiar* systems. At any time those with which we are comfortable provide 'paradigms', or systems against which we compare others. They give us our sense of what would count as a satisfactory explanation. But without the rationalist ideal, we become aware that this sense is perhaps itself changeable. If we replace 'reason' by 'habit and custom', then cannot our customs and habits change? The famous philosopher of science Thomas Kuhn (1922–96) argued that indeed they can. 'Normal' science proceeds in the light of a set of paradigms, or implied views about what kind of explanations we should hope for. Periods of revolutionary science occur when the paradigms are themselves challenged. Science is to be seen as 'a series of peaceful interludes punctuated by intellectually violent revolutions'. After the revolutions, our sense of what makes for a comfortable explanation of why things hang together changes.

Some people get quite excited quite quickly by this kind of thought. They take it to suggest a kind of 'relativism', whereby some people have their 'paradigms' and other people have others, and there is no judging which is better. But that is unwarranted. There may be better or worse paradigms. Looking at the sky as an opaque veil with holes in it through which we see specks of the heavens beyond was once a paradigm or model of the way the heavens are. We believe that we know better, and I hold that belief too. Paradigms can be asked to show their worth, and some of them do not stand up.

Thus, suppose it is true it is that we inevitably approach the world with a particular set of preferred categories, partly set by our culture and history. It still does not follow that all such sets are equally 'good'. Some sets have been discarded for good and sufficient reason. A scientific environment is (ideally) an environment in which the constant process of experimenting, predicting, and testing, weeds out the bad ideas. Only the ones that survive go on into the next generation. This is not to say that actual scientific environments are as ideal as all that: at any time science can no doubt boast its fair share of blinkers, prejudices, and distortions. But the process contains within itself the mechanisms of correction. We might remember here the discussion in Chapter 1, when we criticized Descartes for not taking account of the 'self-corrective' nature of the senses, whereby illusions are detected as such. Science similarly contains within itself the devices for correcting the illusions of science. That is its crowning glory. When we come upon intellectual endeavours that contain no such devices—one might cite psychoanalysis, grand political theories, 'new age' science, creationist science—we need not be interested.

In this chapter we have discovered some of the elements to notice in our reasonings. We have seen the some of the ideas that underlie formal logic. We have distinguished processes of inductive reasoning, and seen how dependent we are on brute faith in the uniformity of nature. We have a sense of how to reason about the probability of things. And we have looked a little at processes of model building and explanation, and been led to mistrust a priori reasonings about cause and effect. All these give us tools to be used as we go on to think about the world and our place in it.

CHAPTER SEVEN

The World

IN THE SIX CHAPTERS so far, we have visited six problem areas. These were: thoughts about our own global reliability, thoughts about mind and body, thoughts about freedom and fate, thoughts about the self, thoughts about God, and thoughts about the order of nature. These are each notorious areas of difficulty, where the structure of our thoughts, or the way to think properly, are hard to discern. We might hope, by comparison, that thinking about the world around us is relatively problem-free. In this chapter, we visit areas in which a little thought generates trouble about that, as well.

COLOURS, SMELLS, SOUNDS, FEELS, AND TASTES

Here is Descartes's great contemporary, the physicist Galileo Galilei (1564–1642):

> *Now I say that whenever I conceive any material or corporeal substance, I immediately feel the need to think of it as bounded, and as having this or that shape; as being large or small in relation to other things, and in some specific place at any given time; as being in motion or at rest; as touching or not touching some other body; and as being one in number, or few, or many. From these conditions I cannot separate such a substance by any stretch of my imagination. But that it must be white or red, bitter or sweet, noisy or silent, and of sweet or foul odor, my mind does not feel compelled to bring in as necessary accompaniments. Without the senses as our guides, reason or imagination unaided would probably never arrive at qualities like these. Hence I think that tastes, odors, colors, and so on are no more than mere names so far as the object in which we place them is concerned, and that they reside only in the consciousness. Hence if the living creature were removed, all these qualities would be wiped away and annihilated.*

Galileo is here expressing what has become called the distinction between the *primary* and the *secondary* qualities of material things. The secondary qualities are the immediate objects of the senses: colours, tastes, sounds, odors, feels. According to Galileo they 'hold their residence' only in the sensitive (i.e. perceiving) animal. Moreover, according to Descartes, there is no reason for supposing them to 'resemble' whatever in nature causes them—the arrival of photons at the eye, in the case of colour, for example.

Descartes similarly had a poor view of the senses as vehicles of truth (remember the ball of wax in Chapter 1):

> *For the proper purpose of the sensory perceptions given me by nature is simply to inform the mind of what is beneficial or harmful for the composite of which the mind is a part . . . but*

I misuse them by treating them as reliable touchstones for im-
mediate judgments abut the essential nature of the bodies lo-
cated outside us.

An example he liked was the perception of a pain as being in the
foot, after the 'animal spirits' had conducted their energy, their 'jet
of flame', up the nerves and into the brain. God devised it that the
mind receives the best sensation that it could (God's good pleasure, again). The particular motion of the brain could have con-
veyed something else to the mind. However, there is 'nothing else
which would have been so conducive to the continued well-being
of the body'. In other words, if God had brought it about that I interpreted the motions in the brain as, for instance, just signalling a
perturbation of my *brain*, then I would be slow to move my foot,
which is being injured, out of harm's way. We might notice that
Descartes's position here contains a denial of epiphenomenalism.
It is *because* the mental events are one thing or another that we
move our foot quickly. If the mental were inert, God could let it fall
out however he wants without affecting our well-being.

Descartes's quaint language conceals a surprisingly modern
point. If we substitute evolution for God, we can put it like this. For
a creature to flourish, it must get information from the environment that tallies with its actual needs. All that is necessary for this
is that the information stimulates it to action in the right way. For
instance, if a predator is coming, it needs some information that
stimulates flight. However, for this function, it does not matter
what experience it gets. If the predator treads on a twig, then the
'motions' this induces in the ear could result in the creature hearing a loud sound, or a discordant sound, or a harmony, or a high

pitch, or a low pitch, or they could result in just a bad smell, but so long as it senses something that frightens it, its senses are doing their job. The senses provide us only 'confused' (as opposed to clear and distinct) data.

This also lets God off the hook. If we ask why the senses sometimes deceive us, making us think that colours lie outside us when they do not, then the answer comes in two parts. First, he created the 'best system that could be devised' for producing a sensation especially conducive to the preservation of the healthy person. The senses, as we have seen, can deceive us. But Descartes insists that it is we, not nature or God's design, who are at fault if we misinterpret the data of the senses, uncorrected by use of intelligence. We should not treat the data of the senses as straightforwardly conveying information about the real properties of things. This would be to treat confused data as if they were clear and distinct.

When we do use our intellects, abstracting away from the data of the senses, what kind of world are we left with? Descartes, the mathematician, believed that the real property of 'res extensa' was, as the name suggests, spatial extension. Everything else was the possibly illusory, sensory 'filling' of spatial volume by things like colours and feels—things that, like Galileo, he believed to have their real residence only in the mind. So as well as opening up dualism of mind and body Descartes and his contemporaries open up a dualism between the world as it is for us (sometimes called the 'manifest image')—the coloured, warm, smelly, noisy, comfortable, familiar world—and the world as it is objectively or absolutely (the 'scientific image')—the world that contains nothing but physical particles and forces spread out across the boundless spaces of the cosmos.

Why is science thought to drive colours and the rest into the mind? The most compelling argument seems to be one from perceptual relativity. People are apt to think of 'relativism' as a particular threat, or temptation, in moral philosophy, where we are uncomfortably familiar with the way situations strike different people differently. But a more general relativism is here raising its head. We can present an argument from relativity concerning tastes, odours, colours, sounds, and 'feels' like this:

> Suppose a part of the world or an object in the world displays a certain smell, etc. to one observer O. How it smells, etc. will be a function of O's particular sensory structures. *So*, there will be or could be another creature O* with different sensory structures, to whom the same part of the world or the same object would smell, etc. quite differently. O and O* may each live equally efficient, adapted lives. *So*, there is no reason for saying that just one of O or O* has got the smells, etc. right. *So*, there is no one correct distribution of smells, etc. in the world. *So*, smells, etc. are better thought of as entirely mind-dependent.

This argument was familiar in the ancient world, before returning to prominence in the seventeenth century. There are a number of points to notice about it.

First, it does not depend on the actual existence of the different creature O*. It is enough that we can see how there *could* be such a creature: one whose colour receptivity is quite different, or whose auditory apparatus sensitizes it to different frequencies of sound, or to different kinds of energy altogether. Of course the argument becomes more graphic when we come across striking instances. Nobody who keeps a dog can believe that the world of smells that dogs inhabit bears much resemblance to our own. And some of us can remember, for instance, how differently beer or dry wine first tasted before we got used to it. Different sensitivities clearly exist: for a start, all mammals except some primates are colour-blind. There are substances (phenol thio-urea is an example) that have a pronounced bitter taste to a high proportion of human beings, but no taste at all to others. And so on.

But quite apart from such actual cases, we can easily see how there could be forms of life that get by perfectly well with quite different sensory 'fillings'. Some people tune their TV sets so that the colours seem garish and glaring to others, but they see the same scenes as a result.

The second premise too seems incontestable. It represents a piece of knowledge we have about the world. We know that certain kinds of condition, for instance, can lead us to taste things very differently. With colds, we lose much of our sense of smell. We know a good deal about how colour vision depends upon the particular sensitivities of three different kinds of receptors in the eye, as described in Chapter 2. We know that bats navigate by acoustic means that are closed to us.

So the initial conclusion seems inevitable. Compare this: two different television sets may receive the same signal. However, what picture appears depends on the particular structure of the television. Hence, there could be televisions that deliver different outputs from the same signal (and of course there are).

The next premise is crucial, and one that is often forgotten in discussions of relativism in other areas, such as ethics. Any argument aiming at something like the final conclusion needs to go via this. It is no good just pointing out that different creatures perceive the world differently, if that allows the interpretation that just one set of them has got the world *right*. The analogy with the televisions makes the point. Sure, someone might say, the way in which a television set shows a picture in response to a signal may vary. If the television is the wrong kind for that signal, then it just shows snowstorms, for instance. But that just means that the television misses information that exists, that is objectively there, carried by the signal. It is no kind of argument that the information is not really there, independently of the receiver, in the first place. If the transmitter is beaming the inaugural speech, a television showing a snowstorm is doing worse than one showing the speech. It is not doing just as well, but in a different way. But that is what this argument from relativity is aiming to show. So, there is a hole in it.

There would be if it were not for premise that the different creatures might live equally well-functioning, adapted lives. This plugs this gap, by asking us to see the different observers as potentially equally well adapted to their worlds. For Descartes, that would have been a belief with theological backing. For us, it may have an evolutionary explanation. Creatures that cannot receive the kind of information they need to live their lives die out. So, unlike the televisions, O and O* may be doing as well as each other, but living lives with different sensory experiences: seeing, smelling, hearing, tasting, and feeling differently. It is this equality that suggests, as

Russell later put it, that it would be 'favouritism' to say that the world is better represented in one of these ways than in any other.

The premise about equal adaptation may not be enough however. We may want to think like this. Certainly, dogs, for instance, are adapted creatures, with sensory systems that meet their natural needs. But let us distinguish the different dimensions of sensory experience. Dogs have marvellous noses. So, let us admit that they can smell smells that we cannot. They are the 'authorities' on the distribution of smells. On the other hand, dogs are colour-blind. Therefore, they are not 'authorities' on the distribution of colours. We can make finer visual discriminations amongst objects in a whole variety of different lights than dogs can. That is what our colour vision is for. So why not say that the real colours are the ones that the creatures best adapted for colour see? And the real smells the ones that creatures best adapted for smell sense? And if we can say this, then the subsequent conclusions will not follow.

This certainly points to a hole in the argument as it is stated. To repair the hole we would need some stronger premise. A repair that would do the job might be to aim for each sensory dimension D (vision, touch, smell, sound, taste), one at a time. There would be five different arguments, and in each of them the crucial premise would read:

> O and O* may each live equally efficient, adapted lives in respect of sensory dimension D.

If this is accepted, the rest of the argument looks like plain sailing. The rationale for the final move is obvious enough. Consider phenol thio-urea. It cannot in itself be both tasty and tasteless. Similarly, the world cannot be thought of as containing as many smells as there are possible sensory apparatuses, adapted for registering just some molecules (or their absence) in some combinations and concentrations. Such a world would contain an infinite number of coexisting smells, since there is no limit to the possible varieties of detector.

The upshot of the argument is called 'secondary quality idealism'. It gives us Galileo's result that the qualities that are the immediate objects of sensory experience are driven 'back into the mind'.

GOOD SOLID SENSE

This did not strike Descartes and many of his successors as too bad. Descartes himself, as we have seen, still had 'reason' to inform him about the properties objects really had. He did not mind the illusory aspects of the world of appearance—the fact that colours are, as it were, due to us, and not to the things we see. His position in this was canonized in English-speaking philosophy by John Locke.

Locke is very explicit. There are

> original *or* primary *qualities of body, which I think we may observe to produce simple ideas in us, viz. solidity, extension, figure, motion or rest, and number.*

There are also

> *such qualities, which in truth are nothing in the objects themselves, but powers to produce various sensations in us by their*

> *primary qualities, i.e. by the bulk, figure, texture, and motion*
> *of their insensible parts, as colours, sounds, tastes, etc. These I*
> *call secondary qualities.*

In this picture there is the scientific world, of objects as they really are in Locke's time, a world of little particles clinging together to form bigger bodies, each having the primary, scientific, properties. This is the scientific picture. There is also the manifest image: the coloured, smelly, tasty, noisy, warm, or cold world we think of ourselves as inhabiting. But the manifest image is either in or at least largely *due* to the mind. The scientific world is not.

Are objects then not really coloured or smelly in Locke's view? There is a sense in which they are: objects have the powers to produce colours and smells in us. Nevertheless, these powers are not the colours and smells themselves.

> *What I have said concerning colours and smells may be*
> *understood also of tastes and sounds, and other the like sens-*
> *ible qualities; which, whatever reality we, by mistake, at-*
> *tribute to them, are in truth nothing in the objects themselves,*
> *but powers to produce various sensations in us, and depend*
> *on those primary qualities, viz. bulk, figure, texture, and mo-*
> *tion of parts; as I have said.*

The various sensations in us do not in any way resemble the powers that give rise to them.

Locke's view is often thought of as a natural, common-sense, scientific realism. We may substitute energies, forces and fields, or sub-atomic particles for his little particles of matter of peculiar figures and bulks. However, the essential opposition between the world of science and the manifest image remains in many people's minds substantially as he presented it.

Well, is there any problem with that?

BERKELEY'S PROBLEMS

A number of writers in France had difficulties with Descartes's world-view. In particular, if God was, after all, a kind of deceiver (although, of course, for our own good) with respect to secondary qualities, might he also be one with respect to primary qualities? If it is good of him to make us see in terms of colours, although seen colours bear no resemblance to anything in physical reality, might it not be good for him to make us see in terms of objects extended in space, although physical reality is not actually spatial? Colours are here a kind of Trojan horse working to reintroduce the general Evil Demon scepticism that Descartes thought he had beaten down.

This is an epistemological problem. However, we can become even uneasier if we think about the metaphysics of the scientific world. Try to think about what actually fills space. Descartes had banished all qualities from physical reality except one, extension. But everyone thought that this was untenable. 'Extension' is entirely abstract. A cubic foot of space is one thing; a cubic foot of space with a body in it quite a different thing. We must conceive of physical reality in terms of things occupying space, not just space itself.

Well, we may think, that is fine. Locke has things with properties like 'solidity' and 'motion'. Motion however will not help unless we have *things* moving. So let us concentrate upon things. Now a volume of space with a thing in it is known by the solidity or resistance the thing offers. That is the difference between a cubic foot of space filled with granite, and a cubic foot of vacuum. So, what is solidity? Locke is very keen on it:

> The idea of solidity we receive by our touch: And it arises from the resistance which we find in body, to the entrance of any other body into the place it possesses, till it has left it. There is no idea, which we receive more constantly from sensation, than solidity. Whether we move, or rest, in what posture soever we are, we always feel some thing under us that supports us, and hinders our farther sinking downwards; and the bodies which we daily handle make us perceive, that, whilst they remain between them, they do by an insurmountable force, hinder the approach of the parts of our hands that press them. That which thus hinders the approach of two bodies, when they are moved one towards another, I call solidity ... [I]f any one think it better to call it impenetrability, he has my consent. Only I have thought the term solidity the more proper to express this idea, not only because of its vulgar use in that sense; but also because it carries some thing more of positive in it than impenetrability, which is negative, and is, perhaps, more a consequence of solidity, than solidity itself. This, of all other, seems the idea most intimately connected with and essential to body, so as no-where else to be found or imagined, but only in matter.

The solidity of objects seems to come down to their 'powers' to exclude other objects from the bit of space they occupy. But can we rest content with a conception of the world in which there are only different regions of space with different powers? Do we not also need something, some substance, to possess the powers?

At least Locke allows that we know about solidity, so perhaps its epistemology is in order. It seems clear that we know about solidity by what we feel. Locke actually emphasizes this:

> *If any one asks me, what this solidity is, I send him to his senses to inform him: Let him put a flint or a foot-ball between his hands, and then endeavour to join them, and he will know. If he thinks this not a sufficient explication of solidity, what it is, and wherein it consists; I promise to tell him what it is, and wherein it consists, when he tells me what thinking is, or wherein it consists; or explains to me what extension or motion is, which perhaps seems much easier.*

Although Locke was not particularly sensitive to it, the problem with this was grumbling in his time, and it erupted at the beginning of the eighteenth century in the writings of Pierre Bayle (1647–1706) in France and the Irish philosopher George Berkeley (1685–1753). Berkeley makes a number of devastating objections to the Cartesian/Lockean world-view. His position is that it does not hold together either metaphysically, or epistemologically. His case is complex and many-layered, but we can appreciate its general strengths under two headings.

(1) Look again at Locke's view of how we know about solidity. If this is all we can say, in that case how is solidity not on all fours with colour, or felt heat, or smell? If those sensations give us no real idea of the qualities of real things, being just excited in us by the 'powers' of real things, how is it any better with solidity? How can you

get from the sensations of solidity in the mind, to any resembling property in the world? Whatever solidity is 'in the mind' it is not the same as solidity in the world. Our ideas are not solid, so what is the sense in saying that they 'resemble' solid things?

And if solidity disappears from the real world, what is left? Berkeley's own answer to this is notorious: nothing. His world retreats entirely into the mind—the doctrine known as subjective idealism.

(2) The Lockean view seems to require at least that we conceive of a world in purely primary-quality terms, bleaching out everything that according to him resides in the mind. But can we? Berkeley says, 'I deny that I can abstract one from another, or conceive separately, those qualities which it is impossible should exist so separated.' Think of an ordinary physical object, say, a tomato. 'Abstract out' its colour, feel, smell, taste, and the sensations you get as you play your hands round it. What is left? An invisible, intangible, undetectable tomato—surely no better than no tomato at all! Hume puts this objection superbly (in the following quotation, 'the modern philosophy' is Locke's position):

> The idea of solidity is that of two objects, which, being impelled by the utmost force, cannot penetrate each other, but still maintain a separate and distinct existence. Solidity therefore is perfectly incomprehensible alone, and without the conception of some bodies which are solid, and maintain this separate and distinct existence. Now, what idea have we of these bodies? The ideas of colours, sounds, and other secondary qualities, are excluded. The idea of motion depends

> *on that of extension, and the idea of extension on that of solid-*
> *ity. It is impossible, therefore, that the idea of solidity can de-*
> *pend on either of them. For that would be to run in a circle,*
> *and make one idea depend on another, while, at the same*
> *time, the latter depends on the former. Our modern phil-*
> *osophy, therefore, leaves us no just nor satisfactory idea of*
> *solidity, nor consequently of matter.*

Or in other words: '[A]fter the exclusion of colour, sounds, heat, and cold, from the rank of external existences, there remains nothing which can afford us a just and consistent idea of body.' Berkeley and Hume deny that we can really understand the alleged properties of the alleged independent world, except in terms drawn from our own experience—our own minds. The 'modern philosophy' or scientific world view requires us to make sense of a 'scientific' or 'absolute' conception of reality, thought of in terms of space-occupying things, independent of us, whose arrangements explain all that can be explained about the entire universe, including us and our experiences. But if this conception is flawed at its heart, we have to look elsewhere.

FORCES, FIELDS, AND THINGS

In the quoted passage Hume asked what conception we had left of the 'bodies' that are impenetrable to each other, and argued that without the 'stuffing' afforded by the secondary qualities, there was no answer. But this raises a more general problem: what conception do we *ever* have of bodies, apart from their powers of interaction with each other, and with us?

This is not the place to enter into details of physical thinking, but we can take up the story in the words of one of the greatest of physicists, Michael Faraday (1791–1867). Suppose we try to distinguish a physical particle *a* from the powers or forces *m* whereby it makes its influence known, then, Faraday writes:

> [T]o my mind . . . the *a* or nucleus vanishes, and the substance consists of the powers, or m, and indeed what notion can we form of the nucleus independent of its powers: what thought remains on which to hang the imagination of an *a* independent of the acknowledged forces? Why then assume the existence of that of which we are ignorant, which we cannot conceive, and for which there is no philosophical necessity?

Hume's protest about bodies apart from solidity is here taken on the chin, as it were. We just do not have to think in terms of things apart from their powers.

In that case the world of physics, the 'scientific image', resolves itself into a vast flux of forces: presumably such things as gravitational forces, electromagnetic attractions and repulsions, or if we turn up the magnification, strong and weak interactions amongst elementary particles. But then there is something very uncomfortable going on. For remember that the argument is entirely general, so that these 'particles' themselves resolve into other 'forces'. This is a problem because normally, when we think of forces, or of things like gravitational or magnetic fields, we take some notion like that of a particle for granted. We understand the existence of a field or force at some point in space in terms of the acceleration that *would* occur *if* some test particle were placed there. If there is a magnet on the table, the existence of the magnetic field around it is a matter of the way in which other 'things' (particles) *would* tend to move *if* they were put at various distances from it. In the familiar school experiments, iron filings take the role of test particles.

But if, following Faraday, we resolve particles themselves into yet further powers, dispositions, or forces, we cannot be satisfied with this kind of image. We have to try to understand what the cosmos contains without the mental crutch afforded by 'things' of any kind whatsoever. Hume's complaint about impenetrability—that we need to know what it is that cannot penetrate what—then returns to haunt us. It is as if the common-sense conception of the difference between space occupied by a body, and space not so occupied, has been displaced in favour of space of which some *ifs* are true, as opposed to space of which other kinds of *ifs* are true. But we hanker after something to really *occupy* space, whose presence explains the differences in *ifs*, the differences in potentials and powers.

We can put the problem in the terms of Chapter 2. If God creates the physical universe, how much does he have to do? Can he get by creating only forces? In that case the universe seems to resolve itself into a giant set of *ifs*. Or does he also have to create objects, both for the forces to act upon, and perhaps to explain how the forces arise? If we plump for the latter, then what conception of those objects can we have? The first conception seems to leave the universe as some kind of huge potential, like a gigantic shimmer. Perhaps Descartes, the mathematician, was happy with this (it is a fascinating question whether he anticipated Faraday's kind of vision). But common-sense thinking seems to demand something (something *solid*) to fill the bits of space that have matter in them.

This is a problem that greatly exercised Kant, himself one of the pioneers of the resolution of matter itself into 'forces'. Kant thought that this conception of things was the best we could ever achieve. He thought this partly because we know of the world by means of the senses, and the senses are essentially *receptive*. That is, all they ever give us are the results of powers and forces. The senses are not adapted to tell us *what* in the world underlies the distribution of powers and forces in space. They simply bring to us the result of that distribution. Anything underlying it would have to be entirely 'noumenal'—lying behind the range of scientific investigation, and for that matter beyond the range of human experience and thought.

Hume thought that his problem with impenetrability cast doubt on the whole metaphysics of 'the modern philosophy', although he also thinks Berkeley's own retreat into subjective idealism is entirely unbelievable. Kant too believed that the problem required an entire rethink of the modern philosophy.

STRAIGHTJACKETS AND LAWS

There is another way of coming to appreciate the problems raised in the last section, which is to think about a different staple of scientific understanding, the concept of a law of nature. It requires revisiting something we met in the last chapter: the lottery for the Golden Harp.

After considering that thought-experiment, we might think something along these lines. The thought-experiment is impressive, but perhaps it is also misleading. For it represents the situation as if the state of the world at each interval is *independent* of its state at any other interval. It is just as if God tosses a six-sided die at the end of each period, so it is a 1 in 6 chance whether one colour or another comes up. Now if that were the situation, it would indeed be a fallacy to argue that since one number (blue) has come up five times, it is more likely to come up next time. Arguing like that is falling for what is called the gambler's fallacy. However, in the world as we have it we do not know that there is this kind of lottery taking place all the time. We do not find the chaos that this would lead us to expect. We find only the uniformities. So it is much more probable that there is something that *guarantees order through time*. There is no independent dice-tossing from time to time: rather it is as if God made the one decision, and stuck to it. There must be a metaphysical solution to the problem of induction, even if there is no purely probabilistic or mathematical solution.

This may seem to help, but does it?

Part of the problem of course is that even if the universe realizes just one law, like one decision of God, it may have been 'Let's have pattern K' rather than 'Let's have pattern S'. The unchanging law may have the kinked character. After all, we are confined to knowing about the segments that have happened so far. And arguing that because nature *has so far* been uniform in some particular way, then it is likely that it *will continue* to be uniform in that particular way, is making just another inductive inference, as Hume pointed out.

But again, there is a metaphysical side to the problem. Let us call whatever guarantees order a *Straightjacket*. A Straightjacket is something like a law of nature operating over time: a directive or guarantee that fixes the order of things. The idea then is that it is because of this directive or guarantee that things keep on keeping on, as we might say, in the old familiar ways. Now the problem becomes: can we have any conception of what such a Straightjacket would be like?

The problem here is extremely similar to the problem with the cosmological argument, discussed in Chapter 5, and indeed can be seen to be a version of it. The things we meet in space and time, including such things as human resolutions, are inherently changeable. They may last for a long time, but in practice they come and go. A Straightjacket is not to be like that. For if it is in principle changeable then its own survival through time requires explanation, and we are launched on a regress.

The situation is that we are hoping to underpin the ordinary continuation of regularities by citing 'something else', something that *makes true* the fact that events must fall out as they do. But then we turn to consider the regular continuation of that something else. If this is just a 'brute fact' then it is no more likely than what we started with—the empirical order. If it needs a different kind of underpinning, then we are launched on a regress again. If we say that it is 'necessary' or contains its own explanation within itself, then we face the same scepticism that was directed at the cosmological argument. We do not understand what we mean by this, and have no principles for saying to what kind of things such a description might apply.

In other words, if a Straightjacket is the kind of thing that comes and goes, we will be left with no reason for expecting its continuation. But have we any conception of something whose existence is *not* subject to time and change? Can we even touch it, let alone embrace it, with our understandings? Aren't we once more left with Wittgenstein's dire saying, '[A] nothing would serve just as well as a something about which nothing could be said'? Or in Hume's words,

> *The scenes of the universe are continually shifting, and one object follows another in an uninterrupted succession; but the power or force, which actuates the whole machine, is entirely concealed from us, and never discovers itself in any of the sensible qualities of body.*

It seems that our understandings are baffled in this too. We can have no conception of what it is for a law of nature to hold. We can understand the ways in which events do fall out, but never obtain any glimmer of a conception of why they *must* fall out as they do.

In the last section, following Faraday and Hume, we found that the 'absolute' scientific conception of an independent reality ran into problems of things versus their powers. We now find that our conception of those powers themselves, underwritten by laws of nature, is as frail as it could possibly be.

KANT'S REVOLUTION

Problems with the 'modern philosophy' led Berkeley to retreat inside his own mind. He decided that the universe of our understanding was confined to our own ideas, and our own nature as 'spirits' or souls. Fortunately we are not quite alone in this subjective universe, for we can be sure (he thought) that our experiences must be injected into us by another greater spirit: God (one can by now anticipate Hume's snort of derision at this a priori piece of causal reasoning). But nobody has ever held that Berkeley's solution was satisfactory: it sounds too much as if Berkeley's God just plays the role of Descartes's Evil Demon, putting us into an entirely delusive virtual reality.

One philosopher who agreed with Berkeley's diagnosis of the situation was Kant. Kant thought that Locke's 'modern philosophy' had attempted what he called a 'transcendental realism', which is untenable. 'Realism', because it insists on a real world of independent objects situated in space and time. 'Transcendental', because this world is outside our own experience, and only an object of inference. But Kant agrees with Berkeley that the inference is too precarious. On the Lockean position:

> *I am not, therefore, in a position to perceive external things, but can only infer their existence from my inner perception, taking the inner perception as the effect of which something external is the proximate cause. Now the inference from a given effect to a determinate cause is always uncertain, since the effect may be due to more than one cause. Accordingly, as regards the relation of the perception to its cause, it always remains doubtful whether the cause be internal or external; whether, that is to say, all the so-called outer perceptions are not a mere play of our inner sense, or whether they stand in relation to actual external objects as their cause. At all events, the existence of the latter is only inferred, and is open to all the*

dangers of inference, whereas the object of inner sense (I my-self with all my representations) is immediately perceived, and its existence does not allow of being doubted.

For Kant the priority is to get away from this 'inner theatre' model. We already met some of his approach in Chapter 4, on the self. There, we saw that various quite complex feats of organization are needed for self-consciousness. We have to organize our experience not as what Kant calls a mere 'rhapsody' or kaleidoscope of percep-tions, but in terms of a temporal and spatial order. Only so can we get a concept of ourselves as moving amongst an independent world of objects situated in a space. How does Kant use this insight to surmount the impasse left by the tradition from Descartes on-wards?

Part of Kant's achievement was seeing that Locke is involved in an untenable conception of understanding. For Locke the para-digm of understanding would be to have something in the mind that 'resembles' the features of things that cause it, like a picture. Berkeley shared this ideal. True, he thought that the resemblance could not really obtain ('An idea can resemble nothing but another idea'). But he drew the consequence that we only understand the world of our own ideas. Kant sees that when it comes to space and time, size, shape, and the objective order, to have a concept is not to have a mental picture. It is to have an organizing principle or rule; a way of handling the flux of data. Having the same organizing principles or rules could give us the same understanding of the world in spite of *differences* of subjective experience.

The implication then is that we got into the problems of the last two sections because we were looking for 'things' to play certain roles: the role of objects standing behind and apart from powers and forces, or the role of something responsible for causal and physical laws. But if we can wean our understandings from this dependency on things, perhaps we can do better. Suppose instead we see thoughts of causation and law, things in space and time, and space and time themselves as necessary *categories* of thought. They provide us with a framework of principles with which to organize or systematize our experience. They do not provide a set of things we 'infer' from our experience. The idea here is very similar to the ideas about the 'self' that we took from Kant, and indeed form the other side of the same coin. If we try to understand the self in sensory terms, as an object of experience, we meet Hume's problem, that it is no such object. But if instead we think of the way a personal or egocentric standpoint *organizes* experience, the role of the self as an element in our thinking becomes clearer—and so do illusions engendered by that role.

Kant's revolution is introduced in a famous passage at the beginning of the *Critique of Pure Reason*:

> Hitherto it has been assumed that all our knowledge must conform to objects. But all attempts to extend our knowledge of objects by establishing something in regard to them a priori, by means of concepts, have, on this assumption, ended in failure. We must therefore make trial whether we may not have more success in the tasks of metaphysics, if we suppose that objects must conform to our knowledge. This would agree better with what is desired, namely, that it should be possible to have knowledge of objects a priori, determining something in regard to them prior to their being given. We should then be proceeding precisely on the lines of Copernicus' primary

hypothesis. Failing of satisfactory progress in explaining the movements of the heavenly bodies on the supposition that they all revolved round the spectator, he tried whether he might not have better success if he made the spectator to revolve and the stars to remain at rest. A similar experiment can be tried in metaphysics, as regards the intuition of objects. If intuition must conform to the constitution of the objects, I do not see how we could know anything of the latter a priori; but if the object (as object of the senses) must conform to the constitution of our faculty of intuition, I have no difficulty in conceiving such a possibility.

This is the element that Kant calls 'transcendental idealism'. He is very keen that it is not the 'subjective idealism' of Berkeley. And obviously, it cannot be the 'transcendental realism' of Locke. So what is it?

It sounds as though in having experience we thereby 'create' a world that must conform to it. That is a very odd idea. It is the universe that created us after some thirteen billion years, not we that create it. Kant is not intending to deny that. What he wants is an understanding of the way in which concepts like those of things, forces, space, time, causation determine the way we think (and have to think) about the world. The intention is not to *deny* some element of scientific understanding, or indeed common sense, but to *explain* how those elements hang together in our thought. It is those thoughts that structure what he calls the 'phenomenal world': the world that is both described by science, and is manifested to us in sense experience.

Kant certainly did not think that all sensory experience somehow 'creates' such a world. He did not think this about secondary qualities, for example:

> *Colours are not properties of the bodies to the intuition of which they are attached, but only modifications of the sense of sight, which is affected in a certain manner by light. Space, on the other hand, as condition of outer objects, necessarily belongs to their appearance or intuition. Taste and colours are not necessary conditions under which alone objects can be for us objects of the senses.*

The idea being that space, unlike colour, is a 'condition' under which alone objects can be objects of the senses. Space has more objectivity going for it than colour.

The central difficulty in interpreting Kant here is whether he actually advances as far as he seems to think beyond Berkeley. Suppose Berkeley thanks Kant for three insights:

(1) We must depart entirely from Locke's sensory view of the understanding, and see the concepts with which we describe the world in terms of rules, principles, and organizing structures rather than as mental images.

(2) Our experience has to be orderly (in the phrase of the contemporary philosopher Jonathan Bennett, there has to be a 'speed limit') for us to be self-conscious at all.

(3) For it to be orderly we have to think of ourselves as occupying a standpoint in space, from which we perceive enduring objects in space and time, whose behaviour falls into patterns determined by laws of nature.

This might all seem grist to Berkeley's mill. Berkeley himself knew that we *interpret* our experience in spatio-temporal, objective terms. But he thought we had to 'speak with the vulgar but think with the learned': in other words, learn to regard that interpretation as a kind of *façon de parler*, rather than the description of a real, independent, objective world.

A factor confusing the picture is that Kant says things showing considerable sympathy with a position not unlike Berkeley's subjective idealism. The 'Copernican revolution' leaves him saying things like this:

> In our system, on the other hand, these external things, namely matter, are in all their configurations and alterations nothing but mere appearances, that is, representations in us, of the reality of which we are immediately conscious.

The ingredient that sets Kant apart from subjective idealism is that he thought that Descartes and his successors got hold of the wrong end of the stick. They thought that 'inner experience' remained rock-solid, while the outside world became problematic. To do better,

> [t]he required proof must, therefore, show that we have experience, and not merely imagination of outer things; and this, it would seem, cannot be achieved save by proof that even our inner experience, which for Descartes is indubitable, is possible only on the assumption of outer experience.

'Outer experience' is here experience in which we are immediately conscious of a reality that extends beyond us. The question of whether, and how, Kant is successful is one of the great issues of modern thought.

THE EYE OF THE BEHOLDER

A true *realist* or opponent of idealism wants to contend for facts and states of affairs that are entirely independent of the mind. The idealist constantly reminds us of the work of the mind in selecting and moulding our conception of the world we inhabit. The mind, for the idealist, *creates* the world we live in, the 'Lebenswelt' of our thoughts, imaginings, and perceptions. Kant, of course, is in this up to the elbows, since the entire framework within which we think, our 'conceptual scheme' of space, time, objects, causes, and selves, is due to organizing principles of the mind.

Now, without being Cartesian dualists, we might still sympathize with this awareness of the work of the mind in generating the only world we understand. In fact, most twentieth-century thinkers (following a nineteenth-century trend) have picked up Kant's ball and run with it even more enthusiastically than he did. In particularly, they have celebrated what we have already met under the heading of 'paradigms': the idea of cultural and historically mutable lenses through which we see things, or conceptual palaces or prisons of our own engineering.

Once more, though, I shall introduce the moderns via a classic, and once more we can start with Berkeley. In the first of the *Three Dialogues* there is this celebrated passage, with Philonous representing Berkeley himself:

> PHILONOUS. . . . *But (to pass by all that hath been hitherto said, and reckon it for nothing, if you will have it so) I am content to put the whole upon this issue. If you can conceive it possible for any mixture or combination of qualities, or any*

sensible object whatever, to exist without the mind, then I will grant it actually to be so.

HYLAS. If it comes to that, the point will soon be decided. What more easy than to conceive a tree or house existing by itself, independent of, and unperceived by any mind whatsoever? I do at this present time conceive them existing after that manner.

PHIL. How say you, Hylas, can you see a thing which is at the same time unseen?

HYL. No, that were a contradiction.

PHIL. Is it not as great a contradiction to talk of conceiving a thing which is unconceived?

HYL. It is.

PHIL. The tree or house therefore which you think of, is conceived by you.

HYL. How should it be otherwise?

PHIL. And what is conceived is surely in the mind.

HYL. Without question, that which is conceived is in the mind.

PHIL. How then came you to say, you conceived a house or tree existing independent and out of all minds whatsoever?

HYL. That was, I own, an oversight; but stay, let me consider what led me into it. It is a pleasant mistake enough. As I was thinking of a tree in a solitary place, where no one was present to see it, methought that was to conceive a tree as existing unperceived or unthought of, not considering that I myself conceived it all the while. But now I plainly see, that all I can do is to frame ideas in my own mind. I may indeed conceive in my own thoughts the idea of a tree, or a house, or a mountain, but that is all. And this is far from proving, that I can conceive them existing out of the minds of all spirits.

PHIL. *You acknowledge then that you cannot possibly conceive how any one corporeal sensible thing should exist otherwise than in a mind.*

HYL. *I do.*

PHIL. *And yet you will earnestly contend for the truth of that which you cannot so much as conceive.*

HYL. *I profess I know not what to think, but still there are some scruples remain with me.*

Hylas is probably right to retain some scruples, for Philonous's argument has attracted a great deal of criticism, and even contempt. We might try applying to it some of the weaponry deployed against the ontological argument, wondering if Philonous is surreptitiously misunderstanding phrases like 'in the mind'. We might also raise the question of the strength of Philonous's conclusion. For although he thinks Hylas cannot conceive how a house or tree should exist otherwise than 'in' *a* mind, the argument looks equally set to prove the appallingly strong conclusion that Hylas cannot conceive how a house or tree should exist otherwise than in Hylas's *own mind*. And this is too radical even for Berkeley.

Nevertheless, as usual with the great thinkers, we might worry that there is some grain of truth in Philonous's position. Here is one way of sympathizing with it. Suppose we think of Hylas as seeking to show that he can understand the realist notion of an object 'independent' of his actual modes of comprehension. He undertakes to 'abstract' away from contingencies of his own perceptual experience or contingencies of his own modes of thought, or his own conceptual choices. Then we can see Berkeley, in the person of Philonous, reminding him that this feat of abstraction is impossible. Whatever he succeeds in imagining or conceiving, he is doomed to bring his own perspective to it.

For example, perhaps Hylas imagines his tree to have a brown trunk and green leaves. Then it is open to Berkeley to insist that this is *not* meeting the challenge of imagining an object from outside the human perspective, since the colours of things are artefacts of that perspective. The point is clearest with secondary qualities, but by this point in the first *Dialogue* Berkeley has softened the reader up for applying it more generally. A nice thought-experiment that illustrates his position is this. Suppose I ask you to imagine a room, with a mirror on one wall, and a table some way in front of it on which there is a bowl of flowers. I warn you not to imagine *yourself* in this room. You believe you can do it. Now I ask you whether the bowl of flowers is in the mirror. If you say 'yes', then you are surreptitiously occupying one perspective, and if you say 'no' you are occupying another (for the flowers will be in the mirror from some angles and not from others). You can hardly say 'neither', and neither can you escape by saying that they come and go, since that corresponds to moving your point of view around the room. You seem to be trapped—the point of view comes in all unbidden, as soon as you exercise your imagination.

Berkeley is reminding us of the universal influence of our own perspective on what we imagine or comprehend. We can see the strength, and the importance, of his position if we consider for a moment a philosopher who ignored it, namely G. E. Moore. Moore undertook to refute the idea that beauty lies in the eye of the beholder—in other words he undertook to defend realism about beauty. He argued for it by an 'isolation' thought-experiment.

Moore asks us to imagine two worlds. One is full of fluffy clouds, green trees, running streams, and other pastoral delights. The other is a heap of cinders and garbage. Now we specify that there is nobody in either of these worlds. They are unobserved. But surely one is more beautiful than the other? And doesn't that show that beauty is independent of the eye of the beholder?

Philonous inoculates us against this specious argument of Moore's. It is *we* who accept the invitation to think of these worlds. And *we* bring to them our own aesthetic responses, which no doubt include a love of the countryside and a dislike of cinders and garbage. But we haven't got *behind* those responses or put them into abeyance as we respond to the imagined worlds. On the contrary, it is these *very* responses that we voice in our verdicts. All that Moore really succeeds in showing is that we can deem things to be beautiful regardless of whether we think they are actually seen, and this does not refute the idealist or subjective view that beauty nevertheless lies in the eye of the beholder.

I suspect most people find Moore's argument fishy, and thus far they sympathize with Philonous. But then most people find Philonous fishy as well. If we want to reject Moore and Philonous together, we will need to work hard to find a stable place to stand. We might think Kant points the way. Concede things like beauty and secondary qualities to Philonous, but hold that the 'eye of the beholder' is not quite so involved with more important categories of thought, such as the notions of space, time, physical objects, the self, causation. But in the next section we glance briefly at ways even this promise of a synthesis runs into choppy water.

RULES, UNIVERSALS

The idealist tradition in philosophy stresses the inescapable and vital place that the shape of our own minds plays in 'constructing' the world as we understand it. It can select different features shaping our minds. Berkeley and the empiricist tradition start with the subjective nature of sense experience, particularly experience of secondary qualities. It is the fact that they 'lie in the eye of the beholder' that proves so bothersome.

At the present time, cultural and especially linguistic factors are more prominent. We worry not so much about the subjectivity of experience as the variations of culture. So, many contemporary philosophers applaud a line of thought found in Wittgenstein: the so-called rule-following considerations. Wittgenstein considers the moment of understanding, when some concept is explained to us, and we realize 'Now I can go on' or 'Now I know what is meant'. We seem to have grasped a rule or principle that separates correct application of a term from incorrect applications. This is a real feat. Some people and animals are too dumb or different to catch on (we have already met the example of the way in which dogs cannot follow the activity of pointing, and incline to look at your finger instead). The way we perform that feat, and the fact that sufficiently often we do so in just the same way is, as it were, a fact of natural history. It makes communication and shared understanding possible. But it is not just a given, or to be taken for granted, that we all do it in the same way, or in any one particular way. It requires that our minds are shaped the same way. But what shapes our minds one way or another?

This is in fact the ancient topic, much pondered by Greek philosophers, of universals. To understand things and describe them requires using concepts that are rule-governed in the minimal way just described. But what is the 'reality' behind these rules? Three main positions are traditionally distinguished:

■ REALISM (sometimes PLATONISM). These rules have a real, objective existence. They determine the proper application of concepts over past, present, future, and possible instances. We grasp them by some mysterious act of apprehension, which cannot easily be understood in natural terms.

■ CONCEPTUALISM. These rules are the creatures of the mind. They are conjured into existence by *our* shared responses arising from our shared human natures, or perhaps our educated and culturally shaped natures. In this way all concepts are 'response dependent': artefacts of our own dispositions to respond to things.

■ NOMINALISM. There aren't really any rules at all. There are just human beings with their dispositions to apply words or withhold them. There is no real 'correctness' or 'incorrectness' in this, although as so often people whose applications diverge from those of the herd will find themselves being called incorrect.

It may help to think of an example, where each position might have its attractions. Consider a rather doubtful concept, such as that of 'hysteria' or 'neurasthenia'. A realist, using the concept, will suppose that there is here a real phenomenon, with real boundaries (some people who carry on are hysterics, and others not). In using the term we 'carve nature at the joints', to use a rather unpleasant metaphor. A conceptualist will reject the metaphor. He may, however, embrace the concept of hysteria itself, supposing that it marks a useful principle or category with which to draw the boundaries around a particular kind of medical or psychological condition. It classes together cases that strike us as similar, and that, at the end of the day, is all that any concept does. Finally a nominalist says that the word is as good as any other. People are disposed to use it; well and good, for that is all there is to the use of any term at all.

Naturally these positions come in slightly different flavours, and each has its apparent strengths and weaknesses. To the realist or Platonist, the others open the door to the pit of idealism: the mind constructing or making up its own reality (if hysteria is not a real unified phenomenon, we have no business describing the world in terms of it. We cannot get at objective truth that way). To both the Platonist and the conceptualist, nominalism is completely untenable: a denial that meaning and concept-application, and in fact thought at all, are real. It is a kind of 'eliminativism' or denial of the very act of thinking. No mind is just as good as a mind that simply blurts out verbal responses to stimuli, with nothing governing truth or correctness. But to the nominalist, Platonism is incredible, and conceptualism simply embraces the rhetoric of rule-following without delivering on the substance. For what is the difference between rules that are 'constituted' by our dispositions or responses, and rules that we make up as we go along? And what is the difference between those and no rules at all? A conceptualist, on this view, is just a nominalist who is too cowardly to admit it.

It is said that the students of medieval Paris came to blows in the streets over the question of universals. The stakes are high, for at issue is our whole conception of our ability to describe the world truly or falsely, and the objectivity of any opinions we frame to ourselves. It is arguable that this is always the deepest, most profound, problem of philosophy. It structures Plato's (realist) reaction to the sophists (nominalists). What is often called 'postmodernism' is really just nominalism, colourfully presented as the doctrine that there is nothing except texts. It is the variety of nominalism represented in many modern humanities, paralysing appeals to reason and truth. 'Analytical' philosophy plays Plato to its sophistry, trying to silence its siren appeals.

In recent years a kind of 'naturalized' realism, avoiding the mysteries of Platonism, has seemed plausible to some philosophers. According to this there really are properties that things have, quite independently of whether we regard them one way or another. And our minds are built in response to these properties. Evolution and success shape us to be responsive to the real causal *kinds* that things fall into. While conceptualists are right to stress the contingent shape of our minds, they are wrong to forget that those minds do not exist in a vacuum. Our minds are naturally shaped by the causal structures of the world we inhabit. In favourable circumstances, we all 'go on in the same way' because, in the context of the world, that is the right way to go on. Such a naturalism might, for instance, make contact with the sketch we gave of colour science in Chapter 2. It would try to show that the way in which even secondary-quality classifications take place is far from arbitrary. And if they regain some 'realistic' status, others ought to follow suit.

This is a comfortable view, and it ties in nicely with the 'natural foundationalism' or evolutionarily inspired defence of harmony between our minds and the world that we met at the end of Chapter 1. We may indeed hope that it survives in the seas of thought I have tried to stir up in this chapter. But it does require confidence that our troubles are over, that the scientific or absolute image of the world is comfortably in place alongside the manifest image. We would need to believe, in effect, that Kant or a sucessor has successfully steered us between Philonous and Moore, or solved Hume's problem with 'the modern philosophy' without giving too much to idealism. Not everyone is convinced of that.

CHAPTER EIGHT

What to Do

So far we have been concerned with our understanding of the world. We have been concerned with the nature of things, and our knowledge of them, and ways of reasoning about them. But much of our reasoning is not so much theoretical, or concerned with how the world *is*, as practical, or concerned with how to act in it. We think about what to do, and muster considerations and arguments in favour of one course or another. How are we to think about that? Whole treatises and encyclopaedias are devoted to this subject— ethics and moral philosophy form its core, although they do not exhaust it, since practical reasonings are by no means exclusively moral in nature. We have technical and aesthetic questions to address as well as moral problems. In this final chapter, I have no intention of covering the ground such treatises occupy. That cannot be done in such a short space. But I think there exist some building blocks of adequate thought in these areas, and I shall try to suggest what these are.

REAL CONCERNS

Much practical thinking is technological in nature. We have a goal, and our problem is how to meet it. We try to adapt means to ends, with the ends given in advance. The end is set: we want to fix the refrigerator or grow flowers or build a bridge. Obviously we can be more or less good at these things. There is no single 'way of thinking' that enables us to achieve our goals across the board, any more than the person who knows how to fix the refrigerator necessarily knows how to grow the flowers or build the bridge. Acquiring the necessary skills requires understanding the system in question, and knowing which changes to effect, and how to effect them, in order to deliver the desired end.

It is commonly said that our goals are fixed by our desires, so that means–ends reasoning is a matter of efficiently satisfying our desires. This is often true, at least as an approximation. But it can be misleading. If desires are thought of as states of enthusiasm for an end—things that put a gleam in our eye—then we often act because we have particular *concerns*, when desire is not the right word. Here I am cutting the grass when I would like to be out sailing. Why? Not really because I *desired* to cut the grass. Perhaps I hate it. But it was time to do it, or it had to be done. I am concerned to get the grass cut. I set about adopting efficient means to that end. Having a concern here means being moved by the thought that the grass needs to be cut. I may think that it is my *role* to cut the grass. Or, I may just think 'It is time to do it', without self-consciously thinking about my role as householder or whatever. Nevertheless,

I typically recognize that someone else's grass needs cutting without being moved to do it myself. So it is my role as householder that has made me especially sensitive to the thought that *my* grass needs cutting, even if I don't self-consciously think about that role.

The difference between acting from some concern and acting because you want to do it is important. It is sometimes deliberately ignored when people argue with one another. Imagine a relationship that is in difficulty. Annie feels bound to leave Bertie because of some cause: perhaps a duty to others or a life plan that requires moving. Bertie can ratchet up the emotional temperature by insisting that Annie would not be leaving if Annie *didn't want to*. 'You must want to otherwise you wouldn't be doing it.' These are hurtful words, since the accusation is that leaving Bertie puts a gleam into Annie's eye or counts as a positive feature of her course of action. And this may be entirely unwarranted. Annie may be completely dejected at the thought of leaving Bertie. But, like cutting the grass, it has to be done.

It might be suggested that when we have a concern there must be something in the offing that we desire. If I am concerned to cut the grass, but do not want to do it, then if I do it, this must be because I do want something else: perhaps just peace of mind, for instance. This introduces another very dangerous mistake, which is that of thinking that whenever a person has a concern, what she 'really' desires is some state of herself, such as her own peace of mind. Psychologists, especially, have been apt to think of desire in terms of a kind of build-up of tension, and what the agent is driven to do is to release the tension. It is then easy to think that the release of tension was the real object of desire all along. This too can introduce hurtful words: 'You weren't really concerned about the starving children, you were just wanting to feel good.' And all behaviour is diagnosed as fundamentally selfish, as though it is always your own state that concerns you, with other goals and aims a kind of mask.

This set of thoughts (sometimes called psychological egoism) is entirely wrong. Suppose you want food. Following the train of thought of the last paragraph, I interpret you as wanting relief from the tension of wanting food. So I punch you in the stomach, making you sick enough to stop wanting food. Did I get you what you wanted? Not at all (even forgetting that the punch may have been painful). You didn't want *any old* relief from the tension. You wanted food. Similarly a normal person aroused by sexual passion does not want any old relief from the passion. A bromide might give him that, but he doesn't want a bromide. He wants sex.

Consider more wide-ranging concerns. Suppose I am a Mafia godfather and believe myself to have been insulted by Luigi. I order you, my henchmen, to rub out Luigi. You go away a little daunted by this dangerous task. But, you reflect, what I really want is relief from the tension that Luigi's existence brings to me. You can relieve me of that in another way: give me a completely successful delusion that you have killed Luigi. So this is what you do, by arranging convincing appearances. Did you do what I wanted? Clearly not. I didn't want to live in a fool's paradise in which I falsely believed that Luigi was dead (and just imagine the upshot if I learned that this was what you had brought about!). I wanted you to kill Luigi.

We might say: one of our concerns is not to be deceived about whether our concerns are met.

Again, we here uncover a central cause of strife and misunderstanding. For communication is often a matter of addressing one another's concerns. This is not done if one side has a concern, and the other regards that concern just as a kind of problem or obstacle in itself—something to be managed or cured. Suppose Annie is concerned about her career and self-development, and Bertie responds not by thinking about ways to nurture her career and self-development, but by thinking about ways to damp that concern. 'Don't get upset, darling, you won't worry about that if we go out to dinner/hold my hand/have a baby . . .' The response is inappropriate in just the way that the punch in the stomach removing hunger was inappropriate. But it is probably not quite so *obvious* that it is inappropriate, at least not to Bertie, and probably not even if Annie walks out on him. In terms I introduced in Chapter 3, we can put this by saying that Bertie has 'objectified' Annie's concern, treating it *itself* as the problem, rather than seeing what it was that concerned Annie. But from Annie's perspective it is Annie's *career* that is the problem, not Annie's concern with her career. In so far as Bertie does not share that perspective, they are not on all fours.

This point has vast repercussions in connection with the whole culture and industry of 'therapy'. I return to this after putting one or two more pieces on the board.

I said that one of our concerns is not to be deceived about whether our concerns are met. A parallel point is that often, but not always, one of our concerns is not just to *lose* our concerns. Suppose the godfather who really wants Luigi dead is told that if he waits ten years this desire will pass over ('So it will all be all right in the end', someone might say). This is like telling the partner concerned about her career that if she waits until she has had a baby that concern will diminish. The person doesn't *want* the concern to diminish. We can express this by saying that the godfather *identifies* with his desire for revenge, and the woman identifies with her concern for her career.

Now there are indeed cases in which we do not identify with our desires and concerns. We might wish ourselves to be rid of them by any means. A person craving a cigarette might not only want the cigarette, but want also to be rid of the craving any way he could. Therapy or a kind of surgical removal of the state of mind would do fine. If you find yourself 'obsessing' about someone or something, you might also come to regard your obsession as something you need to be without, and perhaps set about getting rid of it. Categorizing a desire or concern with which you have been identified as a craving or an obsession is a way of distancing yourself from it, and beginning the process of objectifying it, en route to seeking some strategy for escape. The wife with the concern for her career, in the example above, *might* come to share her husband's perception that it is that ambition that is to be regarded as the problem, and seek with more enthusiasm to rid herself of it by other distractions. But then again she might not do this, and she might make a mistake if she does, for the concern may be more central to her identity than she has been led to think.

This shows that the difference between concerns with which we identify, and concerns that we can objectify, is not always evident. We may not know until we try whether it is possible (or appropriate) to shake ourselves out of some concern, or whether it is only possible, or appropriate, to go ahead and to try to meet it.

What then are concerns? I said that to have a concern is to be

moved by a thought. Some aspect of things engages our motivations and becomes an aspect that *weighs* with us or that matters to
us (it is interesting that the natural metaphors are ones of weight,
or pressure). Aspects of things weigh with us when we are deciding
what to do, obviously. They can also weigh with us by influencing
attitudes, such as admiration or contempt, or emotions, such as
fear or hope. Reading a work of fiction, for example, I can find myself repelled by some character, meaning that the character is described in ways that weigh with me. I am moved to admiration by
the virtues of the hero or to loathing by the vices of the villain.

When we have concerns, the aspects of things to which we are
sensitive can be described as our *reasons* for choosing one thing or
another, or feeling some attitude or emotion. My reason for cutting the grass is that it needed it. Annie's reason for leaving Bertie is
that her career requires that she moves. Our reasons in this sense
are those aspects of a situation that weigh with us as we deliberate
about what to do, or how to feel about something. In a slightly
wider sense our reasons may outrun what we call to mind as we
deliberate. They can include aspects of situations that in fact affect
us, even when we are unaware or only half-aware of what is
happening. In this wider sense, Annie's reason for leaving Bertie
might be that he bores her, even when she does not admit this to
herself.

When we talk of the reasons that move other people, there is an
important distinction to notice. We can speak *descriptively*, or *normatively*. That is, we can describe what it is about a situation that is
moving them. Or we can say that what concerns them is or is not
really a reason, expressing our own endorsement or rejection of the

concern. It is important to keep this distinction in mind. If we say Annie had no reason for leaving Bertie, we may be making a (probably false) remark about Annie's psychology: that she acted entirely on impulse, without thought and without any desires or concerns that she was trying to meet. Or, more likely, we may be *rejecting* the concerns that actually motivated Annie: she went because she was concerned to pursue her career in the ballet, but in the circumstances that was a silly ambition or something that should not have weighed with her. When we speak normatively we should signal what we are doing by words like 'ought' and 'good'. But sometimes, instead of saying 'She had no *good* reason' we say things like 'She had no reason at all', and that can be misinterpreted.

On the face of it, our concerns can be a very mixed bunch. The death of an enemy, the pursuit of a career, the state of the grass, the well-being of family and friends, are common kinds of concern, as are many others: the fact that you gave a promise, the fact that someone once did something for you, the fact that you are a spouse or a doctor or a lawyer. People have different concerns, as many as there are different people and different kinds of people. And we have already rejected one attempt to reduce this diversity to some kind of unity. That attempt tried to see us as always and only concerned with our own states of mind (our own relief from the tension induced by having a concern). But that was a mistake, and it rides roughshod over the distinction between concerns with which we identify, and ones that we can indeed distance ourselves from and wish away.

THE VOICE WITHIN

Many concerns are private and optional. Suppose I am interested in steam engines. Then the feature of a place, that steam trains run there, weighs with me. It is a reason, in my eyes, for going there. It need not weigh with you. And it need not bother me that it does not weigh with you. I might even be glad that it does not, since I get a better view when the crowds are smaller.

But there are other concerns that we *expect* people to have. That is, it is one of our concerns that these things should bother them in a certain way. There are features of things that we expect to influence their decisions and attitudes: the fact that doing something would be deceiving someone, or breaking a promise, or behaving dishonestly or manipulatively, and so on. Similarly we expect the fact that some course of action would cause distress to weigh with people. We would be surprised or even shocked if it did not. This brings us to the traditional domain of ethics. What are the concerns that we can expect from each other?

We can separate two different ways of taking this question. One asks what are the concerns that make up an ideal life. What is the way to live? Different ethical traditions answer this in different ways. The ideal life of a Homeric hero is full of concern for his honour, status, and success in battle. The ideal life of a Christian saint is full of concerns that include the love of God, the suppression of pride, and various ideals of brotherly love. According to Confucianism, the ideal life contains a large dose of respect for traditional ways. All these ideals can be fleshed out and painted in more or less attractive colours. Yet there is something uncomfortable about them, if only because there is little reason to suppose that there is any such thing as *the* ideal life. Since different people have different tastes and interests, and different cultures encourage different concerns, it seems likely that any 'ideal life' will be heavily contextualized: ideal for this person in these circumstances, perhaps, but not much more. Even the components of a good life, rather than an 'ideal' life, are not obvious. Some core components are pretty uncontroversial. Most people will put down health (and the means to secure it), happiness (but of the right sort: not as a result of living in a fool's paradise), achievements (but again, only of the right sort: not the fulfilment of vain or foolish ambitions), dignity, friendships, love, family. Beyond that, things like wealth or leisure would be controversial, and some varieties even of the core elements may count as a curse rather than a blessing. A person might have had a better life if, for instance, he had not been blessed with such rude health that he was unable to sympathize with the frailties of others.

But something more rigid comes into view if we take the question of what we can expect from each other a different way. On this interpretation, it is asking for the right boundaries on conduct. This is the sense in which if we fail to live up to expectations, we have done something *wrong*. We have fallen short, and become targets for various kinds of possible reproach. People expect of each other that they should be honest, cooperative, sensitive to people's needs, fair, well-meaning, and so on, and if we fail in one of these then we have fallen short and may receive censure. Other people have a complaint against us; they are concerned that we should not be like that.

Someone might chafe against that. One might try to shrug off the ill opinion of others. Why should it concern one? Why not be a free spirit, blithely unconcerned with what the world may think? In some cases there is something admirable about this: the visionary or the saint or hero might have to unconcerned with the world's opinion while they seek to change it, perhaps for the better. But the question will be why we are attracting the world's bad opinion. If we attract it because, for instance, we don't care a jot about keeping our promises, or don't care about keeping our hands off other people's money, then it may be harder to shrug off the censure of others. Doing so—being able to look them in the eye and say that you don't see what they have to complain about—requires not only no concern for promises or honesty, but also no recognition of the concerns of others about these things. And in normal people *that* degree of insensitivity is rarely found. It is one thing to be the common-or-garden villain who says, 'I don't care if I have wronged you by breaking my word or stealing your goods.' But it is another to achieve the rather extraordinary pitch of villainy which says, 'I don't even recognize that you have a complaint.' It is usually easier to take that up as a defiant posture than to be comfortable in it, although sexual morality provides areas where people who have behaved badly sometimes cannot see what the other has to complain about—thereby making things worse. A society in which people were all incapable of recognizing the others as having a complaint, whatever they do, would be one without an ethic—but for that very reason it would be hard to recognize it as a society at all.

There are various ways in which thinkers have tried to articulate these ideas. 'Internalizing' a set of values is very close to internalizing the gaze or voice of others. Recognizing that they have a complaint against you is regarding yourself as having fallen short in their eyes, and to have internalized their voice means finding that itself weighing with you. The discomfort comes out in self-reproach, or emotions such as shame and guilt. Most systems of ethics have some version of the Golden Rule near their core: 'Do unto others as you would have them do unto you.' Some thinkers stress the emergence of a 'common point of view'; others stress the sympathy or empathy whereby our view of ourselves resonates with what we can take the view of others to be. To show how easily and naturally we incorporate the views of others into our concerns, Hume gives the splendid example: 'A man will be mortified if you tell him he has a stinking breath; though it is evidently no annoyance to himself.' We see ourselves from the point of view of others, and may be comfortable or uncomfortable as a result.

We can describe this aspect of our psychologies in terms of taking up one another's reasons. If there is a piano on your foot, one of your concerns is to move it quickly. If I am aware of this then I will naturally share that concern—and I would be falling short if I did not. I do not have the same place in this situation, for after all the piano is hurting you, not me. But I am expected to sympathize, to take up your concern, to help, and to treat your problem as mine also. What is a reason for you to act, becomes a reason for me to help. Some moral philosophers like to think that there is a kind of imperative of reason itself here. They think that there would be something defective about my rationality, or my understanding, if

I did not take up your concern and make it my own. I do not counsel this way of looking at it. The person who is indifferent in this situation is bad, certainly. And there may be things wrong with his reasonings, or his ways of understanding the world. He may be a psychopath, unable to comprehend the reality of others. Or he may make some deficient calculation, about whether it is good for you in the long run to suffer. But in the more common case where he averts his gaze, or passes by on the other side, there need be nothing wrong with his understanding of the world, nor his reasonings about it. He is cold-hearted, not wrong-headed. That is just as bad, or worse. But placing the defect in the right place shows that what is needed to improve him is a kind of education of the sentiments, rather than some kind of extra insight into the structure of reasons.

TRUTH AND GOODNESS

However, there is an issue here that divides thinkers into two camps.

Consider this equation:

One of X's concerns is to aim for/promote/endorse ϕ =
X thinks ϕ is good/thinks ϕ is a reason for action.

The division lies between thinkers who read this equation 'left to right', and those who read it 'right to left'. That is, there are thinkers who suppose that the right direction of explanation is from concerns, taken as understood, to 'seeing something as a reason', which is thereby explained. And there are those who think the right direction of explanation is from thinking that something is a reason, considered as a pure belief about the case, to concerns, which are thereby explained.

The difference is sometimes called that between 'non-cognitivism' and 'cognitivism' in the theory of ethics. The idea is that if the equation is read left to right, then talk of something being good, or something being a reason for action, is a kind of reflection of a motivational state of mind: the fact of something weighing with you. This motivational state of mind is not a simple belief. It is not a representation of some aspect of the world. It is a *reaction* to representations of the facts of the matter. It does not itself pick out some fact of the matter. Hence it is not strictly speaking a state of mind that is either true or false, any more than a desire for coffee is either true or false. The non-cognitivist direction is beautifully expressed by St Augustine:

> [T]here is the pull of the will and of love, wherein appears the worth of everything to be sought, or to be avoided, to be esteemed of greater or less value.

If the equation is read the other way, from right to left, then there is at the foundation a belief: the belief that ϕ is a reason for action. It is a special kind of belief, because it picks out or represents *reasons*. But it is a belief that carries concern with it. It is often said that Aristotle believed in this direction of explanation: its slogan is that to desire something is to see it as good. It is as if desire answers to a perceived truth.

The issue here is important to many thinkers, especially on the cognitivist side. They fear that without the backbone injected by cognitivism, all we have in practical reasoning are 'mere' concerns, desires, and attitudes. Whereas if we can somehow bring the whole thing under the control of Truth, we have some kind of basis for the claims of ethics. Concerns that correspond in the right way to these truths are the right ones; they deserve authority over the others.

Myself, I believe this is one of these areas where the advantage is definitely on one side: the non-cognitivist side.

The principal reason for this is that there is bound to be something other than beliefs or cognitions—representations of aspects of things—in the mix. There is also the 'pull of the will and of love'. The person with a concern is someone for whom some feature of a situation matters in practical reasonings. The weight attached to it is measured in motivational strength: in its disposition to cause her to change her actions and attitudes. Can 'seeing that ϕ is a reason for action' have that weight?

There are various suggestions possible about what it is that is seen or cognized. One would be that it is some purely natural fact. For instance 'seeing that the piano is on your foot is a reason to take it off' might be construed as 'seeing that the piano is on your foot is causing you pain'. But the trouble here is that it is obviously *contingent* whether this weighs with the agent. If she is cold-hearted or an enemy or has too robust a sense of humour it may not weigh at all. So it is not equivalent to having the motivation nor with having the concern, which weighs by definition. G. E. Moore summed this up by saying that whatever natural features of things we discern, it is always an 'open question' in what way we think that they form reasons for action. Taking them to do so is taking a step—the very step that leads us into the domain of practice in the first place.

Another tack would suggest that what is cognized is a peculiar, non-natural, 'normative' fact. This was Moore's own view, and it might have been that of Plato. It is as if we get a glimpse of something other than ordinary empirical or scientific features of things. We get a glimpse of the normative order.

This sounds very mysterious. The equation read right to left, if this is what is on the right-hand side, is altogether a strange thing. Suppose the normative order talked of is conceived of on the model of human laws. So it is as if you had come upon a law saying that pianos are to be taken off people's feet. The trouble is that it is always up to us what to feel about a law, just as much as anything else. I could, in principle ignore the law. I could reject it outright. There is no necessary connection between coming upon a law, and having it weigh with me. So it is not clear that moving in this direction gives us any explanatory story at all. The same, incidentally, is true even if the law had 'God's law' written on it. I might not care about that. If I do not, the traditional weapon to beat me with is the Fear of God's Wrath. But the cognitivist does not want to appeal to a contingent emotional state like this, for that is taking the issue outside the domain of reason. She wants what is discerned to be necessarily motivating, necessarily magnetic.

Faced with this a cognitivist might panic. She might respond by denying the equation with which we started. She would say: 'All right, I concede that there is a gap between truly perceiving the normative order, and being motivated. But that is fine: it takes a good will or a good heart to be motivated to do what you see you have reason to do.' The reason I call this a panic is that it allows the cognitivist to protect her cherished involvement with the idea of Truth—but only at the cost of taking its motivational force *outside* the domain of truth. For on this line, whatever it is that is wrong with people without good will or good hearts, it is not that they see the wrong truths. But the whole point of cognitivism was to bring practical reasoning *within* the purview of truth, enabling us to say that the person with the wrong concerns or bad concerns is flying in the face of reason, getting the world wrong. If the cognitivist cannot say this at the end of the day, there is no point in winning individual battles by conceding it.

My own view is that all these problems disappear if we read the equation the other way. When people have concerns, they express themselves by talking of reasons, and seeing the features that weigh with them as desirable or good. They do this in the 'pull of the will and of love'. I believe we invent the normative propositions ('This is good'; 'That is a reason for action'; 'You ought to do this') in order to think about the concerns to demand of ourselves and others. We talk in these terms in order to clarify our motivational states, to lay them out for admiration or criticism and improvement. There is no mysterious normative order into which we are plugged.

So is no set of concerns better than any other? Certainly they are. But their superiority does not lie in conformity to an independent normative order. Their superiority lies in the ways of life embodying them. A set of concerns that leads to lives that are loyal, friendly, grateful, prudent, sympathetic, fair is indeed superior to one that leads to lives that are treacherous, suspicious, malicious, careless, hard-hearted, unjust. Our lives go better when we can be described the first way, than when we are described the second way. And we should be concerned that lives go better.

GOOD BAD FEELINGS

Many writings on ethics introduce the subject rather differently. They introduce a dualism. On the one hand there is the seething mass of desire. On the other hand, above it and separate, there are the lordly principles of ethics, which exist to control it. I believe nothing but confusion comes from this picture. It makes the lordly principles of ethics seem utterly mysterious: things that perhaps require a divine origin or some kind of Platonic ability to resonate in harmony with the Nature of Things. I substitute for this a model in which there is just a plurality of concerns. But among these concerns are ones that have the kind of status that leads us to talk of virtue and vice, duty and obligation. These are the concerns we expect of each other, so that if we do not share them, or weigh them properly, we are regarded as having fallen short. We can usually say that these are the concerns that we regard people as owing to each other. If someone does me a great kindness, then I *owe* him a sentiment of gratitude: it is his *due* and it is my *duty* to feel it or express it. If I am callous or careless, I have fallen short. I will forfeit admiration in the eyes of others, and in so far as I have a voice within myself echoing the voice of others, I will feel bad about myself. If I do not, that itself can become a cause of censure, and sometimes a more important one than the original failing. If someone overlooks a debt of gratitude, that can be bad. But if when it is pointed out, he shrugs it off or doesn't see what the fuss is about, that can be more shocking than the original fault. Hence the importance we attach to contrition and, in serious cases, repentance. These bad feelings are good.

Here we might return to the complaint above against the contemporary obsession with 'therapy'. In our example, Annie's concern was her career, and that concern was not met nor shared by Bertie, who took the concern itself as the problem. Moral cases are similar. Feeling bad about ourselves or our conduct is indeed unpleasant. We might wish such feelings away. But in cases in which they are justified, wishing the feelings away involves a self-alienation, and is not the right response. Suppose Annie knows she has hurt or insulted Bertie. She might be grateful to a therapist, who tells her that some neat process can dissolve away her self-reproach. But it is not clear that she ought to be grateful. In the first place, her concern is to put things right with Bertie; to apologize or make amends, or assure him how much it matters, and so on. Or her concern might be with the depravity of her own character or conduct, which she wishes were better. But her concern is not with those concerns themselves. And if a therapist could give her a pill that took them away, she is not necessarily helping Annie. She is not putting things right with Bertie, nor for that matter improving Annie's character. In fact, she is making Annie the kind of person who attracted the extra degree of censure, not only for behaving badly, but also for failing to have within herself the awareness that she has. She is alienating Annie from her awareness of what she has done, and her wish not to have done it.

Of course, in time or with bad luck there can indeed come cases in which the self-reproach is festering. It is doing no good, it is an obsession, and Annie could well wish herself to be without it. But the point is that this is not the typical or straightforward case. It is a case when things have got out of hand. When things are in hand, it is not guilt or shame that is the problem, but the actions that invited them.

Our concerns weigh with us (that is a tautology; that is what makes them concerns). But their weights are susceptible to change, and one of the things that can sometimes change them are discussions, arguments, and an awareness of the direction of pull of other concerns. Hence we have practical argument, taking the form of wondering what is to be done, or what principles to endorse, or what features of character to admire or reject. How are we to think about that?

PRACTICAL REASONING

At the beginning of the chapter we mentioned technological reasonings, in which an aim is given and the problem is one of finding means to it. But of course much practical reasoning is concerned to alter people's aims. We seek to put the situation in a different light, so that they come to share aims we approve of, or abandon aims of which we disapprove.

A great deal of such reasoning is, of course, sheer persuasion. Its arts are those of the salesman and the advertising agency. We deploy rhetoric to excite people's emotions and direct them in the desired channels. The preacher painting the horrors of hell or the politician painting the virtues of his party and the vices of the other are not really seeking to improve anyone's understanding of anything. We might say that the concern here is to manipulate rather than to instruct. Their aim to attach emotional weights to various courses of action, so leading people in a desired direction. At its lowest level this might be a matter of attaching penalties and threats to courses of conduct, rather than other less overt kinds of persuasive pressures.

When we take up this kind of stance to each other, we are in effect treating others as means to our own ends. For some reason, we want them to have an aim. We want them to buy our product or vote for our party or come to our church. If we are prepared to pursue any course we can think of to get them to do this, we are treating them as what Kant called 'mere means' to our own ends. By manipulating them—which might include deception as well as other persuasive arts—we hope to divert their course, just as we might hope to divert any other obstacle to our own goals.

A lot of life may be like that, but not its best parts. For we can take up a more cooperative and respectful stance towards each other. If I am convinced that your life is setting out down the wrong path, I may not want to manipulate you into a different course just by any old means. If I had a magic injection that would change you in the direction I desire, then unlike the salesman or the preacher, I would not give it you. Doing so would be failing to respect your point of view, or failing to respect you as a person. I want you to come to share my understanding of your situation in the *right* way, not by means of manipulation or subterfuge or threats or brute force. So what is this right way?

Roughly, it is going to be one which addresses and takes account of your point of view. There are clearly things this rules out: deception and manipulation. And there are clearly things it rules in: improved understanding of the situation, for example. If I know how things stand and you do not, I cooperate with you while seeking to change you if I share that understanding with you.

We might think that this is all, so that reason as opposed to rhetoric must be entirely confined to pointing out the facts of the situation. An argument to that conclusion would be something like this. Suppose we each understand the situation as it is, and in the same way. Then suppose I have a set of concerns that eventually resolve themselves in my having one aim. How can you seek to change me except by some process of persuasion or manipulation? However much you profess a cooperative stance, aren't we really in conflict, since my concerns define my take on the situation, and you are wishing one of them away. You can't get me to change by *addressing* those concerns, since the assumption was that they issue in the direction you dislike.

Fortunately, there are two gaps in this argument. The first arises because our concerns are not always evident to ourselves. So your take on the situation may not adequately reflect everything that in fact matters to you. When we 'turn things over' in our own minds, we are as it were prowling round to see if there are aspects of things that we haven't brought to mind, which engage our motivations. And we are the same time exploring whether there are unrecognized forces at work: whether we care more or less about one thing or another than we admit to ourselves. We can be blind to our own natures, as well as to aspects of the world around us. A conversation seeking to uncover motivations that we may have suppressed or discounted is cooperative, not manipulative.

Second, even when you understand your situation properly, and your concerns are sufficiently transparent to yourself, I need not be manipulating you or merely trying to persuade you of something if I lay out my own take on things for you to consider. Consider the case in which there is a moral dimension. You are bent on a course of action, say, which in my view does not adequately reflect the duty of gratitude or loyalty that you have to some third party. I tell you this. I am putting my cards on the table: there is no manipulation or deception going on. I may change you, for if you respect me sufficiently my good opinion matters, and if you are likely to forfeit that opinion by maintaining your course, this becomes a factor for you to know.

This second mechanism is in a sense a way of presenting to you another factor in your situation: that your course of action attracts my disapproval. But of course it is not intended to stop there. If it did, then my disapproval would be functioning as an 'object': a mere obstacle to your preferred course, to be factored into a cost-benefit analysis. But this is not what is intended. In cooperative moral discussion, it is intended that we come to common ground, where that includes common approval and disapproval. My disapproval is put on the table as something for you to share or undermine, but in either event as something that you are to engage on its own terms. Otherwise it is being objectified, like Annie's concern for her career, in the example above.

So discussion turns to whether my insistence on the duty of gratitude or loyalty should be respected, or whether it represents something else: perhaps a fetish to be ignored or brushed aside. To answer this question we turn over yet *other* things that weigh with us. We might try to bring to bear, for example, considerations of how well or badly the world would go without people having that concern. Or we might try to relate it to other things that matter to us, such as friendship or honesty.

Underlying the method here will be another fundamental concern: that our practical stances should be *coherent*. And perhaps they should be other things as well, such as imaginative and objective.

COHERENCE, OBJECTIVITY, IMAGINATION

A lot of practical reasoning proceeds by looking for the general features that matter to us. When we advance a reason or justification to one another, we are trying to show the favourable light in which the action or attitude appeared. Some writers are suspicious of any requirement that this process should be systematic or ordered. They want to deny that practical life is a matter of 'rules' or 'principles'. It may be more like aesthetics. We can look at a painting and pronounce upon it without any articulated, general principles that we could cite to defend our verdicts. We might also remember the example, from Chapter 1, of our ability to recognize things and our ability to certify a sentence as grammatical, both of which seem to go on with our using any general principles or rules, at least consciously.

But practical reasoning is not in general like that. This is because we need to *know where we stand*. The constraint is here the same as with a system of law. It would be no good having a system of law that refused to articulate general principles and rules, but insisted on 'treating each case on its merits'. If it were not predictable in advance what would actually *count* as the merits then we could not regulate our lives by such a 'system'. It would be no law at all. Similarly in ethics. We need to know where we stand, which means being able to discern features of a choice situation or a scenario that count in favour or against practical decisions and attitudes. This means that while our desires and wishes can presumably be as fickle as we please, the concerns we exact from each other cannot be. They need to fall into some kind of defensible system.

We saw in Chapter 6 how logic prizes consistency above all else. There has to be a way in which our beliefs can be true. In practical life, the equivalent virtue is that there has to be a way in which our values could all be implemented. A system of law is inconsistent if it is impossible to obey its constraints (suppose, for example, that it forbids the consumption of alcohol on Sunday but also mandates attendance at mass, which has to include wine). Now life throws up plenty of cases where there is an apparent inconsistency between simple values. Always tell the truth; never hurt anyone. But on this occasion the truth is hurtful. Always respect property; never put the State in danger. But on this occasion protecting the State requires requisitioning someone's property. So a great deal of practical thinking consists in adjusting the simple obligations and boundaries that we are apt to require of each other, to accommodate clashes and complexities, and to get some sense of which adjustments best work towards a comprehensive and consistent system of living. This is not an easy process, and the results tend to be tentative and provisional and hostage to new cases and problems.

Fortunately we have devices to help us. One is history, thought of in terms of the survival of the fittest. The adjustments and solutions embodied in our inherited form of life have this much going for them, that they have survived some test of time. We have to be careful of the kind of conservative worship of inherited forms that is associated with thinkers like Edmund Burke (1729–97). But it is much less intelligent to lurch to the other extreme, and believe that the test of time shows nothing. At the very least it gives us a datum point from which to think about change. Another device to help us is imagination. We do not have to wait for crises to come along, when fiction and imagination and the sheer resolution to *think through* our values and their relative importance can be had more or less for free. And this thinking can occur when we have a relatively objective view of our situation—we can see ourselves as others see us—when in the heat of passion or action this is much harder to achieve. With this kind of reflection, we can learn some understanding of our ideologies and our disguises.

RELATIVISM

So at the end of the day is it 'just us'? Do all our vaunted moral imperatives and values come down to a contingent, situated, perhaps variable set of concerns, that we happen to exact from one another?

Well, it is indeed us, but it may not be 'just' us. The 'just' insinuates that other solutions are equally good, or equally 'valid' or valuable. In particular cases we may well come to think this. The British drive on the left and Americans on the right. Each has hit upon an equally good solution to the essential problem of coordinating traffic. Driving on the one side is 'just us'. But it is not just us that we *do* drive exclusively on the one or the other. Driving at random or in the middle is not an equally good solution—it is no solution at all—to the problem of coordination.

Once we see a solution as one of many equally good solutions to some problem, we can appreciate that it is 'just ours'. And we are no longer minded to moralize against the others. Different languages have different words for different things, and different grammars and word orders, but so far as that goes they may all serve the purposes of communication equally well. Different customs, rites, observances, social arrangements of all kinds can be seen as different solutions to problems of public expression, coordination, and communication. We do not have to rank them. When in Rome, do as the Romans do.

But suppose a society solves its problems in ways that do grate upon our concerns. Suppose, like the Taliban in contemporary Afghanistan, they deny education to women. Or suppose the ages have bequeathed them a caste system that denies equal opportunities of health, education, or even sustenance to whole classes of people, according to their birth. Or even that the ages have bequeathed them a system in which some people are owned body and soul by others. These systems are some kind of solution to problems of how to live. But we do not have to see them as equally good ('just different') or even as tolerable at all. We can properly see them as trespassing against boundaries that matter to us. They offend against boundaries of concern and respect that we believe ought to be protected. Here it is natural to look to the language of 'rights', meaning not only that it is good or nice of people to show concern and respect, but that if they do not, the injured parties may rightly feel resentment and call upon the world to rectify their state.

In saying these things, we voice our own sympathies and concerns and values. But that is what practical reasoning is bound to be. There is no reason to feel guilty about it, as if it would only be with a certificate from God, or from the Normative Truth (what Plato called the Forms) that we have any right to hold our opinions. Our ethical concerns are well seen on the model of Neurath's boat (Chapter 1). We must inspect each part, and we have to do so while relying on other parts. But the result of that inspection may, if we are coherent and imaginative, be perfectly seaworthy. And if, relying upon it, we find ourselves in conflict with other boats sailing in different directions, there is no reason to lament that we are not seated in some kind of dry dock, certified by Reason or God. They are not in any such place, either.

FAREWELL

This book has tried to introduce some of the great themes, and the things to think about them, and the things other people have thought about them. I have not tried to coerce people into one set of doctrines or views. In fact, the sensitive reader may have noticed that the upshot of the arguments is often a kind of pessimism. The harmony between our thoughts and the world, the bridge we build between past and future, the sense of what the physical world contains and how our minds fit into it, are all topics on which the finest thinkers have hurled themselves, only to be frustrated. There always seem to be better words, if only we could find them, just over the horizon.

It would be possible to be cynical about this—professional philosophers have been known to be so—as if the defence of critical reflection I tried to give in the Introduction had been shown to be hollow. I do not think that would be justified. I believe the process of understanding the problems is itself a good. If the upshot is what Hume called a 'mitigated scepticism' or sense of how much a decent modesty becomes us in our intellectual speculations, that is surely no bad thing. The world is full of ideas, and a becoming sense of their power, their difficulty, their frailties, and their fallibility cannot be the least of the things it needs.

Notes

1. KNOWLEDGE

18 'prudent never to trust'. Descartes, *Meditations on First Philosophy*, p. 12.

19 'I will suppose therefore'. Ibid. p. 15.

19 'Does it now follow that I'. Ibid. p. 16.

20 'Thinking? At last I have discovered it'. Ibid. p. 18.

21 '[T]he residual taste is eliminated'. Ibid. p. 20.

21 'I now know that even bodies'. Ibid. p. 22.

26 Brains in vats. This thought-experiment is due to Hilary Putnam, *Reason, Truth and History*, ch. 1.

30 Lichtenberg is quoted in J. P. Stern, *Lichtenberg: A Doctrine of Scattered Occasions*, p. 270.

34 The trademark argument occurs in Descartes, *Meditation* 3, pp. 31–3.

36 '[W]e can touch'. This is from a letter to Marin Mersenne, referenced at *Meditations*, p. 32, footnote.

38 Arnauld's objection is in the Fourth Set of *Objections and Replies*, in *Descartes: Selected Philosophical Writings*, p. 142.

40 'There is a species'. Hume, *Enquiry Concerning Human Understanding*, Section XII, p. 149.

44 'We are like sailors'. Neurath's image is presented in his *Anti-Spengler*.

46 Russell's example of scepticism about time occurs in *An Outline of Philosophy*, pp. 171–2.

46 The issue of probability and entropy is discussed in Huw Price, *Time's Arrow and Archimedes' Point*, ch. 2.

2. MIND

50 For Descartes on the nervous system, see especially the sixth *Meditation*, pp. 59–60.

51 'ghost in a machine'. Ryle used this phrase in his *Concept of Mind*. It ought to be said that Descartes himself denied that on his account the soul was lodged in the body 'like a pilot in a ship', so there is a scholarly issue of whether he was reaching for a more sophisticated view.

54 'And how can I generalize'. Wittgenstein, *Philosophical Investigations*, 293, p. 100.

58 'Let us suppose at present'. Locke, *Essay Concerning Human Understanding*, II. viii. 13, p. 136. Here and elsewhere when quoting Locke I have modernized capitalization.

60 'Now, when certain particles'. Leibniz, *New Essays on Human Understanding*, 131.

64 'For unthinking particles of matter'. Locke, *Essay*, IV. x. 16, p. 627.

65 A good source for the current cautious revival of techniques of analysis is Jackson, *From Metaphysics to Ethics*.

74 'Always get rid of the idea'. Wittgenstein, *Investigations*, Pt II. xi, p. 207.

75 The best source for recent colour science is C. L. Hardin, *Color for Philosophers*.

3. FREE WILL

81 'Again, if movement'. Lucretius, *De Rerum Natura (Of the Nature of Things)*, Bk. II, ll. 251–7, p. 43.

86 'Let us imagine'. Schopenhauer, *On the Freedom of the Will*, p. 43.

97 'freedom of clockwork'. Kant, *Critique of Practical Reason*, pp. 99–101.

101 For Spinoza, see *Ethics*, Pt. IV, p. 187; Pt. V, pp. 199–224.

102 For Aristotle, see *Nicomachean Ethics*, III. 5 (1114a4).

107 Strawson's point was made in his celebrated essay, 'Freedom and Resentment'.

110 The Sufi story is adapted from Shah, *Tales of the Dervishes*.

118 'It is humiliating'. Wittgenstein, *Culture and Value*, p. 11.

4. THE SELF

122 'For my part, when'. Hume, *Treatise*, I. iv. 6, p. 252.

123 'A part of a person'. Reid, *Essays on the Intellectual Powers of Man*, p. 202.

125 'That being then one plant'. Locke, *Essay*, II. xxvii. 4, p. 331.

128 'But the question is'. Locke, *Essay*, II. xxvii. 12, p. 337.

129 'An elastic ball'. Kant, *Critique of Pure Reason,* A 364, p. 342.

131 'Suppose a brave officer'. Reid, *Essays on the Intellectual Powers of Man*, p. 213.

132 'But yet possibly'. Locke, *Essay*, II. xxvii. 20, p. 342.

137 'We feel then that in the cases'. Wittgenstein, *The Blue Book*, p. 69.

140 Kant's great move. The central passages in the *Critique of Pure Reason* are in the section entitled 'Transcendental Deduction of the Pure Concepts of the Understanding', B 130–B 170.

148 Kant. See preceding note.

5. GOD

154 'But when this same fool'. Anselm, *Proslogion*, pp. 99–100.

159 'Whatever exists must have'. Hume, *Dialogues*, Pt. 9, p. 54.

161 'It is pretended that'. Ibid. Pt. 9, p. 55.

163 'Look round the world'. Ibid. Pt 2, p. 15.

165 'But, allowing that we were'. Ibid. Pt. 2, p. 19.

166 'The world plainly resembles'. Ibid. Pt. 7, p. 44.

166 'If I rest my system'. Ibid. Pt. 7, p. 47.

168 'In a word, Cleanthes'. Ibid. Pt. 7, p. 37.

169 'His power, we allow, is infinite'. Ibid. Pt. 10, p. 63.

171 'The true conclusion is that'. Ibid. Pt. 11, p. 75.

172 'a nothing will serve'. Wittgenstein, *Investigations*, 304, p. 102.

172 'If the whole of Natural Theology'. Hume, *Dialogues*, Pt. 12, p. 88.

178 'This contrariety of evidence'. Hume, *Enquiry Concerning Human Understanding*, X, Pt. 1, p. 112.

178 'The very same principle'. Ibid. X, Pt. 1, p. 113.

178 'The plain consequence is'. Ibid. X, Pt. 1, pp. 115–16.

180 'The wise lend a very academic faith'. Ibid. X , Pt. 2, p. 125.

181 'The passion of *surprise* and *wonder*'. Ibid. X, Pt. 2, p. 117.

181 '[L]et us consider, that'. Ibid. X , Pt. 2, p. 121.

186 Pascal's wager is found in his *Pensées*, pp. 149–55.

190 'is but one superstition'. Mill, *On Liberty*, p. 41.

190 Clifford makes the comparison in 'The Ethics of Belief', collected in his *Lectures and Essays*. See p. 346.

190 'He who begins'. Coleridge, *Aids to Reflection*, Aphorism XV, p. 107.

6. REASONING

207 The notions introduced here were extensively studied by Paul Grice. His papers are collected in *Studies in the Way of Words*.

212 'As to past *Experience*'. Hume, *Enquiry Concerning Human Understanding*, IV, Pt. 2, pp. 33–4.

217 'It is impossible'. Ibid. IV, Pt. 2, p. 38.

228 'That gravity should be innate'. This is from a letter from Newton to Bentley. It is quoted in Kemp Smith, *The Philosophy of David Hume*, p. 61.

228 'I shall venture to affirm'. Hume, *Enquiry Concerning Human Understanding*, IV, Pt. 1, p. 27.

229 'We fancy, that were we'. Ibid. IV, Pt. 1, p. 28.

229 'Hence we may discover the reason'. Ibid. IV, Pt. 1, p. 30.

230 Kuhn's masterwork was *The Structure of Scientific Revolutions*, published in 1962.

7. THE WORLD

234 'Now I say that whenever'. Galileo, *The Assayer*, in *Discoveries and Opinions of Galileo*, p. 274.

234 'For the proper purpose'. Descartes, *Meditation* 6, p. 57.

240 Russell raises the charge of 'favouritism' briefly in *The Problems of Philosophy*, ch. 1, p. 10.

241 '*original* or *primary* qualities'. Locke, *Essay*, II. viii. 9 and 10, p. 135.

242 'What I have said concerning colours'. Ibid. II. vii. 14, p. 137.

244 'The idea of solidity we receive'. Ibid. II. iv. 1, p. 122.

245 'If anyone asks me'. Ibid. II. iv. 6, p. 126.

246 'The idea of solidity is that'. Hume, *Treatise*, I. iv. 4, p. 228.

247 '[A]fter the exclusion of colour'. Ibid. I. iv. 4, p. 229.

248 '[T]o my mind'. Faraday, 'A Speculation touching Electrical Conduction and the Nature of Matter'. I owe the quotation to Langton, *Kantian Humility*, p. 101.

253 'The scenes of the universe'. Hume, *Enquiry Concerning Human Understanding*, VII, Pt. 1, p. 63.

254 'I am not, therefore, in a position'. Kant, *Critique of Pure Reason*, A 368, p. 345.

255 'rhapsody' of perceptions. Ibid. A 137/B196, p. 193.

256 'Hitherto it has been assumed'. Ibid. Preface to the 2nd edn., p. 22.

258 'Colours are not properties'. Ibid. A 29, p. 73.

259 'In our system'. Ibid. A 372, p. 347.

259 '[t]he required proof must'. Ibid. B 275, p. 244.

260 'But (to pass by all …)'. Berkeley, *Three Dialogues*, Dialogue 1, para. 398, p. 35.

263 Moore's isolation argument occurs throughout *Principia Ethica*, ch. 6.

265 The rule-following considerations are presented in Wittgenstein's *Philosophical Investigations*, from (roughly: the discussion blends into other material) § 137 to § 203.

8. WHAT TO DO

273 Psychological egoism. It is difficult to find a pure psychological egoist, but Thomas Hobbes is sometimes claimed to have been one. The classic discussion is given by Joseph Butler in his *Fifteen Sermons Preached at the Rolls Chapel* in 1726, especially Sermon XI. I discuss the whole issue further in my *Ruling Passions*, chs. 5 and 6.

281 'A man will be mortified'. Hume, *Treatise*, III. iii. I, p. 589.

283 '[T]here is the pull of the will and of love'. St Augustine, *The Literal Meaning of Genesis*, Bk. 4, ch. 4, para. 8. I have slightly altered the translation.

284 Moore's 'open question' argument is from his *Principia Ethica*, pp. 10–20.

285 Plato extols glimpses of the normative and ideal order in terms of insight into the 'Forms'. But there is intense scholarly debate over what he meant by this, and to what extent his opinions remained the same from one dialogue to another.

290 Kant's polemic against treating others as 'mere means' is most easily accessed in the *Groundwork of the Metaphysics of Morals*.

295 Burke's conservatism is expressed in his *Reflections on the Revolution in France*.

298 Hume talks approvingly of mitigated scepticism in the *Enquiry Concerning Human Understanding*, XII, p. 161.

Bibliography

Anselm. *Monologion and Proslogion*, trans. Thomas Williams. Indianapolis: Hackett, 1995.

Aristotle. *Nicomachean Ethics*, in *The Works of Aristotle Translated into English*, vol. ix, trans. W. D. Ross. Oxford: Oxford University Press, 1925.

Augustine, St. *The Literal Meaning of Genesis*, trans. John H. Taylor. Ancient Christian Writers, vols. 41 and 42. New York: Newman Press.

Berkeley, George. *Three Dialogues*, ed. Robert Merrihew Adams. Indianapolis: Hackett, 1979.

Blackburn, Simon. *Ruling Passions*. Oxford: Oxford University Press, 1998.

Burke, Edmund. *Reflections on the Revolution in France*. Oxford: Oxford University Press, 1993.

Clifford, W. K. *Lectures and Essays*. London: Macmillan, 1886.

Coleridge, Samuel Taylor. *Aids to Reflection*, ed. John Beer. Princeton: Princeton University Press, 1993.

Descartes, René. *Meditations on First Philosophy*, trans. John Cottingham. Cambridge: Cambridge University Press, 1986.

—— *Selected Philosophical Writings*, trans. John Cottingham, Robert Stoothoff, and Dugald Murdoch. Cambridge: Cambridge University Press, 1988.

Faraday, Michael. 'A Speculation Touching Electrical Conduction and the Nature of Matter', in *Experimental Researches in Electricity*, vol. 2. London: Richard and John Edward Taylor, 1844.

Frege, Gottlob. '*Begriffsschrift*, A Formula Language, Modeled upon that of Arithmetic, for Pure Thought', in J. van Heijenoort (ed.), *From Frege to Gödel: A Sourcebook in Mathematical Logic, 1879–1931*. Cambridge, Mass.: Harvard University Press, 1967.

Galileo Galilei. *Discoveries and Opinions of Galileo*, trans. Stillman Drake. New York: Doubleday, 1957.

Grice, Paul. *Studies in the Way of Words*. Cambridge, Mass.: Harvard University Press, 1989.

Hardin, C. L. *Color for Philosophers*. Indianapolis: Hackett, 1988.

Hume, David. *Dialogues Concerning Natural Religion*, ed. Richard H. Popkin. Indianapolis: Hackett, 1980.

—— *Enquiries Concerning Human Understanding and Concerning the Principles of Morals*, ed. L. A. Selby-Bigge, 3rd edn. revised by P. H. Nidditch. Oxford: Oxford University Press, 1975.

—— *Treatise of Human Nature*, ed. L. A. Selby-Bigge. Oxford: Oxford University Press, 1888.

Jackson, Frank. *From Metaphysics to Ethics*. Oxford: Oxford University Press, 1998.

Kant, Immanuel. *Critique of Practical Reason*, trans. Lewis White Beck. New York: Macmillan, 1956.

—— *Critique of Pure Reason*, trans. Norman Kemp Smith. London: Macmillan, 1929.

—— *Groundwork of the Metaphysic of Morals*, trans. H. J. Paton. New York: Harper Torchbooks, 1964.

Kemp Smith, Norman. *The Philosophy of David Hume*. London: Macmillan, 1941.

Kuhn, Thomas. *The Structure of Scientific Revolutions* (first published as the *International Encyclopedia of Unified Science*, vol. 2, no. 2), 2nd edn. Chicago: University of Chicago Press, 1970.

Langton, Rae. *Kantian Humility*. Oxford: Oxford University Press, 1998.

Leibniz, Gottfried Wilhelm. *New Essays on Human Understanding*, ed. Peter Remnant and Jonathan Bennett. Cambridge: Cambridge University Press, 1996.

Locke, John. *An Essay Concerning Human Understanding*, ed. Peter H. Nidditch. Oxford: Oxford University Press, 1975.

Lucretius. *De Rerum Natura (Of the Nature of Things)*, trans. Sir Ronald Melville. Oxford: Oxford University Press, 1997.

Mill, John Stuart. 'On Liberty', in *On Liberty and Other Essays*, ed. John Gray. Oxford: Oxford University Press, 1991.

Moore, G. E. *Principia Ethica*. Cambridge: Cambridge University Press, 1903.

Neurath, Otto. *Anti-Spengler*. Munich: G. D. W. Callwey, 1921.

Pascal, Blaise. *Pensées*, trans A. J. Krailsheimer. Harmondsworth: Penguin Books, 1966.

Price, Huw. *Time's Arrow and Archimedes' Point*. New York: Oxford University Press, 1996.

Putnam, Hilary. *Reason, Truth and History*. Cambridge: Cambridge University Press, 1981.

Reid, Thomas. *Essays on the Intellectual Powers of Man*, ed. A. D. Woozley. London: Macmillan, 1941.

Russell, Bertrand. *An Outline of Philosophy*. London: George Allen & Unwin, 1927; also published in the United States as *Philosophy*. New York: W. W. Norton, 1927.

—— *The Problems of Philosophy*. Buffalo, N.Y.: Prometheus Books, 1988.

Ryle, Gilbert. *The Concept of Mind*. London: Hutchinson, 1949.

Schopenhauer, Arthur. *On the Freedom of the Will*. Oxford: Blackwell, 1985.

Shah, Idries. *Tales of the Dervishes*. London: Jonathan Cape, 1967.

Spinoza, Benedict. *Ethics*, trans. Andrew Boyle. London: J. M. Dent, 1979.

Stern, J. P. *Lichtenberg: A Doctrine of Scattered Occasions*. Bloomington: Indiana University Press, 1959.

Strawson, Peter. 'Freedom and Resentment', in Gary Watson (ed.), *Free Will*. Oxford: Oxford University Press, 1982.

Wittgenstein, Ludwig. *The Blue and Brown Books*. Oxford: Blackwell, 1964.

—— *Culture and Value*, trans. Peter Winch. Oxford: Blackwell, 1978.

—— *Philosophical Investigations*, trans. G. E. M. Anscombe. Oxford: Blackwell, 1953.

Index